Issues in Religion and Theology

10

Prophecy in Israel

D0793138

Issues in Religion and Theology 10

Prophecy in Israel
Search for an Identity

Edited with an Introduction by
DAVID L. PETERSEN

FORTRESS PRESS | SPCK
Philadelphia | London

First published in Great Britain 1987
SPCK
Holy Trinity Church
Marylebone Road
London NW1 4DU

First published in the USA 1987
Fortress Press
2900 Queen Lane
Philadelphia
Pennsylvania 19129

Library of Congress Cataloging in Publication Data

Prophecy in Israel.
  (Issues in religion and theology; 10)
  Bibliography: p.
  1. Prophets.   I. Petersen, David L.   II. Series.
BS1198.P75   1986   224′.06   85–45584
ISBN 0–8006–1773–8

British Library Cataloguing in Publication Data

Prophecy in Israel: search for an identity.
  —(Issues in religion and theology; 10)
  1. Prophets
  I. Petersen, David L.   II. Series
  220.8′2916′3   BS1505
  ISBN 0–281–04275–6

Made and printed in Great Britain by Richard Clay Ltd, Bungay, Suffolk

Contents

Acknowledgments

Hermann Gunkel, "The Prophets as Writers and Poets", was first published as "Die Propheten als Schriftsteller und Dichter" in *Die Propheten* (Göttingen: Vandenhoeck & Ruprecht, 1923) 34–70.

Sigmund Mowinckel, "Cult and Prophecy", was first published in *Psalmenstudien III: Kultprophetie und prophetische Psalmen* (Kristiana: Jacob Dybwad, 1922) 4–29.

Max Weber, "The Prophet", is reprinted from *The Sociology of Religion* by Max Weber, English translation from the 4th edition (Boston: Beacon Press, 1963) 46–59. It is used by permission of Beacon Press. Copyright © 1963 by Beacon Press.

James F. Ross, "The Prophet as Yahweh's Messenger", was first published in *Israel's Prophetic Heritage: Essays in Honor of James Muilenburg* (ed. Bernhard W. Anderson and Walter Harrelson; New York: Harper & Row, 1962) 98–107. The essay is reprinted by permission of Harper & Row, Publishers, Inc. Copyright © 1962 by Bernhard W. Anderson and Walter Harrelson.

John S. Holladay, Jr., "Assyrian Statecraft and the Prophets of Israel", is reprinted from *Harvard Theological Review* 63 (1970) 29–51 by permission of the author and *HTR*. Copyright © 1970 by the President and Fellows of Harvard College.

James L. Mays, "Justice: Perspectives from the Prophetic Tradition", is reprinted from *Interpretation* 37 (1983) 5–17 by permission of the author and *Int*. Copyright © 1983 by *Interpretation*.

Gene M. Tucker, "The Role of the Prophets and the Role of the Church", is reprinted from *Quarterly Review: A Scholarly Journal for Reflection on Ministry* 1 (Spring 1981) 5–22 by permission of the author and *Quarterly Review*. Copyright © 1981, The United Methodist Publishing House and the United Methodist Board of Higher Education and Ministry.

The editor and the publishers gratefully acknowledge the help of James L. Schaaf (Trinity Lutheran Theological Seminary, Columbus, Ohio), who translated the Gunkel and Mowinckel selections.

The Contributors

DAVID L. PETERSEN, Professor of Old Testament at the Iliff School of Theology, is the author of *Late Israelite Prophecy, The Roles of Israel's Prophets*, and *Haggai-Zechariah 1–8* (OTL).

HERMANN GUNKEL (1862–1932) held positions in Old Testament at the University of Halle (1889–1894) and Berlin (1894–1907). Apart from his introduction to the prophetic corpus in *Die Schriften des Alten Testaments*, part of which is translated in this collection, he is best known for his article on Psalms in *RGG*, his commentary on Genesis, and his early, programmatic work, *Schöpfung und Chaos*.

SIGMUND MOWINCKEL (1884–1965), whose first publication (in 1909) was devoted to Israel's prophets, taught at the University of Oslo for his entire career. While most influential for his multivolume *Psalmenstudien*, and other works on psalms, his *oeuvre* includes studies devoted to Ezra-Nehemiah, Jeremiah, and Pentateuchal problems.

MAX WEBER (1864–1920) taught at the Universities of Berlin, Freiburg, Heidelberg, and Munich, though for much of his life he was not employed in a university position because of illness. For the student of religion, his most prominent works are his *Sociology of Religion, Ancient Judaism*, and *The Protestant Ethic and the Spirit of Capitalism*.

JAMES F. ROSS is Professor of Old Testament at the Protestant Episcopal Theological Seminary in Virginia. He is coauthor of *Basic Sources of the Judaeo-Christian Tradition* and author of numerous articles in the areas of archaeology and biblical studies.

JOHN S. HOLLADAY, JR., Professor of Near Eastern Studies at the University of Toronto, was involved in the Gezer excavation and publication program and has published other work devoted to archaeology and biblical studies.

JAMES L. MAYS, Professor of Hebrew and Old Testament at Union Theological Seminary in Virginia, is long-time editor of *Interpretation* and author of commentaries on Hosea, Amos, and Micah (OTL).

GENE M. TUCKER is Professor of Old Testament at the Candler School of Theology, Emory University. He authored the influential *Form Criticism of the Old Testament* (GBSOTS), coedits FOTL, and is a member of the RSV committee.

Series Foreword

The Issues in Religion and Theology series intends to encompass a variety of topics within the general disciplines of religious and theological studies. Subjects are drawn from any of the component fields, such as biblical studies, systematic theology, ethics, history of Christian thought, and history of religion.

The series aims to address these issues by collecting and reproducing key studies, all previously published, which have contributed significantly to our present understandings. In each case, the volume editor introduces the discussion with an original essay which describes the subject and its treatment in religious and theological studies. To this editor has fallen the responsibility of selecting items for inclusion. Together the essays are intended to present a balanced overview of the problem and various approaches to it. Each piece is important in the current debate, and any older publication included normally stands as a classical or seminal work which is still worth careful study. Readers unfamiliar with the issue should find that these discussions provide a good entrée, while more advanced students will appreciate having studies by some of the best specialists on the subject gathered together in one volume.

The editor has, of course, faced certain constraints: analyses too lengthy or too technical could not be included, except perhaps in excerpt form; the bibliography is not exhaustive; and the volumes in this series are being kept to a reasonable, uniform length. On the other hand, the editor is able to overcome the real problem of inaccessibility. Much of the best literature on a subject is often not readily available to readers, whether because it was first published in journals or books not widely circulated or because it was originally written in a language not read by all who would benefit from it. By bringing these and other studies together in this series, we hope to contribute to the general understanding of these key topics.

The series editors and the publishers wish to express their gratitude to the authors and their original publishers whose works are reprinted or translated here, often with corrections from living authors. We are also conscious of our debt to members of the editorial advisory board, who have been prepared to spare much time and thought for the project.

DOUGLAS A. KNIGHT   ROBERT MORGAN

Abbreviations

AB	Anchor Bible
ABL	*Assyrian and Babylonian Letters*, ed. Robert F. Harper
AfO	*Archiv für Orientforschung*
ANET	*Ancient Near Eastern Texts*, ed. J. B. Pritchard
ASR	*American Sociological Review*
BA	*Biblical Archeologist*
BETL	Bibliotheca ephemeridum theologicarum lovaniensium
BEvT	Beiträge zur evangelischen Theologie
Bib	*Biblica*
BJRL	*Bulletin of the John Rylands University Library of Manchester*
BK	Biblischer Kommentar
BLS	Bible and Literature Series
BZAW	Beihefte zur *Zeitschrift für die alttestamentliche Wissenschaft*
CBQ	*Catholic Biblical Quarterly*
DBSup	*Dictionnaire de la Bible, Supplément*
EA	*El-Amarna-Tafeln*
EB	Études bibliques
EncJud	*Encyclopaedia judaica* (1971)
ETL	*Ephemerides theologicae lovanienses*
EvT	*Evangelische Theologie*
EVV	English versions
FOTL	The Forms of the Old Testament Literature
FTL	Forum theologiae linguisticae
GBSOTS	Guides to Biblical Scholarship: Old Testament Series
HKAT	Handkommentar zum Alten Testament
HSM	Harvard Semitic Monographs
HTR	*Harvard Theological Review*
HUCA	*Hebrew Union College Annual*
IB	*The Interpreter's Bible*
ICC	International Critical Commentary
IDBSup	Supplementary Volume to *The Interpreter's Dictionary of the Bible*
Int	*Interpretation*
IRT	Issues in Religion and Theology
JAAR	*Journal of the American Academy of Religion*
JAOS	*Journal of the American Oriental Society*
JBL	*Journal of Biblical Literature*
JNES	*Journal of Near Eastern Studies*
JRAS	*Journal of the Royal Anthropological Society*
JSOT	*Journal for the Study of the Old Testament*

JSOTSup	Journal for the Study of the Old Testament—Supplement Series
JSS	*Journal of Semitic Studies*
JTS	*Journal of Theological Studies*
KUB	*Keilschrifturkunden aus Boghazkoi*
MVAG	Mitteilungen der vorder-asiatisch-ägyptischen Gesellschaft
ND	field numbers of tablets excavated at Nimrud
NTT	*Norsk teologisk tidsskrift*
OTL	The Old Testament Library
PRU	*Le Palais royal d'Ugarit*
RB	*Revue biblique*
RCA	*Royal Correspondence of the Assyrian Empire*, ed. L. Waterman
RGG	*Religion in Geschichte und Gegenwart*
RS	field numbers of tablets excavated at Ras Shamra
RSV	Revised Standard Version
SBB	Stuttgarter biblische Beiträge
SBLDS	Society of Biblical Literature Dissertation Series
SBLMS	Society of Biblical Literature Monograph Series
SBLSBS	Society of Biblical Literature Sources for Biblical Study
SBLSP	*Society of Biblical Literature Seminar Papers*
SBT	Studies in Biblical Theology
TBü	Theologische Bücherei
TDNT	*Theological Dictionary of the New Testament*, ed. G. Kittel and G. Friedrich
TLZ	*Theologische Literaturzeitung*
TRu	*Theologische Rundschau*
TUMSR	Trinity University Monograph Series in Religion
UUÅ	Uppsala universitetsårsskrift
VAB	Vorderasiatische Bibliothek
VT	*Vetus Testamentum*
VTSup	Vetus Testamentum, Supplements
WdF	Wege der Forschung
WMANT	Wissenschaftliche Monographien zum Alten und Neuen Testament
ZAW	*Zeitschrift für die alttestamentliche Wissenschaft*
ZRGG	*Zeitschrift für Religions- und Geistesgeschichte*
ZTK	*Zeitschrift für Theologie und Kirche*

Introduction:
Ways of Thinking about Israel's Prophets

DAVID L. PETERSEN

What is a prophet? This question recurs explicitly or implicitly throughout virtually all volumes and essays devoted to Israel's prophets. Moreover, the question is of importance to both the academic and the religious professional—whether the interest lies primarily in understanding the prophets in their own context or in appropriating the prophets for present application. Both parties have a stake in determining what was at the core of prophetic activity in ancient Israel.

It is perhaps not surprising that various definitions of prophets and prophecy have arisen. Typically, biblical prophets have been positively evaluated in Western society, and this positive assessment is usually articulated in a way that expresses something about a particular society. In late eighteenth-century Germany, prophets were understood to be romanticists, expressing the spirit of natural poetry. In nineteenth-century England and Holland, prophets were understood as sober rationalists expressing strict moralisms, and in the 1960s in the United States, prophets were often viewed as counterculture figures. Stated differently, the role of the prophet has been malleable in a manner that our understanding of other roles, for example, king and priest, has not. Each society in which prophets are read and pondered has tended to inject its own value structures and models when speaking about Israel's prophets.

This situation is no less true of the scholarly than the popular culture. In the scholarly discussions prophets have been understood as priests, charismatics, ecstatics, poets, theologians, politicians—the list could go on almost without limit. There are quite simply a myriad of ways to identify what it was to be a prophet, and the use of such models—whether the use is explicit or implicit—influences profoundly our understanding and appropriation of Israel's prophets.

1

   Concentrating a relatively brief volume of essays on the topic of Israelite prophecy is not an easy task. Such a volume must not only offer specific and important selections, but should establish as well, in the Introduction, the larger field of vision in order for the discrete selections to appear in sharper focus. Scholarship on prophecy has always been a vital and sizable element in Old Testament studies. With the explosion of academic publishing in the second half of the twentieth century, there has been a concomitant increase in books and articles devoted to things prophetic. Rather than attempting to survey and summarize all that has been published, it has become even more necessary to think critically, not simply historically or in a *Forschungsbericht* mentality, about prophecy in Israel.[1] What are the central issues that require study, and what have been the major advances in our understanding of prophetic phenomena? This volume is one contribution to the task of critical thinking. One of its hallmarks is the conviction that the essays provided herein are not so much comprehensive, that is, representing all that has been said, as influential and excellent, worth study and reflection.

   As a part of the task of reflecting critically about prophecy in Israel and at the risk of oversimplification, two questions that drive the study of Israelite prophecy must be raised: How does one think about the identity of the prophet, and how does one understand prophetic literature? Having made this statement, however, I must immediately moderate it and allow that certain topics in the study of prophecy do not fit neatly under either of these questions. By way of dealing with this analytical complexity, I suggest the use of the following map to help us understand what the issues are in the study of Israel's prophecy.

A Map for Scholarship on Israelite Prophecy

Prophetic Identity		*Prophetic Literature*
Models:	*General Issues:*	*Methods:*
1. religious experience	1. comparative perspectives	1. philology
2. speaker/writer	a. ancient Near East	2. form criticism
3. social/political context	b. anthropological data	3. redaction criticism
4. personal qualities	2. thematic traditions	4. literary criticism
5. intermediary message	3. theology of the prophets	5. rhetorical criticism
6. distinctive message	4. true vs. false prophecy	6. canonical criticism

   The essays in this volume deal essentially with the left side of this chart, that is to say, with the identity of the prophet. However, in order to set the context for the essays included here, I propose in this introduction to move from the literature, the right-hand side of the map, to the left, that is, the prophet.

I

The Hebrew Bible contains prophetic literature, not prophets. Hence it should not be surprising that rigorous and methodologically controlled work has been done on the prophetic texts. That is not, of course, to suggest that unanimity has been achieved on literary issues. In fact, the consensus on one of the methodological issues, form criticism, is not as cohesive now as it was ten years ago. Those who do research on the prophetic texts perform such work from a discrete variety of methodological perspectives. Sensitivity to the text as text is, however, a common denominator. I will now indicate precisely what these methods include.

It is fair, I think, to speak first of philological approaches to the text. Philology as it has been traditionally understood involves grammar, that is to say, morphology, phonology, syntax, lexicography, as well as text criticism. This work, as the ingenuity of commentators continually demonstrates, is never finished.[2] Moreover, new data provide the impetus for new solutions, as is clearly the case with recent study in the book of Jeremiah.[3]

Then, of course, various forms of higher criticism have been tremendously influential. Form criticism takes pride of place.[4] This is a literary method that has influenced profoundly one model for understanding the prophets, namely, the prophet as a person who produces literature. Form criticism of the prophetic literature is properly associated with the name of Hermann Gunkel. The genius of Gunkel, a key example of whose work appears here in English for the first time (chap. 1), was the ability to observe that the primary literary units of prophetic discourse were not book, chapter, and verse; nor were they lyric poems. They were instead short poems, created with considerable formal and stylistic variety. Moreover, Gunkel maintained that the prophets utilized forms of discourse that had been created and preserved in other sectors of the society, for example, the law court. The search for this original setting in life, the *Sitz im Leben*, became as essential a part of the form-critical enterprise as reading the prophetic texts themselves. Equally impressive in this regard was the search for the various types of forms to be found in the prophetic literature.

Much form-critical work in the post-Gunkel period crystallized in the influential synthesis of Claus Westermann.[5] Westermann was dissatisfied with earlier form-critical work since, in his judgment, it had not successfully delineated the central form of prophetic discourse. Westermann appealed to a "secular" text, Genesis 32, for the source of a formula that occurs there and in a number of prophetic texts: "Thus says Yahweh," the so-called messenger formula, a feature that Westermann claimed was paralleled in the Mari texts. The basic form of the messenger proclamation was, in Westermann's view, the so-called announcement of judgment which had two basic parts: the accusation, which delineated the reasons, and the announcement, which specified what would happen in the future. The essay by James Ross in this volume appeared only two years after Westermann's book was published in German and represents well the synthesis effected by Westermann. Ross maintained that if the prophets used the messenger formula, then it makes sense to consider the prophets not so much as authors or poets, as Gunkel had done, but as messengers of the deity. In this view the character of the prophetic literature as messages communicated by the prophet from the deity to an individual or to the people, and the identity of the prophet as messenger, are inextricably linked. Although the form-critical arguments of Westermann and Ross have been the subject of considerable criticism, their basic arguments—that the prophetic literature could be conceived as God's and not the prophet's words to society and that the prophets may be construed as messengers of the deity—are likely to remain as part of our vocabulary for some time to come.[6] Put another way, even if we reject the notion of the "This says Yahweh" formula as a messenger formula and reject the notion of all prophetic speech as messenger speeches, the notion that the prophets are communicating something from the deity seems more on than off target.

Although philological and form-critical work tend to atomize the prophetic literature, other more recently articulated approaches attempt to provide a more synthetic or holistic perspective: redaction criticism, literary criticism, rhetorical criticism, and canonical criticism.

Redaction criticism is a natural outgrowth of form criticism. If one argues that a book is made up of a series of originally disparate and independent short speeches, then at some point it becomes necessary to ask about the process of collecting and editing that resulted in the final form of the book. A related question was raised in its most vigorous form prior to the time of Gunkel by Bernhard Duhm. On metrical and other grounds, Duhm argued that certain texts in the prophetic books, especially Isaiah, do not represent the prophet's own words but were instead later additions.[7] For Duhm, and for others of his and ensuing periods, the judgment of certain prophetic texts as secondary rested on literary grounds: form and meter. Form-critical insights could weigh in here as well, though; if one identified a certain form as typical of a prophetic book and then discovered a second form, a critic would be inclined to identify that second and deviant material as secondary. However, redaction criticism, while specifying that certain materials in a text may be nongenuine, does not do so in a way that dismisses it. Redaction criticism at its best enables the student to identify various literary materials as strata that represent the prophetic word speaking to new and different contexts.[8] Redaction criticism does, however, presuppose the prior form-critical work.

Not so with the rest of the literary perspectives mentioned here. Literary criticism, rhetorical criticism, and canonical criticism may be integrally tied to the exegetical procedures I have just mentioned, though they need not be. Literary criticism of prose biblical texts has come into prominence in the last decade.[9] Similar forces are now at work on poetic texts. For example, attention to tropes such as metaphor, irony, and symbolism will materially assist the reader in attempting to understand prophetic texts.[10] Of similar importance is the work of rhetorical criticism. Though some rhetorical criticism is virtually identical to what we know as literary criticism (so the work of James Muilenburg), some work done under the rubric of rhetorical criticism really does represent an attempt to apply theories of rhetoric, classical and contemporary, to Hebrew Bible texts.[11] The work of Y. Gitay is particularly prominent in this regard.[12]

The reader of this introduction will have an opportunity in the next decade to observe the growing prominence of literary and rhetorical studies, and these studies will have a concomitant development on reflection concerning the identity of the prophet. The prophet will, no doubt, appear as poet and rhetorician, respectively.

On the literary side of the ledger one issue remains, the issue that has come to be described as canonical criticism.[13] There is some similarity between redactional and canonical perspectives, to the extent that both methods are interested in the final literary product. However, canonical criticism assesses the final, that is, canonical literary product, and, one might add, especially the theological significance of the literary process that has created the prophetic books. Brevard Childs encapsulates this process in the following way:

"Prophetic oracles which were directed to one generation were fashioned into sacred scripture by a canonical process to be used by another generation."[14] Childs provides an example of such a canonical perspective on prophetic literature in the following reflection on Deutero-Isaiah:

> Critical scholarship has made out a convincing case for dating chapters 40—55 . . . to the period of the Babylonian exile. Yet in their present canonical position these chapters have been consciously loosened from their original setting and placed within the context of the eighth century prophet, Isaiah of Jerusalem. Moreover, the original historical background of the exilic prophet has been drained of its historical particularity—Cyrus has become a theological construct almost indistinguishable from Abraham (cf. Kissane)—and the prophetic message has been rendered suitable for use by later generations by transmitting it as a purely eschatological word.[15]

On the basis of this quotation it should be clear that the focus of attention in canonical criticism is literary/theological. Moreover, this perspective, unlike that of formal literary criticism, has few direct implications for the other major questions in our discussion, namely, the identity of the prophet.

II

The middle ground of the map is made up of a variety of issues, some of which are related to both central questions—prophetic identity and prophetic literature—and several of which are more general in character. Comparative data, both from the ancient Near East and from societies examined by anthropologists, relate to both sides of our map. Cuneiform texts that portray prophetic individuals have informed our understanding of the identity of the prophet as well as the nature of prophetic literature.[16] Some of the individuals at ancient Mari were clearly part of the ritual establishment; others were not. Moreover, the texts themselves suggest that individual prophetic oracles or prophetic events could circulate independently. So, too, the neo-Assyrian oracles represent a variety of prophetic types.[17] In addition, the neo-Assyrian material is especially important in regard to the literary question since it is there, and not in the Mari texts, that we find collections of oracles. Analysis of these collections when they become readily available will facilitate considerably the work of redaction criticism. Not dissimilarly, the recently published Deir 'Alla inscriptions describing the activity of Balaam, son of Be'or, will also be of significant value for the redaction-critical enterprise. This text provides a simple narrative in which Balaam's oracles and visions are re-counted for the population. As a result of the Mari letters, the neo-Assyrian oracles, and the Balaam texts, our knowledge of both the prophet's identity and the prophetic literature has been materially enhanced.

In this volume the comparative Near Eastern material is prom-inent in two ways. The essay of Ross (chap. 4) has incorporated the Mari evidence as part of this endeavor to describe the identity of the prophet as a messenger. Moreover, John Holladay (chap. 5) introduces nonprophetic material, evidence of ancient Near Eastern diplomatic practice and royal protocol, in order to specify the role of the prophet as herald and to locate the activity of that herald in a covenant-style context.

Evidence garnered from anthropological reports entails a second way of dealing with Israelite prophecy. The work of Robert Wilson, Burke Long, and Thomas Overholt is exemplary here.[18] Wilson's book emphasizes several important ways in which intermediaries may have functioned in ancient Israel. With anthropological studies providing some control for such categories as peripheral and central intermediation, Wilson maintains that these categories may be used fruitfully to analyze Israelite prophetic behavior. Such analysis enables Wilson to identify several different forms of intermediation in Israel. Works like this one point us in the direction of the identity of the prophet.

Anthropological perspectives, however, can point to the other side of the ledger as well, that is, the literary question. After reflecting on the issues of power and legitimacy and legitimating the role of an intermediary, Long points out that the so-called prophetic call narratives are not to be read as accounts that buttress a prophet's position in a concrete social conflict. Rather, he contends, on the basis of anthropological material, that the authority of the prophet is proved in acts rather than through more general assertions of power or authority. Hence, "the vocational accounts of Isaiah, Jeremiah, and Ezekiel are balanced presentations of reflective material far removed from direct conflict and any immediate need to justify. They function most directly in relation to the edited form of the book."[19] Here the anthropological perspectives provide signifi-cant interpretive guidelines in the understanding of the prophetic literature in its final literary form.

Another important aspect of the prophetic literature is the origi-nal context in which it was recorded. Overholt has dealt incisively with this issue, "The Sociology of Story Telling," in *Prophecy in Cross-Cultural Perspectives*,[20] which provides considerable insight concerning the points of origin, both oral and literary, of the prophetic literature as well as the final form of the text.

In sum, both the comparative ancient Near Eastern work and the anthropological treatments of Israelite prophecy help us gain significant leverage as we reflect on the two critical questions of our map: what is the identity of the prophet, and how are we to understand the makeup of Israelite prophetic literature?

The situation with the other three topics in the central part of our map is considerably different. These three issues—thematic traditions, theology of the prophets, true versus false prophecy— are more conceptual and, especially the last two, less open to definition by particular method or perspective. First, the method of studying thematic traditions.[21] Here we may be rather brief since there are two quintessentially representative works. In 1956, Edzard Rohland completed a dissertation at Heidelberg which demonstrated the importance of delineating specific theological traditions, the election traditions, in the various prophetic books.[22] It was this perspective that influenced materially the magisterial treatment of prophets by Gerhard von Rad.[23] Von Rad argued that one incisive way to study the prophets, to think about the prophets, was to construe them as conservators of discrete religious, and for that matter, political traditions.[24] Isaiah, a parade example, is best read from the perspective of the Zion and David traditions, which we know elsewhere in the Bible through the so-called Zion psalms. This was a way of looking at the prophets that emphasized not so much their creativity as their dialectical relationship to tradition. The prophets updated the religious heritage of Israel for a new time. If form critics emphasize certain rhetorical givens in the prophetic literature, historians of themes and traditions emphasize certain theological givens, though neither form critics nor tradition historians deny the freedom and creativity used by the prophets. The traditio-historical impulse has worked itself out in a variety of ways, most notably in the commentaries of Hans Walter Wolff on Hosea, Joel, and Amos.[25]

The penultimate topic in the middle of the map is the theology or thought of the prophets. There are many treatments of the thought of the prophets from a comprehensive theological or thematic perspective, the most successful of which have typically proceeded in historical fashion outlining the notions of Amos, Hosea, Isaiah, and those following. One of the decisive variables in such volumes is the extent to which the prophets are perceived as creative theologians and innovative thinkers, or the extent to which they are perceived as preserving and conserving earlier Israelite traditions. Works as old as those of Julius Wellhausen and as new as Klaus Koch's recent two-volume work have emphasized the theological creativity of the prophets.[26] The work of von Rad mentioned earlier represents something of a middle ground. On the far side of the sheet, one would include work that argues that the prophets are covenant spokesmen, essentially conservators of a given theological tradition, that of the covenant.

Traditio-historical and form-critical insights have played a significant role in these theological discussions. As we have seen, von Rad was able to chart certain theological traditions throughout the prophetic books, and form critics have argued that certain elements of covenantal theology appear prominently in the prophetic rhetoric. Whether or not the prophets were theologians—and it is probably an anachronism to maintain that they were in the contemporary sense of that term—they did use language about the deity, and we are, therefore, likely to continue to hear about the theology of the prophets.

Another and final conceptual issue that belongs in the middle of our map is often referred to as true versus false prophecy. Approaches to this topic have varied considerably, although most typically it has been addressed in theological terms. More so than perhaps any other topic broached in this Introduction, the topic of true versus false prophecy is less methodologically controlled and more open to the theological predilections or creative insights of the contemporary interpreter. It is, therefore, no accident that von Rad defined false prophecy in a way consistent with his notion of what true prophecy involved. False prophets were false for him because they did not perceive how Yahweh was active in the historical scene, whereas true prophets, though informed by the older traditions, perceived Yahweh as doing a new thing.[27]

Such formulations, however, exist at a fairly high level of generality, and the issue of false prophecy for Israel was hardly a general problem. If someone spoke as a prophet, should that person be heeded, and if two prophets spoke and disagreed, which of those two should be obeyed? This is one of the fundamental problems that is subsumed under the larger rubric of true versus false prophecy. G. Quell, to his credit, maintained that there was no easy or single way for an observer of prophetic performance to determine whether or not the prophet should be believed; it is therefore not surprising that in his recent survey of research on the matter, P. Neumann concludes: "There are no absolute criteria for judging true and false prophecy."[28] This remains as true for us, in attempting to decide which prophets of Israel should have been believed, as it was for ancient Israelites when they wrestled with the same question.

The language of true versus false prophecy is, of course, not language of the Hebrew Bible. The book of Deuteronomy spoke negatively about prophets that should be put to death or prophets that should not be feared (Deut. 18:15–22). 1 Kings 22 and Jer. 23:16–17 also speak negatively about certain prophets, but there is great variety in the negatively assessed prophets, just as there is in the positively assessed prophets of ancient Israel. One senses that conflict between prophets was a given within prophetic behavior. Because of the rhetorical claims of prophets, that is, the claims that they spoke the word of God, there was no easy way to adjudicate differing prophetic messages. Moreover, prophetic conflict might not always be easily reducible to true versus false prophecy but might also manifest itself as true versus true or false versus false prophecy. In sum, the matter of true versus false prophecy is a difficult issue.[29]

III

We are now able to turn to the central question that provides the primary focus for this volume: What is a prophet? The very vocabulary scholars have used to articulate this question has served to muddy rather than clarify the waters. For example, it has been a commonplace to speak of the prophetic institution or office, as if the notions of institution or office offer significant explanatory power. I have argued elsewhere that we should speak more discretely of the role(s) of the prophet, the more so since that vocabulary has been refined considerably by social scientists.[30] The category "role" has analytical significance in a way the terms of "office" or "institution" simply do not. It is therefore imperative that we choose carefully the analytical categories we use to define essential features of Israelite prophecy.

The essays in this volume either express or stand in dialogue with some of the important and influential positions on the identity of the prophet. In my judgment, there are at least six such positions that have been influential in the twentieth-century critical discussion of prophecy.

1. *The prophet is a person who has had a special sort of religious experience and/or a special sort of relationship to the deity.* This notion has worked itself out in a variety of ways. The most influential early proponents of this view were Hermann Gunkel and Gustav Hölscher. Gunkel published several versions of his view,

the first appearing in 1903.[31] He maintained that the prophets had had certain peculiar, usually private or inner, experiences in which the deity was revealed to them. These experiences were, in theory, hidden from others, but they could involve certain external behaviour manifestations. Gunkel used the term ecstasy to describe this experience, and this term has remained prominent in discussions of prophetic behavior to this day. In his most thoroughly worked out presentation of this thesis, Gunkel was able to refer to the work of Hölscher in maintaining that ecstasy was a phenomenon attested outside Israel. However, it is important to recognize that Gunkel was using the vocabulary of ecstasy prior to Hölscher's influential work.

Hölscher, influenced as he was by the writings of Wilhelm Wundt, maintained that the key to understanding Israel's prophets was to place them within the context of a certain type of behavior, namely, ecstasy.[32] However, this was not simply a comparative perspective; it was genetic as well. Hölscher argued that Israel inherited this form of religious activity from the Syro-Palestinian cultures with which they came in contact when they entered that region.

Probably the most influential version of this approach, which views prophecy as an especially intense form of religious behaviour, has been that of Johannes Lindblom. As did Hölscher, Lindblom noted affinities between the experiences of Israel's prophets and certain individuals who have "supernormal experiences." Lindblom's work is truly comparative, adducing evidence from cultures with which Israel was not in contact. As a result, Lindblom defines the prophet as:

> . . . a person who, because he is conscious of having been specially chosen and called, feels forced to perform actions and proclaim ideas which, in a mental state of intense inspiration or real ecstasy, have been indicated to him in the form of divine revelations.[33]

Recently Robert Wilson has helped refine the language of inspiration and/or ecstasy on the basis of an assessment of data gathered and analyzed by anthropologists.[34] He has contended that it is more appropriate to speak of possession behavior than of ecstasy. The emphasis here is on observable, that is, studied behavior, and not inner or secret experiences as advocated by Gunkel.

Serious questions have been raised, however, about whether possession behavior is a common denominator for prophetic behavior. One must ask if it is an essential feature or simply one thing an Israelite prophet could do. There is much that Israel's prophets did that does not seem to fall within this general range of behavior.[35]

2. *The prophet is a person who speaks or writes in a distinctive way.* Here the focus of attention is on literature attributed to the prophets, much of it, of course, poetic. Attention to Old Testament poetic literature has, perforce, had an impact on notions of prophecy; note especially the influential work of Johann Gottfried Herder.[36] However, it was the incisive analysis of Gunkel, translated and included in this volume, which sparked a mode of inquiry that continues in a vital fashion today. Gunkel maintained that the prophets are to be understood, at least initially, as speakers, not writers. Their speeches were short. Some, namely the oracles against non-Israelite nations, appear to describe future actions. These oracles against the nations Gunkel took to be original with the prophets. However, most other speeches represent the utilization by the prophets of a way of discoursing that had been borrowed from another social context, that is, another *Sitz im Leben*: the cult, law court, school, family institution, et al. Hence part of the literary-historical task involved identifying the limits of discrete speeches that populate the prophetic books and identifying their genres.

This was only part of the task, however. Gunkel was also interested in the evolution of the prophetic literature, how it moved from short speeches to short collections and then to the prophetic books with which we are confronted today. It is not too much to suggest that this one essay presents the birth of what we know today as form and redaction criticism. This line of inquiry established by Gunkel has been pursued by any number of scholars. It is a style of research that populates virtually all of the recent commentaries on prophetic books and that will appear as the raison d'être for the forthcoming FOTL treatments of the prophetic books.

The form-critical effort, depending as it does on essentially literary observations, has, following the lead of Gunkel in this seminal piece, led to two different but related pictures of the prophet: the speaker and the writer. Gunkel's use of this distinction, that is, speaker become writer, betrays his evolutionary bias; long and complex literature is the result of a writing rather than a speaking process. Since the time of Gunkel much has been learned about oral literature and the process of its composition, so much so that we are also able to think about the prophets in the role of either speaker or writer when they compose something other than the very briefest oracle.[37] Nonetheless, Gunkel's emphasis on the prophets as significant creators of literature, whether oral or written, remains fundamentally important.

3. *The prophet is a person who acts as a prophet in a particular social setting.* This notion initially grew directly out of form-critical observations and, in the current discussion, may be traced to the vigorous logic of Sigmund Mowinckel.[38] Mowinckel thought Gunkel had correctly identified much stereotypic discourse in the prophetic literature. Moreover, Gunkel had, in another essay, identified so-called prophetic elements in the psalms.[39] Mowinckel maintained, in the study translated here for the first time into English (chap. 2), that Gunkel had not pursued consistently the lines of research that he himself had established. What Gunkel had thought of as a literary relationship was, for Mowinckel, cultic reality. Mowinckel contended that the prophets did not simply borrow cultic speech; the prophets were in fact cultic officials, active as priests in a primary institution of Israel's society, the temple.

Mowinckel's studies sparked what has come to be known as the cultic prophecy thesis, a way of looking at the prophets that has been influential, especially in Scandinavia and Great Britain. In this vein, A. Johnson, among others, has argued that prophets were personnel of the Israelite cultus.[40] In surveys of scholarship on Israelite prophecy, cultic prophecy is often treated as a discrete topic and yet, of course, it is not. The notion of cultic prophecy provides one of several possible answers to the question: In which Israelite social institution did the prophets work, if they worked in such an institution?

Other answers suggest that the prophets were active within the royal institution. Frank Cross's model of the early activity of the prophet pictures the prophet involved in war, in designating kings, and in providing judgment upon royal individuals.[41] Moreover, the article by Holladay included in this volume emphasizes the political-religious reality in which certain of the classical prophets acted. Holladay maintains that these particular prophets were heralds whose action was substantively affected by political modes of behavior in the ancient Near East, especially neo-Assyrian models. This way of looking at the prophets, namely, that of Cross, Holladay, and others, provides a different model, a political one, rather than the model of the cultic prophet, which locates prophetic activity in the ritual sphere.[42] Both theses find adherents today, and the issue of the social context in which the prophet acts is one that generates much discussion.[43]

4. *The prophet is a person who possesses distinctive personal quali-*

ties, namely, charisma. This model sounds at first blush to be psychological. However, Max Weber, whom we may consider responsible for the powerful articulation of this notion, was speaking in a distinctly sociological vein. Weber, when outlining his various notions of authority, spoke of traditional, bureaucratic, and prophetic types. Prophetic authority involves the articulation of certain personal leadership characteristics that eventuate in the individual's attracting a following. Put another way, charisma is attested by the presence of a group around the putative charismatic individual or prophet. The prophet so defined is presented in Weber's widely influential presentation (chap. 3 in this volume). The clear implication of Weber's programmatic statement is that the prophet will not work out his charisma within the context of either a traditional institution, for example, a family, or a bureaucratic institution, the temple. Hence it would be difficult to contemplate using Weber's notion of the prophet together with the notion of the cultic prophet as understood by Mowinckel.[44]

Weber's work, of course, depended upon the Hebrew Bible scholarship of his time. Needless to say, the arguments of Mowinckel and others had a profound impact upon ensuing scholarship by pointing to at least one institutional context, the cult, in which the prophets were active. P. Berger, a sociologist who was cognizant of the implications of Mowinckel's insights, recognized that the analysis of Weber stood in need of refinement.[45] If prophets could be related integrally to certain social institutions of ancient Israel, then to define them, as Weber had, in a way that would preclude their participation, as prophets, in either traditional or bureaucratic authority structures was simply illegitimate. Hence, Berger noted that, although the model of charismatic authority was potentially useful as an ideal type, it should not be viewed as a historical statement about Israel's prophets.[46]

The critical issue, of course, is whether or not charisma, in Weber's understanding, is applicable to those whom we normally term prophets. Dorothy Emmett has, in my judgment, provided an incisive statement:

> Weber, we have seen, connects charismatic authority particularly with the kind of people he calls prophets. But if we are to follow him and define a prophet as a person who binds his followers into personal allegiance to himself as bearer of some mission or new revelation, then we shall surely need some other name for other types of inspirational leadership which do not follow this pattern. Moreover, we should have to restrict the notion of prophet to a type of messianic or millenarian preacher or religious revolutionary. This would be to deny it to many of

the kinds of people who are generally known as prophets—the Hebrew prophets, for instance—and this would seem unnatural.[47]

The key issue here is the existence of a group of followers around a putative prophet. Such a group is attested in the case of Elisha, "the sons of the prophets" (e.g., 2 Kings 4:38). And there is some indication of such a group in Isa. 8:16, "Bind up the testimony, seal the teaching among my disciples." But apart from this limited evidence, there is little warrant for arguing that Israel's prophets exercised charismatic authority through the creation of a disciple band.[48]

5. *The prophet is an intermediary between the divine and human worlds.* This notion of the role of the prophet is articulated in a variety of ways and has been argued from a variety of perspectives. I note three such arguments here. First, the brief though seminal essay by Ross included here represents the form-critical method and its implications. The clause, "Thus says Yahweh," had been identified as the messenger formula by Köhler.[49] It was not a major leap to argue that the prophets as ones who use the messenger formula were themselves messengers. Ross then argued that the source of the prophetic authority was the deity and the divine council from which the prophets were sent as messengers. Now, although some legitimate questions have been raised about the warrant for describing "Thus says Yahweh" as the messenger formula, the notion of the prophet as messenger, one who conveys the deity's message to the human world, has remained significant in the critical discussion of the work of the prophet.

A second and more specialized notion of the intermediary role is that of the mediator. This view received powerful articulation in the essay of Muilenburg and reflects essentially traditio-historical concerns.[50] By focusing on Northern traditions, especially those embedded in the Deuteronomic history and those associated with the figure of Moses, Muilenburg was able to link the prophetic role as messenger with one of the theological traditions in Israel, the covenant. Hence Moses, and for that matter other people, could be appelled "covenant mediators," individuals who represented the covenant demands to the people from the perspective of the deity. Here, too, the prophets stood between the human and the divine realms. For Muilenburg, to say that the prophet was a covenant mediator was to refine, not to deny, the assertion that Israel's prophets were Yahweh's messengers. This view has been very influential. However, as Wilson has recognized, this picture of the prophet is especially prominent in the Northern or Ephraimitic tradition.[51] Hence, one must take seriously the notion of geographic variation: the conception of prophet in Israel and that in Judah. Prophets as covenant mediators in the Mosaic model are, according to Wilson, more applicable to Israel than to Judahite prophets, and another model may be more important for that Southern sphere.[52]

A third way of analyzing the prophets as those who stand between human and divine realms is offered by the anthropological materials, especially as these data have been adduced by Robert Wilson. To think about the prophets is to think about a class of people in various societies who may be viewed as standing between the deity and human beings. These individuals are, in Wilson's judgment, best understood as intermediaries, a rather general term that allows for different forms of intermediation within it. Use of this notion enables Wilson to adduce evidence not only from the Near East but from the full history of human culture, including modern society.

It would give a false impression of agreement to suggest that Ross, Muilenburg, and Wilson's positions are fundamentally alike. Nonetheless, all three of these positions do share the supposition that prophets are individuals with the role of standing between the divine and the human, usually communicating something from the divine to the human realm, whether word or perspective.

6. *The prophet is a person who has a distinctive message.* This category is almost a logical corollary to the notion of the prophet as messenger. If one subscribes to the view of the prophet as messenger, one naturally asks: What messages did these prophets articulate? Were there discrete words or perspectives the individual prophets had to offer, or was there an overarching message or several prominent themes common to all prophets? The latter question has been answered affirmatively by worthy proponents. Wellhausen's contention that the prophets instigated the inception of ethical monotheism is a notable example. The problem with this approach, of course, is that the attempt to find a common denominator often eventuates in the identification of a lowest common denominator, that is, a vague statement about prophets and God.

James Mays' essay (chap. 6) is a more concrete attempt to delineate one theme that many of Israel's prophets share, though the data here are garnered from eighth-century Judahite prophets: Amos, Micah, and Isaiah. The essay is forceful, however, since it moves beyond the specific statement, Amos on justice, but remains less general than all prophets on justice. This sort of middle-range thematic approach is one way of moving beyond single-figure descriptions without attempting to find one element common to all prophets. Including this type of essay is especially important. If we construe the prophets as messengers or intermediaries, we must ask at some point about the content of the message of the Yahwistic intermediaries. These messengers, at least the ones assessed by Mays, do have a message. The reader of this volume is invited to engage in a similar exercise as regards other Israelite prophets to determine whether the theme that Mays highlights in eighth-century prophets is an essential feature of other prophetic literature as well.

Having surveyed these six rather distinct models of what it is to be a prophet, we need to admit that it is unlikely that we will ever achieve consensus on a single notion on the nature of prophecy. This is, of course, not to deny the importance of highlighting certain motifs: for example, the notion of prophet as herald. Nonetheless, because of the complexity of the prophetic roles in ancient Israel, attempting to identify individuals as prophets in our own time—especially if this identification presumes one fundamental feature, for example, spokesperson for social justice, or messenger—is risky indeed. Moreover, it is equally risky for individuals today, especially those within religious communities, to select *the* prophetic role as something to emulate, since that role in ancient Israel entailed such significant variety. Hence, it is not appropriate to think about *being* a prophet. One should rather speak of having a prophetic perspective, or better, of having one prophetic perspective.

The final essay in this volume, that by Gene M. Tucker (chap. 7), provides a similar sort of caveat. He warns against simplistic or one-sided notions of prophecy in ancient Israel. But—and this is why the essay is especially helpful—this caveat does not prevent Tucker from highlighting certain ways in which the prophets and their message can be understood and appropriated by those working out of the context of the religious communities, church, and synagogue, institutions that continue to preserve, as uniquely authoritative, the prophets' words and the memory of the prophets.

This volume will have served its purpose if the reader has felt the force of the classical positions of Gunkel, Mowinckel, and Weber, if the reader has understood the way in which Ross's and Holladay's essays contribute to our understanding of one model for the prophetic identity, if the reader takes Mays' essay as an occasion to reflect on what it might be to speak of a prophetic message that is larger than the message of one prophet, and finally, after having read Tucker's article, to ask again the question: What is central in

Israelite prophecy, and what might it be to think or act from a prophetic perspective in one's own time?

NOTES

1 Cf. G. Fohrer's *Forschungsberichte* which have been published in *TRU*. I sense that it is no longer possible to write a coherent and truly comprehensive essay in this style.

2 For a recent example of a thoroughgoing philological approach to a prophetic book, see F. Andersen and D. Freedman, *Hosea* (AB 24; Garden City, N.Y.: Doubleday & Co., 1983).

3 The Dead Sea scrolls have provided major impetus for text- and redaction-critical work on Jeremiah, e.g., E. Tov, "Some Aspects of the Textual and Literary History of the Book of Jeremiah," *Le Livre de Jérémie: Le prophète et son milieu, Les oracles et leur transmission* (BETL 54; ed. P.-M. Bogaert; Leuven: Leuven University, 1981) 145–67.

4 The works of J. Hayes (1973), W. E. March (1974), and G. Tucker (1978), as cited in the bibliography, present excellent overviews of this method as applied to the prophetic literature. The articles of N. Habel (1965), H. Huffmon (1959), and A. Rofé (1970), listed in the bibliography, are classical form-critical statements.

5 C. Westermann, *Basic Forms of Prophetic Speech* (Philadelphia: Westminster Press, 1967).

6 See the incisive analysis of the form-critical warrant for the use of the category "messenger" by R. Wilson, "Form Critical Investigation of the Prophetic Literature: The Present Situation," *SBLSP 1973*, (ed. G. MacRae; Cambridge, Mass.: Society of Biblical Literature, 1973) 1:100–21.

7 B. Duhm, *Das Buch Jesaja*, (HKAT; Göttingen: Vandenhoeck & Ruprecht, 1892; 5th ed., 1968).

8 Three eminent examples may serve to exemplify the redaction-critical method: H. Barth, *Die Jesaja-Worte in der Josiazeit: Israel und Assur als Thema einer produktiven Neuinterpretation der Jesajaüberlieferung* (WMANT 48; Neukirchen-Vluyn: Neukirchener Verlag, 1977); J. Vermeylen. *Du prophète Isaie à l'apocalyptique: Isaie, 1–35, miroir d'un demi-millénaire d'expérience religieuse en Israel*, 2 vols. (EB; Paris: Gabalda, 1973, 1978); W. Zimmerli, *Ezekiel*, 2 vols. (Hermeneia; Philadelphia: Fortress Press, 1979, 1983).

9 See, e.g., R. Alter, *The Art of Biblical Narrative* (New York: Basic Books, 1971); A. Berlin, *Poetics and Interpretation of Biblical Narrative* (BLS; Sheffield: Almond Press, 1983).

10 The recent commentary by M. Greenberg, *Ezekiel 1—20* (AB 22; Garden City, N.Y.: Doubleday & Co., 1983), represents work in this direction.

11 J. Muilenburg's theoretical statement is best exemplified in "Form Criticism and Beyond," *JBL* 88 (1969) 1–19; and well worked out in his contribution to *The Interpreter's Bible*, "The Book of Isaiah, ch. 40—66," *IB* 5 (Nashville: Abingdon Press, 1956) 381–773.

12 Y. Gitay, *Prophecy and Persuasion: A Study of Isaiah 40—48* (FTL 14; Bonn: Lingustica Biblica, 1981).

13 See, for an introductory statement, J. Sanders, *Canon and Community: A Guide to Canonical Criticism* (GBSOTS; Philadelphia: Fortress Press, 1984).

14 B. Childs, "The Canonical Shape of the Prophetic Literature," *Int* 32 (1978) 47.

15 Ibid., 50.

16 See the bibliography for works of F. Ellermeier (1968), H. Huffmon (1968), W. Moran (1969), and R. Wilson (1980, 98–110) for a presentation of the Mari evidence and an assessment of its importance for the study of Israelite prophecy.

17 See Wilson's (1980) survey of the neo-Assyrian material, pp. 111–19.

18 See the works by those authors as cited in the bibliography.

19 So B. Long, "Prophetic Authority as Social Reality," in *Canon and Authority*, (ed. G. Coats and B. Long; Philadelphia: Fortress Press, 1977) 11.

20 T. Overholt, *Prophecy in Cross-Cultural Perspective: A Sourcebook for Biblical Researchers* (SBLSBS; Atlanta: Scholars Press, 1986).

21 On this method, see D. Knight, *Rediscovering the Traditions of Israel: The Development of the Traditio-Historical Research of the Old Testament, with Special Consideration of Scandinavian Contributions* (SBLDS 9; Missoula, Mont: Scholars Press, 1975).

22 E. Rohland, "Die Bedeutung der Erwählungstraditionen Israels für die Eschatologie der alttestamentlichen Propheten" (Diss. Heidelberg, 1956).

23 G. von Rad, *Old Testament Theology*, vol. 2 (New York: Harper & Row, 1965).

24 G. Fohrer, "Remarks on Modern Interpretation of the Prophets," *JBL* 80 (1961) 309–19, argued vigorously against this notion.

25 All these, which originally appeared in German, have been translated into English: *Hosea* (Hermeneia; Philadelphia: Fortress Press, 1974); *Joel and Amos* (Hermeneia; Philadelphia: Fortress Press, 1977). See also the excellent traditio-historical work in W. Zimmerli, *The Law and the Prophets: A Study of the Meaning of the Old Testament* (New York: Harper & Row, 1963; and his "Prophetic Proclamation and Reinterpretation," in *Tradition and Theology in the Old Testament* (ed. D. Knight; Philadelphia: Fortress Press; London: SPCK, 1977) 69–100.

26 Despite the prominence of the phrase "ethical monotheism" in connection with prophets as well as Wellhausen's notion that the prophets represented a towering and creative movement in Israelite religion, Wellhausen's work has not been influential in the study of Israelite prophecy. For a brief statement of Wellhausen on Israel's prophets, see, e.g., *Prolegomena to the History of Ancient Israel*. (Cleveland: Meridian, 1957) 397–99. K. Koch, *The Prophets*, vol. 1: *The Assyrian Period*, vol. 2: *The Babylonian and Persian Periods* (Philadelphia: Fortress Press, 1983, 1984).

27 G. von Rad, "Die falschen Propheten," *ZAW* 51 (1933) 109–20.

28 G. Quell, *Wahre und falsche Propheten* (Gütersloh: Bertelmann, 1952); P. Neumann, *Das Prophetenverständnis in der deutschsprachigen Forschung seit Heinrich Ewald* (WdF 307; Darmstadt: Wissenschaftliche Buchgesellschaft, 1979) 39.

29 J. Crenshaw, *Prophetic Conflict: Its Effect upon Israelite Religion* (BZAW 124;

Berlin: Walter de Gruyter, 1971); and more recently, R. Wilson, *Sociological Approaches to the Old Testament* (Philadelphia: Fortress Press, 1984) 67–80.

30 D. Petersen, *The Roles of Israel's Prophets* (JSOTSup 17; Sheffield: JSOT, 1981).

31 H. Gunkel, "Die geheimen Erfahrungen der Propheten Israels: Eine religionspsychologische Studie," *Das Suchen der Zeit: Blätter Deutscher Zukunft* 1 (1903) 112–53.

32 G. Hölscher, *Die Profeten: Untersuchungen zur Religionsgeschichte Israels* (Leipzig: J. Hinrichs, 1914), as influenced by W. Wundt, *Völkerpsychologie: Eine Untersuchung der Entwicklungsgesetze von Sprache, Mythus und Sitte* (2nd ed.; Leipzig: W. Engelmann, 1904–1908).

33 J. Lindblom, *Prophecy in Ancient Israel* (Philadelphia: Fortress Press, 1962).

34 R. Wilson, *Prophecy and Society in Ancient Israel* (Philadelphia: Fortress Press, 1980) 46.

35 So S. Parker, "Possession Trance and Prophecy in Pre-Exilic Israel, *VT* 28 (1978) 271–85; D. Petersen, *The Roles of Israel's Prophets*, 25–30.

36 J. G. Herder, *The Spirit of Hebrew Poetry*, 2 vols. (Burlington, Va.: E. Smith, 1833; originally published 1782–83).

37 So A. B. Lord, *The Singer of Tales* (New York: Atheneum, 1968).

38 This work is best exemplified by S. Mowinckel, *Psalmenstudien* (Kristiana: Jacob Dybwad, 1921–24).

39 This study, originally published in *RGG*, has been translated and is available as H. Gunkel, *The Psalms: A Form-Critical Introduction* (Facet Books, Biblical Series, 19; Philadelphia: Fortress Press, 1967).

40 A. Johnson, *The Cultic Prophet in Ancient Israel* (Cardiff: University of Wales, 1962).

41 F. Cross, *Canaanite Myth and Hebrew Epic* (Cambridge: Harvard Univ. Press, 1973) 223–29.

42 Recent work addressing the political role of individual prophets includes: W. Dietrich, *Jesaja und die Politik* (BEvT 74; Munich: Kaiser, 1976); B. Lang, *Kein Aufstand in Jerusalem: Die Politik des Propheten Ezechiel* (SBB; Stuttgart: Katholisches Bibelwerk, 1978).

43 There are, of course, those who maintain that something inherent in the prophetic role prevents any enactment of that role in social institutions; so H. Gross, "Gab es in Israel 'ein prophetisches Amt'?" *ETL* 41 (1965) 5–19.

44 The relation of Weber's notion of the prophet as an ideal type, as this is explored in his *Sociology of Religion*, to his comments on Israel's prophets in *Ancient Judaism* (Glencoe, Ill.: Free Press, 1952; originally published in German in 1917–19) is not always clear. For a discussion of this issue, see F. Raphaël, "Max Weber et le judaisme antique," *Archives européenes de sociologie* 11 (1971) 297–336, especially 309–18; D. Petersen, "Max Weber and the Sociological Study of Ancient Israel," *Religious Change and Continuity*, ed. H. Johnson (San Francisco: Jossey-Bass, 1979) 117–49; B. Lang, "Max Weber und Israels Propheten," *ZRGG* 36 (1984) 156–65.

45 P. Berger, "Charisma and Religious Innovation: The Social Location of Israelite Prophecy," *ASR* 28 (1963) 940–50.

46 Berger has been criticized by J. Williams, "The Social Location of Israelite Prophecy," *JAAR* 37 (1969) 153–65, for overemphasizing the importance of prophetic institutional performance within Hebrew Bible scholarship.

47 D. Emmett, "Prophets and their Societies," *JRAS* 86 (1956) 16.

48 A. Malamat has maintained that Weber's notion of charismatic authority is attested in the activity of the judges; "Charismatic leadership in the Book of Judges," *Magnalia Dei: The Mighty Acts of God: Essays on the Bible and Archaeology in Memory of G. Ernest Wright*, ed. F. Cross et al. (Garden City, N.Y.: Doubleday, 1976) 152–68.

49 L. Köhler, "Der Botenspruch," *Kleine Lichter* (Zwingli Bücherei, 47; Zürich: Zwingli, 1945) 13–17.

50 J. Muilenburg, "The 'Office' of the Prophet in Ancient Israel," *The Bible in Modern Scholarship*, ed. J. Hyatt (Nashville: Abingdon Press, 1967) 74–97.

51 For R. Wilson's assessment of the Northern traditions, see *Prophecy and Society in Ancient Israel*, 135–252.

52 So D. Petersen, *The Roles of Israel's Prophets*, 70–88.

1

*The Prophets as Writers and Poets**

HERMANN GUNKEL

I

The first question that must be asked when examining an ancient writing in a literary, historical way concerns the genre of the writing. Perhaps the modern reader will be surprised that we place this task at the beginning. Therefore we need to explain why this problem is the initial and basic one and why recognizing that it is causes difficulties for contemporary interpretation. In treating modern literature one deals predominately with outstanding individual poets and writers. A discussion of the persons who are writing seems so important that literary history, at its height, takes the form of biography. Thus literary history of the German classical period is basically concerned with studying the great classical authors, principally Goethe. That those authors themselves made use of certain genres that had developed before they came along is so obvious that it is scarcely considered. Literary history is not written for someone who is so unlearned as to be unable to distinguish between drama and narrative or between historical narrative and a novel. In addition, the genres that once existed have been so obscured in the poetry of modern peoples that in many cases it is senseless to distinguish them. But the matter is quite different with ancient writings like those of Israel. Here there are many genres that are completely unknown to modern readers initially—genres to which modern readers can become accustomed only with a great deal of difficulty. This is especially true of the prophets, who have scarcely any parallel in contemporary literature and whose style of speaking is thus at first completely foreign to us. Moreover, we must further recognize that genres played a far greater role in the literature of an ancient people than they do today, and that in antiquity the

*First published in *Die Propheten* by H. Gunkel (1923) 34–70. Translated by James L. Schaaf.

22

individual author-personalities, which are or appear to dominate modern literature, recede into the background in a manner that is initially strange to us. This phenomenon has its foundation in the characteristics of the intellectual life of ancient culture. At that time individuals were more bound by custom and much less distinguishable from one another than they are today. Ancient customs that guided the life of the individual in prescribed paths also controlled the poet and the writer. Writers chose as their material that with which they were otherwise occupied, and they talked about it in the "style" that had long been traditional; that is, they spoke about it in the genres that had been implanted in them from their youth and that appeared to them to be the natural expression of their thought and sensitivity. And they were more bound to the style than to the thought. Even when they were able to think and utter something new, they were still bound to the traditional forms of expressing it. Out of this situation comes what is for us the strange monotony dominating such genres. As a result, the prophetic writings have surprising similarities to one another. For example, we can insert passages from Isaiah into Amos or Micah, and no one but the specialist will notice. Moreover, the sorts of speeches that spring from lesser intellects are often related so closely that frequently no individual peculiarity is apparent at all. Now, to be sure, ancient Israel also had great writers with personal—indeed the most personal—characteristics. That it did produce such authors makes it famous among the peoples of the ancient Orient. And among them the most original were surely some of the prophets. Here in Israel something characteristic took place which was unknown elsewhere in the Orient: the individual came to the fore. Powerful personalities arose, grasped by the storms of the age, trembling with passion, who, touched by the divinity in secret hours, attained the sublime courage to proclaim thoughts that they, they completely alone, perceived within themselves. And the form in which the prophets wrote must naturally also bear witness to this originality. But great as the originality of the prophets as authors may be, these writers cannot be recognized apart from the genres that preceded them: they began with the traditional genres, and these they used and modified. Until we know that *Faust* is a drama and that *Werthers Leiden* is in the form of a diary, anything that we say about Goethe's literary activity is uninformed. Anyone investigating an author without knowing the genre he uses is building a house beginning with the roof. Thus we conclude that the first task in examining the literary history of the prophets is to describe the prophetic genres and their style. Not until this is done can we begin to recognize the special quality an individual prophet has as a writer.

II

The prophets were not originally writers but speakers. Anyone who thinks of ink and paper while reading their writings is in error from the outset. "Hear!" is the way they begin their works, not "Read!" Above all, however, if contemporary readers wish to understand the prophets, they must entirely forget that the writings were collected in a sacred book centuries after the prophets' work. The contemporary reader must not read their words as portions of the Bible but must attempt to place them in the context of the life of the people of Israel in which they were first spoken. Here the prophet stands in the forecourt of the temple; around him are the men of Judah who have come to Jerusalem for a festival worship service (Jeremiah 26). Or the king and his court have gone out into the open in order to supervise the work on the city's water conduit. The curious people crowd around; then the prophet steps into their midst (Isa. 7:3). A delegation from afar comes to Jerusalem to offer an alliance to Judah; Isaiah speaks to them on the street as the procession of foreign figures approaches the royal court (Isaiah 18). Another time he meets the girls and women of Jerusalem at the Feast of Tabernacles, perhaps while they are performing their dances (Isa. 32:9–13), or he speaks to priests and prophets who delight in imbibing wine at the sacrifices (Isa. 28:7–8). Amos may have slipped his frightful funeral oration over Israel's fall into the jubilee festival at Bethel (Amos 5:2–4). Such situations of prophetic activity are still reported about Zechariah (Zech. 6:10–15; 7:1–14) and Haggai (Hag. 2:10–14). Not infrequently the people themselves sought out a prophet: thus, after the death of Gedaliah the leaders of the army and the people asked Jeremiah for advice, and King Zedekiah secretly summoned the prophet in order to ascertain from him his personal fate (Jer. 38:14–23). The elders of the people who were carried off to Babylon came to Ezekiel's house (Ezek. 8:1, 14:1), and crowds of ordinary people also marveled at this strange figure (Ezek. 33:31). Wherever possible, one should picture in his mind's eye a similar situation for every prophetic word, even when one is not expressly stated. Wherever it is impossible to conceive of the prophet himself delivering a prophetic word to an audience, such a word certainly belongs to a later time of prophecy. For example, when Deutero-Isaiah addresses the heathen (Isa. 49:1), this is no longer an actual but a contrived speech. In addition, the precise description of the temple and the land at the close of the Book of Ezekiel (chaps. 40—48) was certainly never delivered to the people but was a written composition. Previously it was thought that among the major prophets, public activity was least visible in Deutero-Isaiah; but even here some things indicate it: descriptions such as Isa. 49:2–4; 50:4–6 are inconceivable without personal experiences. To be sure, in the Babylonian exile, public activity was to a great extent no longer possible.

III

Now we turn our gaze from the audience to the prophet himself and visualize the manner in which he spoke. Here, too, it is difficult to perceive the matter correctly. We hear the texts of the prophets read formally in a liturgical framework in our worship services and we may easily be led into thinking that they were speaking like our preachers, with whom we are apt to compare them. Those Israelite prophets, however, spoke much differently. There an ecstatic man shouted his wild threats among the people; there his speech often was a strange stammering, a marvelous gibberish. And we see how he conducted himself! He collapsed in bitter pain, weeping and wailing about the coming disaster (Ezek. 21:11); he beat his breast and clapped his hands; he wobbled like a drunk; he stood there naked or with a yoke around his neck or madly swinging a sword in his hand (Ezek. 5:1–17; 21:13–22)! We must especially keep the "signs" of these men before our eyes when we read their words. Men who did such exceptional things could not have spoken calmly and prudently. When we constantly find things in their speeches that are foreign, powerful, and baroque, we then may hope that we are comprehending them correctly. The normal beginning of their speeches "So Yahweh spoke to me" certainly shows us that they typically spoke not during their ecstasy but later when they had become calmer. But one should not make a law of this, as was done in the struggle against the Montanists! For we also have texts that, at least in form, were spoken immediately during the prophetic experience (Jer. 4:19; Isa. 21:1–4; 63:1–6; and the Balaam oracles). In the passages before us, there is a continuum from a passionate way of speaking to a very quiet and thoughtful style, such as we find, for example, in the concluding passages of Ezekiel.

IV

The history of the prophets' development from speakers to writers is a long one. The first ecstatic *nebiim*, whom we meet with Saul, wrote nothing and had nothing to write, for nothing is written in such wild conditions. Even men like Elijah and Elisha were not writers: they acted through their own person and did not contemplate an impact in the future. In addition, the people they addressed read little. To be sure, we learn from the later literary prophets that the prophetic style was already clearly developed at this time; but that does not mean much was written at this time: the style can take definite form in oral speech. Nonetheless, we do have individual writings from this period; there are the blessings of Jacob (Genesis 49), Moses (Deuteronomy 33), and Balaam (Numbers 23—24), whose style combines the emulation of the prophetic artistic form with the form of the praising and blessing of an ancient ancestor or a man of God. We may regard it as typical that these extant fragments appeared under other names and that no writings have been preserved from the renowned prophets of ancient time. We may assume that the recording of prophetic utterances began in this manner, under a name from ancient times or perhaps without any name at all.

Men like Amos and Isaiah were not originally writers. But the real reason that these men increasingly used paper is that times had changed. More was being written in other fields than it had been in previous days. Isaiah complains as if it were something new that treaties were being written at that time (Isa. 10:1). Specific reasons for such literary activity of the prophets are also transmitted to us. Jeremiah began dictating to Baruch, his loyal friend, when he was prevented from speaking personally to the people (Jeremiah 36). Amos became a writer when he was expelled from the Northern Kingdom by royal decree. In other places we hear that it was their contemporaries' unbelief that provoked the prophets to write: Isaiah relates an oracle before witnesses in order to be able to prove even to the unbelievers that he prophesied a certain event (Isa. 8:16; 30:8). Or he publicly exhibits a tablet with an inscription (Isa. 8:1). Or the prophets, when living far away from those to whom their prophecies pertain, send them a letter: such prophetic letters must have passed back and forth between the Jews in Babylon and Jerusalem in the final years before Judah's fall (Jeremiah 29). On another occasion, Jeremiah had an oracle about Babylon written down and given to a man who was going there so that he might read it aloud there and cast it into the Euphrates (Jer. 51:59–64).

We can trace how this literary activity began in a small way and finally eventuated in large books. It began with brief words such as Isaiah wrote or sealed, or with a few extensive proverbs or poems. A paper such as this, comparable perhaps to our political ditties, then circulated through the land as a tract, was read, discussed, and copied everywhere, and if it was relevant, could surely have had a powerful effect. An example of this sort of prophetic word is Isaiah's irate poem against the steward Shebna whom he addresses without respect and threatens with banishment to Babylon (Isa. 22:15–19). One might well suppose that for months such a poem was the talk of Jerusalem, where it echoed on every street corner, to the bitter consternation of the high and mighty. Oracles of this sort often bore on their brow the name of the prophet who witnessed in his person to their truth. But very frequently they were nameless: the same sort of anonymous oracles were later given the names of known prophets and incorporated into their books.

The prophets themselves treated these pages, which are so precious to us, quite casually: they thought only of momentary results and not at all of later generations. They were convinced that their prophecies were not related to a far distant future but that they would soon be fulfilled. And also when, in order to sharpen their effect, primitive collections were made by the prophet himself or by the reverential hand of a student, there was scarcely any thought of arranging things logically or chronologically. It is a weakness of Israelite literature that the collected works it produced generally give very little evidence of organization, or none at all. Anyone collecting such a "book" hardly felt that he was creating a carefully organized work of art, but he was rather writing down whatever was at hand. This explains why, for example, the "genuine" portions of the prophet Isaiah were currently in complete disorder. Thus a poem's refrain is divided into two parts,[1] while in contrast we find in chapter 22 two passages whose contents have nothing to do with each other placed together only because they both begin with similar words;[2] or in chapter 28 an oracle against Samaria, contrary to all chronology, comes directly before much later ones against Judah and Jerusalem. Too, the prophets themselves were not concerned about writing down the passages in their original form, but they subtracted from and added to them entirely as they saw fit. A clear example of such subsequent expansion by the prophet himself is the oracle about the steward Shebna mentioned above: when Isaiah republished this passage, perhaps in a collection, he added to the threat against this hated man a brief (certainly genuine, by the way) appendix in which he, in Yahweh's name, appointed Eliakim, Yahweh's faithful one, as Shebna's successor (Isa. 22:20–23). This oracle must have been fulfilled later, but the new minister practised such nepotism that the prophet felt constrained to add a second appendix in which the successor too was to be deposed (Isa. 22:24–25).

No doubt people were fairly casual in dealing with anonymous fragments. These must have appeared throughout the years, and people must have waited continually for their fulfillment. Again and again the fragments must have been copied, but with each copying they were almost certainly altered and new elements were added to them. Thus, for example, in Isa. 19:1–14 we have an old poem about Egypt's defeat to which a fifth-century Egyptian Jew added a continuation (vv. 15–25) that corresponds to it in form and content. In the first passage, there are wrath and fury over the foreign land, in the latter, a worldwide universalism. In the first passage, there is a clearly metrical organization,[3] in the latter, an "exalted prose." The prophetic word of uncertain provenience in Isa. 2:2–4 is handed down in Micah 4:1–3 as well, but the final lines do not agree in both versions and obviously are additions (Isa. 2:5; Micah 4:4–5). So too, other words from later prophets are taken over; Jeremiah scorns the way the "lying prophets" have "stolen" from one another (Jer. 23:30). This is how words from more ancient and from more recent times can happen to stand right next to one other in the later prophetic books: thus Zech. 9:10 says that the chariot and war horse have been driven out of Ephraim and Jerusalem—an oracle that can be understood only as coming from the time when Israel's two kingdoms were independent—but it is immediately followed by mention of a future war for Judah's independence from Greece (Zech. 9:13).

Accordingly, it is understandable that our present "books" of the prophets, which originated earlier or later—sometimes by many centuries—after their appearance or death, and which passed through the hands of many "redactors," depict a variegated world. Sometimes they contain many things that do not come from the old prophets, so that, for example, the Book of Isaiah can more accurately be termed an overview of Hebrew prophecy than a "book of Isaiah." Not until Ezekiel are things different: this man, accustomed as priest and jurist to scrupulous order, and convinced that his prophecies about Israel would be fulfilled only after centuries, wrote what was the first book of prophecy.

V

This history of the growth of the prophetic books belongs together with the history of the gradual development of the individual units of which they are composed. It is one of the inherent laws of a genre that its units have definite limits that are traditionally prescribed. Moreover, one of the fundamental preconditions for aesthetically evaluating as well as for factually understanding a genre is that one keep in mind the whole that the writer himself intended. However, the tradition, which we have received in fragmentary form, leaves us almost completely at a loss. The prophetic words and speeches have come to us virtually without any formal dividers. The superscriptions, which come from ancient time and which are found here and there, and the chapter divisions, which come from much later, sometimes give us a correct starting point; but in general the fragments that are separated from one another by chapter divisions are much too large. In order to comprehend the deplorable condition in which our prophetic books are found we should imagine something like Goethe's poems written one after another without any indication of where one poem ends and another begins, with only larger chapter breaks indicated, and then with the verses chopped up into individual sayings. In such a situation the scholar's first task must be to lift out the individual, original, independent portions—a task that in no way has yet been accomplished with the prophetic writings. Contemporary scholars especially, following the modern German feeling for style, continue to identify far too many units, and they otherwise show a great deal of uncertainty in identifying the fragments.[4]

This is not the place to explore with the reader that vast enterprise. It must suffice to mention that one must pay special attention to certain beginnings and endings that are repeated frequently. Examples of such beginnings include the well-known words "Thus says Yahweh" and "Hear!"; examples of endings include "says Yahweh," "Thus spoke the mouth of Yahweh," "I, Yahweh, have spoken it," and "And they shall know that I am Yahweh."

The oldest units of prophetic style are also the briefest; they are the puzzling words and collections of words that echo the odd cries of the ancient *nebiim*. The prophets of a higher sort adopted such a way of speaking in order to give their thoughts a sharp and impressive expression. Such words are then publicly displayed by these men on something like a sign or are given as names to their children (Hosea 1; Isa. 7:3; 8:3).

The next stage following this is for the prophets to express themselves with great clarity in brief statements, made up of two, three, or a few more long lines. Examples of this are Isa. 1:2–3; 3:12–15; 14:24–27; 17:12–14; 40:1–2, 3–5, 6–8, 9–11; Amos 1:2; 3:1–2; 5:1–3; 9:7; Jer. 2:1–3, 4–9, 10–13, 14–19.

Later the prophets learned to compose longer "speeches," about a chapter in length. These, too, are rarely organized as a unit in a way that corresponds to our feeling for style as it has been informed by the Greeks, but they consist rather of statements that are more or less loosely piled up one after another. The prophet turns from one thing to another, according to whatever his eye lights upon, and he stops when he thinks he has exhausted the subject. Thus it is often very difficult to recognize whether, according to the prophet, a new "speech" is beginning, or whether it is only a part of one, that is, a "word." Such a "piecemeal" style also naturally opens the door for later additions that outwardly can hardly be distinguished from the original text.[5] Yet the outstanding stylists among the prophetic writers possessed the art of assembling the smaller, relatively independent fragments into a larger whole that may be compared to a cyclopean wall. An example of such a style is Isaiah 13, a chapter that comes from the time of the exile, one that is composed of many more or less strongly differentiated fragments. Yet when taken as a whole it forms a unit: in the beginning is the summons, in the middle, the battle, in the end, the destruction; at the beginning, apparent confusion and darkness, at the conclusion, clarity.

Such an organization stands out very impressively from the whole when it is couched in the artistic form of a "refrain" which comes from lyric poetry; poems with refrains are in Amos 1:3—2:16; 4:6–12; in Amos 7:1–9; 8:1–3; in Isa. 2:6–21; and in Isa. 9:7—10:4; 5:24–30. The seven woes in Isa. 5:8–23 were probably first compiled by a collector. The most artistic are those prophetic units in which fragments of different genres are brought together in the form of a "liturgy."

Finally, entire books were produced. But even in them a logical organization is less evident than a chronological one: a day, month, and year of composition is presupposed for every oracle, so that the entire book takes the form of a collection of documents. A painfully exact organization is obviously foreign to the prophetic way of thinking; it is clear that the spirit of priestly legal scholarship is at work here. And the first who really chose this sort of organization for the whole was Ezekiel, a man of priestly ancestry. The later prophets then copied Ezekiel: Zechariah 1—8 and the Book of Haggai are arranged in the same way. In contrast, Deutero-Isaiah was written without any organization: his work can be compared to a diary in which he wrote the words that came to him every day without any further organization.

From all of this we conclude that in interpreting as well as in criticizing the prophetic books one must use the criterion of "context" only with great caution; and also that in attempting to indicate the structure of prophetic books such as Amos or Deutero-Isaiah one must first investigate whether such a thing exists at all.

The complete picture of the history we have just outlined shows us that the number of units gradually increased. This is a manifestation that also has many counterparts in other Israelite genres, and the explanation for it lies in the development of culture and the increasing artistic ability evident therein.

VI

Another line of development in the prophetic passages leads from poetry to prose. By its nature, enthusiasm speaks in prophetic form; rational reflection, in prose. Prophetic "speech," therefore, was originally in the form of poetry. Men like the prophets who received their thoughts in hours of great inspiration and who now, filled with overflowing emotions, proclaim them are capable of speaking only in poetic rhythms. Thus the clearer the prophetic element is in the content, the more pronounced is the poetic form. To be sure, once again here our traditional Greek feeling for style is different from the Hebraic, in which speech and poetry are not mutually exclusive. It was not odd in ancient Israel for the prophetic oracle to speak in verse; after all, the style of oracles was otherwise poetic in form. In the sanctuary, Yahweh's reply was given in verse (e.g., Gen. 25:23) no differently than were the words of the Delphic Apollo.

Two genres can be distinguished in the metric form of poetic prophecy: the strict style, in which the same verse dominates the entire poem, and the freer style, which is expressed in different verses according to the ebb and flow of the sentiment. The first style appears to belong more to sung poetry, while the second more to spoken poetry. Examples of the former genre are Isa. 1:10–17; Jer. 2:1–3; Isa. 2:2–4; 3:12–15; 28:1–4. Examples of the latter genre are Isa. 1:2–3; 29:1–7. Future scholars will have a great deal more work to do in establishing the metrical organization of the prophetic poems; thus the six-colon poem $(2 + 2 + 2)$ which was discovered long ago by E. Sievers is still far too little known. Yet one has to guard against wanting to alter the texts in order to create an overall regularity. Perhaps someday it will be concluded that the freer style appears more frequently in the prophets than the stricter one, and that in general the formation of regular "stanzas," that is, conjunctions of long lines, appears rather infrequently.[6]

Judged according to aesthetic standards, many of the prophetic speeches are beyond comparison and they are among the most powerful passages of the Old Testament, which is so rich in powerful words. Hardly anywhere in the entire world is there religious poetry that is comparable in force and power to these prophetic writings.

From the beginning, some individual elements in the prophetic passages were prose. The narratives are almost always so, regardless of whether the prophet is speaking about himself or others are speaking about him. But prose has also crept into prophetic speech itself. The speeches in Zechariah 1—8 and those in Haggai are in prose, but in the Books of Jeremiah and Ezekiel prose and poetry stand alongside each other. We may assume that this transition from poetry to prose can be explained by the fact that at this time the prophets were starting to be transformed from ecstatics into preachers and religious thinkers. Accordingly, the manner in which they spoke gradually became calmer: the rhythm of their words became freer and freer until it finally became prose. When Jeremiah proclams the law of divine activity (Jer. 18:1–12), or when Ezekiel describes the temple buildings in the most minute detail (Ezekiel 40—48), that cannot have been done in any but a tone of clear, precise description, that is, in prose. Contributing to this was the fact that the later prophets—in the Torah or when recording history—used genres that were by nature prose. This does not mean, of course, that the later prophets did not also continue using the old poetic genres.

VII

As we now attempt to delineate the material of the prophetic books and to arrange it according to genres, we face a difficulty that apparently is almost insurmountable. For what meets our gaze is an infinite diversity that appears to defy any sort of organization. Here we find narratives of the prophets' deeds and fates reported by contemporary students or by later ones, and alongside them are passages that come from the prophets themselves; among these are compositions written for themselves and for their God, as well as others they intended for their people.

We shall examine the latter first, for they form the real foundation of the prophetic writings. These prophetic oracles are divided into two groups, according to the manner in which the revelation came: visions and auditions, that is, what was seen and what was heard, the images and the "words" that are characteristically introduced with "Thus Yahweh showed me" and "Thus Yahweh said to me."

Looked at as a whole, the words by far outnumber the visions. Thereby they reveal the uniqueness of our prophets. In the final analysis what is significant about them is that they present God's thoughts. It is much easier and more convenient, however, for a thought to take the form of an audible word than that of a visible image. It is noteworthy that visions came so strongly to the fore in later times when the old ecstatic forms of prophecy experienced a revival: so it was with Ezekiel and Zechariah. But it is strange that at the same time visions played a minor role in Jeremiah, and none at all in Deutero-Isaiah.

VIII

The visions of the prophets are of the most varied sort. Sometimes they are brief and simple, as when Amos sees a fruit basket (Amos 8:1) or Jeremiah the branch of an almond tree (Jer. 1:11), and sometimes they are longer and more detailed, as in Zechariah and Ezekiel. And their contents are very different. There are, for example, faraway things the prophet cannot see by his own powers: before the eyes of the "lookout" appears the Persian army, approaching two by two, as it traverses the pass (Isa. 21:6–10); Ezekiel, while in Babylon, sees a vision of things that are happening in the temple in Jerusalem (Ezekiel 11). He claims to have experienced the death there of a prominent man, whom he names specifically (Ezek. 11:13). Then a figure appears to him that looks like a man but is made up entirely of fire and brightness; it stretches out its hand, grasps him by a lock of hair, and transports him from Babylon to Jerusalem (Ezekiel 8). Commonly the prophet sees beings of an invisible world. Thus Isaiah saw Yahweh on his heavenly throne with the frightening seraphim hovering before him (Isa. 6:1–7). Zechariah saw the mounted messengers Yahweh sends throughout the world and who then return before him to bring him reports of how things are on earth (Zech. 1:7–11), the chariots which go forth from him to visit his wrath on the earth (Zech. 6:1–8), the form of "wickedness" enclosed in an ephah borne by two women with wings like those of storks (Zech. 5:5–11), and among all these fantastic figures also the pathetic Satan who wants to accuse the high priest before the divine tribunal (Zech. 3:1). Ezekiel sees the miraculous throne borne by cherubim on which God travels (Ezekiel 1), the seven spirits who carry out Yahweh's commands, and in the midst a figure clothed in linen with a writing case in his hand (Ezek. 9:2). The way the details of such a vision are depicted is naturally dependent on the beliefs of the time: the prophet sees the heavenly things the way he himself and his people believe that they are. Here mythological elements too may intrude to the extent that the faith of Israel had adopted individual mythological elements: the seven spirits of Yahweh are originally the seven Babylonian gods of the planets and the one in the center is Nabû, the god of the art of writing; the messengers of God riding on horses of four different colors and the heavenly chariots drawn by similar horses are really the four winds (Zech. 6:4–8), and the four colors signify the regions of heaven.[7] But our explanation is frequently in error when we interpret such visions, the stuff of which is not created anew by the prophets but rather transformed by them, as if they simply went back to the writer's experience or fantasy.

The style of the visions is almost always a narrative one—the prophet reports what he saw in the hour of revelation—but narrative in the Old Testament is almost always given in prose form.[8] More rarely there are poetic visionary accounts that come directly out of experience.[9]

Characteristic of such presentations of visions is a certain secretive tone that we see most beautifully in Balaam's discourses as described by David in Num. 24:17. David's name is not mentioned; it is only from afar that we have in changing images the description of a great conqueror who will crush Moab. Thus the poet hides what he saw behind a secretive veil. All prophetic visions, however, must be read in this way. An example is the glorious vision of Isaiah 6. Human eyes had glimpsed the Lord, but the human mouth falls dumb when it attempts to express the unspeakable. The prophet describes God's throne and his long train; his gaze lights on the beings who stand before God, and his ear listens to the hymn that they sing with loud voices. But how the Lord himself appears he does not say. And only for a moment does he see the heavenly vision; then smoke ascends and obscures it from his view.

Much less delicate is Ezekiel's vision of the wheels, in which the writer attempts to depict God's "glory" in detail; but here too the writer is concerned about not saying too much. He is aware that he dare not describe the divine reality, attempting to approach it only by making comparisons: "And above the firmament over their heads there was the likeness of a throne, in appearance like sapphire; and seated above the likeness of a throne was a likeness as it were of a human form" (Ezek. 1:26). The fact that this chaste reticence is lacking in Ezekiel's vision of the temple (Ezekiel 40—48) proves that it was not a vision that was actually experienced. This veil of secrecy through which the bright colors of oriental mythology glimmer is what gives genuine visions their unique aesthetic charm.

Such visions are ordinarily connected with verbal revelations. The prophet sees Yahweh sitting on his high and elevated throne, and then he hears the spirits surrounding him who themselves speak (Isa. 6:1–8). He sees Yahweh's messengers riding and receives the tidings they bring him (Zech. 1:8–11). Ezekiel sees Yahweh's marvelous chariot-throne and then he hears a "voice," that is, Yahweh's voice, speaking to him (Ezekiel 1). It is significant that the chief emphasis on such a connection between what is seen and what is heard almost always, especially in older times, lies on the words: the chief thing for the prophet is not Yahweh's appearance but rather what he says, not the description of the messengers' appearance but rather their message. Thus it frequently happens with the prophets that their visions end with more or less lengthy speeches set either in the mouths of the divine persons who appear in the vision or in the mouth of the prophet (e.g., Isaiah 6; Zechariah 1). This matter of the visions' receding behind the auditions largely corresponds to the fact, which we have already established, that in general there are far fewer visions than auditions, and moreover, that for those words that appear most frequently the text provides no specific indication of how they might have been received. From this we recognize that the prophets put all emphasis on the thoughts that they contained, not on the miraculous way in which they came.

An especially noteworthy connection exists between vision and verbal revelation when the prophet sees something in front of him and simultaneously hears a voice asking him what it is. Thus he sees something indefinite and at the same time has a strong desire to penetrate the mystery surrounding it. Then, however, he recognizes what is presenting itself to him. It is an object of ordinary life, a fruit basket or the branch of an almond tree or a cookpot. At once, however, he hears again the voice proclaiming to him the meaning of the revelation; what he sees and its significance are connected by a play on words: the almond branch (*šāqēd*) is supposed to mean that Yahweh is watching (*šōqēd*; Jer. 1:11–12, 13–14; Amos 8:1–3). Perhaps one may assume that the thought "He watches" was already unconsciously present in the prophet until it finally presented itself perceptually as the almond branch.

In other places where supernatural forms appear to the prophet in a vision, their nature is revealed to him by the "angel who talks with him," but the interpretation is occasionally still mysterious and unclear:[10] it would be unseemly to speak more definitely about divine things. This is usually the case in the later "apocalypses" as well.

But do these visions refer to real occurrences, or are they only embodiments of thoughts in one's fantasy? This is a question that cannot be answered definitely for each case. For on the one hand, it is certain that the whole genre originates in actual events, for its existence is inconceivable without them. But on the other hand, such experiences are so difficult to put into words that the prophet, as soon as he states them, becomes a poet and an interpreter. Thus, at any rate, these descriptions are not to be taken in the sense of juridical proof of factual events. Moreover, imitation surely does not play an insignificant role (any more, by the way, than it does in the verbal revelations). It is certainly no coincidence that the call vision of Jeremiah agrees so precisely, even in wording, with some visions in Amos. This does not need to be conscious imitation, of course; there is also an unconscious dependency that lies deeper and that causes people of the same age and circle—who not only say the same things but also experience, think, feel, and desire the same things—to have an internal dependency. This is the real reason that we can speak so much about a people's intellectual history. Finally, however, we also have to reckon with an artificial embodiment of something in the form of a vision, a case that is revealed especially clearly in Ezekiel's vision of the temple (Ezekiel 40—48): in the very nature of things such precise measurement of a building would not be revealed in the vision, and Ezekiel, who surely knew these things from the earliest days of his childhood as a priest's son in the temple, would have needed no revelation to teach him what he already knew well. Thus he here adopted the style of a poem and filled it with content of a completely different sort. In the visions, accordingly, we catch a glimpse of a history that begins with real experiences but that is also presented and interpreted poetically and then replicated by others so that finally an artistic style arises which can also be used by conscious imitators. Where in the entire process each individual vision belongs, however, is something that will be very difficult to determine.

IX

Much more important than the visions are the words the prophet proclaims. But in our prophetic books these are almost all originally spoken by Yahweh himself: what the prophet hears from Yahweh in his solitary room he declares as his "message" to the people. The "I" speaking from him and through him is not he himself but rather God, just as the royal messenger literally carrying out his commission says, "I [the king]" (e.g., 2 Sam. 3:14; 19:12), or as the demoniac of the New Testament period might answer a question about his name by saying, "My name is legion" (Mark 5:9). But sometimes the prophet has such a strong sense of such words being given by God that in his own speech, for example, he is capable of ascribing other words to God so that what results is a two-way conversation between God and the prophet: we might think of the intercessory prayers of Amos (7:2, 4), Habakkuk (1:12–17), and Jeremiah. In this way it is possible for God to answer just the opposite of what one wishes and hopes (Jer. 11:14; 12:5; 14:10; 15:1; 19). In the Jewish "apocalypse," 4 Esdras, the entire first part is filled with such conversations between man and the revealing angel.

There is a fluid transition between this form, in which the Divine reveals himself through the mouth of the prophet as an "I", and another, in which the prophet speaks about Yahweh's thoughts and plans and therefore calls Yahweh "he." But even in such cases the prophet is convinced that the inner assurance filling him is of divine origin. Alongside these is a third form of prophetic speech, which we especially see in Deutero-Isaiah, where the man of God adds his own observations, speeches, and poems to God's words.

X

Though classifying these forms has so far presented no particular difficulties, when we examine the content of the words more closely we are confronted with an almost incomprehensible diversity: here we find promises and threats, descriptions of sins, exhortations, priestly sayings, historical reminiscences, disputes, songs of all sorts, religious poems and parodies of profane poems, laments and songs of joy, short poetical passages and entire liturgies, parables, allegories, and so on. But it is the task of the interpreter to put the individual passages in order according to genre, for only when we explain their original context may we hope to understand the individual scattered elements. But literary history, if it is to be worthy of its name, must have as its goal the examination of the history that has caused such a diversity.

The fundamental understanding for this history, however, is the recognition that most of the genres mentioned were not originally prophetic: from the outset the prophets were not composers of songs, tellers of stories, or proclaimers of the torah. Only in retrospect did they become such. This means that prophecy adopted foreign genres in the course of its development. And the motivating cause of this history is also clear: it is the burning desire of the prophets to gain power over their people's soul. Just as the recognition by contemporary Christianity that traditional forms of preaching and religious instruction (*Kinderlehre*) no longer go far enough has led to the adoption of genres that originally were not actually religious (e.g., Christian calendars, lectures, periodicals, newspapers, and novels; in fact, even "Christian bookstores"), so did prophecy, when its original manner of speaking no longer sufficed, adopt other genres through which it hoped to reach the people. The fact that the prophets used so many of them is a sign of the zeal with which they contended for their people's heart.

But then the question arises about the actual prophetic genre from which all others must have come. It must be that genre in which what is really prophetic in content and form is most clearly evident. Now, originally, as we have seen, the chief task of the prophets was to announce the future. Therefore we should expect to find the oldest prophetic style in those passages that depict the future and that we call promises or threats, depending on whether they foretell good or evil. Notably enough, particularly clear examples of this style are the oracles about foreign peoples, such as those in Isaiah 13—21; Jeremiah 46—51; and Ezekiel 25—32. Since the prophets always feel themselves sent in the first instance to Israel, the new forms they use appear principally in the passages addressed to Israel, and the speeches against the foreign peoples resemble a now-dry watercourse that shows us where water previously flowed. If this is correct, then in this really prophetic depiction of the future we should see most clearly the characteristically prophetic, ecstatic form of revelation. That this is largely the case is what we shall see as we now attempt to delineate the style of these prophecies.

XI

Revelations are received in secret hours: only in darkness and shadow do they appear in the prophet's soul. This style of foreseeing the future is faithfully mirrored in the literature. Thus we have the virtually demonic tone that is characteristic of prophecies as well as of history. As much as possible, names are avoided; even the very well known are unnamed. Thus the threatening enemy is not mentioned by name in the oracles about Edom in Obadiah, about Moab in Isaiah 15—16 and Jeremiah 48, about Egypt in Isaiah 19, about Philistia in Isa. 14:29–32 and Jeremiah 47, about Tyre in Isaiah 23, and about Nineveh in Nahum 1:15—3:19. Not even in Habakkuk 3 are those who are to be overcome named. Jeremiah prophesied for decades about an enemy from the north without himself knowing who it was going to be, until finally the Chaldeans appeared and he became certain that it was they Yahweh had meant. Amos, and Isaiah in his early period, both avoided using the name Assyria. Even the later imitations of prophetic oracles, in their common spuriousness, name no names whenever they speak like a prophet.[11] And it is completely unprophetic and thus probably to be explained as an addition when a legend prophesies about a God-man: one day a son will be born to David, Josiah by name (1 Kings 13:2).

Rarely do the prophets give exact numbers, but instead they give very general ones: in three (Isa. 16:14), forty (Ezek. 29:11), or seventy (Jer. 25:11–12) years; when a child that now is conceived is born (Isa. 7:14); when the boy can say father and mother (Isa. 8:4). For this reason it is impossible to put the word of Isa. 7:8, "Within sixty-five years Ephraim will be broken to pieces," in Isaiah's mouth; instead it must read, "In six or five years . . ."

The prophet avoids definite expressions even in ordinary prose, and instead employs an indefinite form of words. Assyria, he says, is sent "against a godless nation" (he means against Israel; Isa. 10:6). Hosea is commanded to love again "a woman who is an adulteress" (it is his own unfaithful wife he is to remarry; Hosea 3:1). Shebna, according to Isaiah's prophecy, will be thrown by Yahweh "into a wide land" (the prophet is probably thinking of Babylonia, but he does not say so; Isa. 22:18). Isaiah describes the frightful land where people carry their treasures on the humps of camels; but he disdains to utter the name aloud, although at that time he knows it well (Isa. 30:6–7).

Likewise the prophet prefers to use images that reveal something but at the same time conceal it. He says "harvest" when he means judgment; "yoke" when he means slavery. "His yoke shall depart from them" means that they will be free from his domination (Isa. 14:25); "Your silver has become dross" means "Your noble customs have degenerated" (Isa. 1:22). Thus, ultimately an entire

prophetic imagery developed. Joel 4:13 is an example. The un-
initiated person will think that the prophet is speaking of the
coming harvest; the initiate, however, knows that he is describing
judgment upon the nations. One speaking in a mystical manner
loves to put together images taken from several different areas in
order to indicate thereby that the words contain a secret:

> A star shall come forth out of Jacob,
> and a scepter shall rise out of Israel.[12]

Much more, however, do the prophets enjoy embellishing an
individual image so that it approaches the "allegorical" manner of
speaking. In Ezek. 21:1–3 there is a prophecy of Egypt's fall under
Nebuchadnezzar in the words "Son of man, set your face toward
the south and preach at noon and prophesy against the woods in
the land of the south. Say to the woods in the land of the south,
Hear the word of the Lord! Thus Yahweh the Lord has spoken: I
will set a fire in you. It shall burn every green tree in you and
destroy every dry tree. The blaze will not go out. And all the faces
from the land of the south to the north will be singed by it."
Understandably enough, the contemporaries of these words did not
comprehend them and jeered at the prophet's "riddles" (Ezek.
21:5).

Another way of keeping the secret was by using certain words
that were clear only to initiates. Thus later apocalyptic speaks of
the "man" and of the "abomination of desolation"; but prophecy
also speaks about the "northerner" (Joel 2:20), the "valley of
Jehoshaphat" (Joel 4:12), the "servant of Yahweh," and "Ariel."[13]
It compresses entire schemes of thought into short, obscure names
such as Shearjashub, "a remnant shall return" (Isa. 7:3), or Rahab-
hammosbath, "the restrained chaos" (Isa. 30:7). Sometimes such
words are employed indiscriminately in a mystical, interpretive way:
Shearjashub includes a threat, but at the same time it is a promise
(Isa. 10:20–23). Jezreel is the name of the place of the blood guilti-
ness of the house of Jehu and the divine judgment upon it (Hosea
1:4–5)—therefore Israel will be destroyed in Jezreel—but at the
same time Jezreel is the place where Israel's new kingdom will one
day arise (Hosea 2:2), and because it literally means "God sows,"
it is the name of the future Israel planted anew by Yahweh (Hosea
2:24–25).

Such obscurity commonly appears at the beginning of the oracle
and then it becomes clearer toward its conclusion: so, for example,
Isaiah 13 starts in a completely mysterious fashion and not until
vv. 17 and 19 do the words "Medes" and "Babylon" occur. In Isa.

17:12—14, three successive scenes are depicted without any names: first, the approach of a powerful, frightened crowd of people; then, the sudden appearance of one who rebukes; finally, a headlong flight throughout the land. And only a brief concluding word indicates that all of this will take place in a single night, and shows, although still semi-obscured, those whom this will affect:

> This is the portion of those who despoil us,
>   and the lot of those who plunder us. (Isa. 17:14).

In Isa. 21:1–10 all the anguish of uncertainty that torments the prophet is depicted, until the redeeming revelation comes at the conclusion: "Fallen, fallen is Babylon."

This secretive tone seems especially appropriate when the appearance of the Divine in history is to be portrayed. Suddenly a voice sounds; the prophet thinks that it is Yahweh's voice, but he is too modest to say so (Isa. 17:13; 13:3). Isaiah (10:28–34) uses especially bright colors to depict Assyria's coming campaign against Jerusalem; he names place after place through which the invasion is coming. Then, however, comes the great moment when the miracle enters the world. Then the curtain falls. An image must suffice:

> Behold, the Lord, Yahweh Sabaoth
>   will lop the boughs with terrifying power;
> the great in height will be hewn down,
>   and the lofty will be brought low.
> He will cut down the thickets of the forest with an ax,
>   and Lebanon with its majestic trees will fall.

Anyone able to penetrate the obscurity of this image will know what Yahweh will do then.

Again, Isa. 40:3–5 speaks about a way leading over mountain and valley, through the midst of the desert, that is to be leveled for Yahweh. Will God come through the desert? He who understands it, understands it; and he who does not recognize it, will someday recognize it when his eyes behold it!

And precisely when the prophets, as they so often do, adopt the most ancient material of mythological origin, themselves trembling inwardly at what is to come, the only thing allowed is a hint from afar. Thus the prophet speaks in deepest secrecy of the child that is to be born for us (Isa. 9:5). But can a child bear the great name of "Wonderful Counselor, Mighty God, Everlasting Father, Prince of Peace"? Can a boy help us in the storms of this time? Yes, that is the great, divine mystery!

The marvelous passage about the future ruler who comes from Bethlehem, "whose origin is from old, from ancient days," leads even deeper into the world of mystery (Micah 5:1–4). But here too there are a multitude of questions: How can the one who comes from ancient days return? How can the dead become alive? Who are those who are given up until "she who is in travail" gives birth? Who gives them up and to whom? And who is "she who is in travail" herself? And when what follows mentions the "rest of his brethren" who one day shall return, who is "he" of whom it speaks? Only one thing is certain: the prophet is not thinking about answering such questions. In similarly obscure passages in the New Testament one finds, "Let the reader understand" (Mark 13:14); the prophet does not make it easier.

And now the miraculous "servant of Yahweh" is even to lead Israel out of captivity and to preach to the heathen—the one whose mouth proclaims the word of God and yet accomplishes nothing, the one who is abused and dishonored but who does not despair, indeed, the one who ultimately is given up to rejection and loathing, to death and burial, but who still attains his glorious goal! We might guess that the prophet is doing something more than describing himself in terms of human sensitivity, but nowhere does he clearly explain the secret of this image. No wonder that in every age those who read this text have pondered that question, especially when even the prophet's contemporaries could not have been entirely clear.

No doubt it was with all deliberateness that the prophets hid even that which was completely clear to themselves: Isaiah thinks that Assyria will plunder Damascus and Samaria, but he says so quite indirectly: "The spoil speeds, the prey hastes." He explains this word only to the extent of saying, "The wealth of Damascus and the spoil of Samaria will be carried away";[14] he does not name the plunderer himself, whom he knows full well. He is content to speak about the roar of nations when he means the masses of people who are approaching Jerusalem in the Assyrian armies (Isa. 17:12). The modern interpreter, when knowing the time and circumstances of an oracle, is in a position to replace the unknown elements with known ones, but when the tradition is lacking, we often fumble in complete uncertainty for an explanation.[15] In such cases may we be preserved from cheap guesses that do not improve after they become fashionable! May we also not proceed to accept additions and glosses too soon, before we really understand the text! We should generally read such passages with an attitude completely different from that with which they have usually been read: we should recognize that we are hardly in a position to penetrate all these secrets without further ado, and we should guard against precipitately destroying by our interpretation the impression that the prophet wanted to achieve.

XII

Another feature of prophetic predictions is their peculiarly disconnected style. Prophetic recognition is not something that is coherent and complete but is rather a sudden, lightninglike illumination. This observation is also important for reproducing the prophets' thoughts, which the modern theologian, using his own thought patterns, too often tries to comprehend and reproduce in some sort of systematic arrangement. Thus even a man like Isaiah is aware that he has proclaimed different things at different times (Isa. 28:23–29). And this abrupt, sudden manner is echoed in the style of the prophetic oracle.

Therefore the prophet loves to begin a speech with a powerful opening: he jumps into the middle of a subject with both feet, often without introduction, without any concern for whether the hearers understand a thought that may perhaps be quite alien to them: let them open ears and eyes (Isa. 6:9) and regard it as madness!

> Go not forth into the field,
> nor walk on the road;
> for the enemy has a sword,
> terror is on every side!
>
> (Jer. 6:25)

Thus Jeremiah once began. How one would have looked at these words with amazement: where is the enemy from whom we should flee, now that we are at peace?

Similar beginnings are "Blow the horn in Gibeah!" (Hosea 5:8), "On a bare hill raise a signal!" (Isa. 13:2), "Get you up to a high mountain, O Zion, herald of good tidings!" (Isa. 40:9). These are all interjections that at first are totally unintelligible. It is equally powerful when the passage begins with a question [16] that is a question for no one but the prophet. "Now why do you cry aloud?" the prophet begins (Micah 4:9), but none of the bystanders hear any cry. Likewise, Isa. 63:1, "Who is this that comes from Edom?" and Jer. 46:7, "Who is this, rising like the Nile?"

And the way the prophets continue is often just as disjointed as their beginning. Purely individual features, taken out of context, are piled up one on another. Block is piled upon block, mere fragments, which, however, when one looks at the whole, present the impression of a skilfully created picture. It is thus that we read such a magnificent passage as Nahum 3:1–3. First, as with Nineveh, so now:

> Woe to the bloody city,
>> all full of lies and booty—
> no end to all the plunder!

Then the attack of the enemy:

> The crack of whip, and rumble of wheel,
>> galloping horse and bounding chariot!
> Horsemen charging, flashing sword and glittering spear!

And then, in conclusion, how it will be:

> Hosts of slain,
>> heaps of corpses,
> dead bodies without end—
>> they stumble over the bodies!

In Jeremiah 46, we observe a magnificent poem portraying things without any transitions: Egypt's expedition, its defeat on the Euphrates, its absolute destruction.

This defeat is emphasized when the prophet's speech turns from proclaiming doom to proclaiming salvation, thereby giving the impression that Yahweh is creating something new. Examples of this are Isa. 29:5 and especially the brilliant conclusion of the vision of the calling of Isaiah, where the final threatening word that only a stump will remain of Israel's oak is powerfully and cleverly turned around: "The holy seed is its stump"; someday a new, holy shoot will spring from this stump (Isa. 6:12). But let no one conclude from such alleged "noncontextualness" that things are spurious, as certainly is often done!

XIII

A further conclusion to be drawn from the style of the prophets' revelation, as well as from the nature of Hebraic thought in general, is that their prophecies are extraordinarily concrete, abounding with the most specific and extremely vivid elements. The prophet does not say, "The desolate Babylon will be inhabited by swamp animals," but he uses the word "hedgehogs" (Isa. 14:23). He depicts the manner in which the discarded idols will someday be thrown "to the moles and to the bats" (Isa. 2:20). He calls the high trees the "cedars of Lebanon" and the "oaks of Bashan" (Isa. 2:13); the large ships, the "ships of Tarshish" (Isa. 2:16). He makes it clear that the princes of the royal house are following strange customs, by saying that they wear foreign attire (Zeph. 1:8). If the matter itself is not graphic, a clear picture is introduced: years whose time is limited are "the years of a hireling" (Isa. 16:14); Israel's faithfulness to Yahweh at the beginning of its history is its honeymoon (Jer. 2:2); someday Israel will be as few as ears remaining in the valley of Rephaim, as fruit remaining after the olive harvest: "two or three berries in the top of the highest bough, four or five on the branches of a fruit tree" (Isa. 17:4–6). That is what it is to speak concretely! The prophet does not depict the entire context, but he knows how to lift a small scene out of the whole and paint it in such a lively way that it reveals everything else. We may think of mood pictures like Isa. 3:6–8, where the total collapse of a state is depicted in a gruesome manner (one who still has a mantle must become king, something against which he protests with all his might), or Isa. 4:1, which depicts the lack of men after the destruction (seven women will take hold of one man), or Zech. 8:23, where it is made clear how, in the last times, the heathen will long for Yahweh (ten men of the heathen shall take hold of a Jew's robe, saying, We want to go with you!).

It is especially in accord with the prophets' bold spirit, which always penetrates to ultimates, for them to depict with particular vividness the final state of the place or person about which they are prophesying: Babylon is pools of water (Isa. 14:23), the mount of Zion a joy of wild asses (Isa. 32:14); a deathly stillness dominates the land (Isa. 6–12); a piece of ground that now is planted with valuable vines is briers and thorns (Isa. 7:23); where once was cultivated land there is nothing being raised but cattle: then a man will have a cow and two sheep, and because they give so much milk he will be able to eat curds (Isa. 7:21). Then one will haul bodies out of the houses in silence in order not to provoke Yahweh's anger once more (Amos 6:9–10). Then Zion will be a plowed field (Micah 3:12). Or the body of the one-time king of the world lies there, a terror or a reproach to the people, and even the dead are stirred up when the one who has been overcome enters Sheol (Isa. 14:9–11). Thus the prophets understand how to let a whole series of events reveal what is to occur from the perspective of the final outcome.

XIV

But there is no characteristic in them that comes to the fore more clearly than the enormous force of their passion. It is religious passion, as we have seen, that motivates them; and such passion streams out in torrents from their words to anyone who reads them. It is almost impossible for us reserved Nordic people, who have an inborn sense of propriety and moderation, who have been trained by the Christian religion to be gentle, and who admire the golden mean exemplified in the Greeks, to match the exuberance of this perception. But the prophets are completely different from us! They all are impressed that the coming one they proclaim is colossal, shocking, frightening, or conversely, gloriously inspiring, thrilling, wonderful. And the intent of much in their oracles is to kindle this ardor in their hearer's heart. The prophet of doom wants to trouble a proud, self-satisfied people; the prophet of salvation wants to encourage the despondent. This tension with the recalcitrant populace causes in the prophets a boiling heat to which the sharpest expressions appear still insufficient. To the prophets of doom no picture is too horrible, too cruel for them not to use it—in fact, apparently to use it with special affection. Those who are murdered lie around like dung (Jer. 8:2), one stumbles over bodies (Nahum 3:3); children are dashed in pieces (Hosea 14:1), women are ravished (Isa. 13:16), pregnant women are ripped open (Hosea 14:1); terrible fear grasps the army, no one can flee (Amos 2:14–16); even the body of the dead king is abused (Ezek. 32:4–8), buried like an ass (Jer. 22:19); his name is forgotten (Isa. 14:20), his sons are slaughtered (Isa. 14:21); the field is laid waste (Isa. 6:11), the vineyard is a thorn hedge (Isa. 7:23); "and though a tenth remain in it, it will be burned again, like a terebinth or an oak, whose stump remains standing when it is felled" (Isa. 6:13).

These men also rage against the sanctuaries of their people: no sympathy, no mercy, no patience, nothing but furious wrath! The people are abruptly scolded for abandoning the national Yahweh-religion for the worship of Baal. The prophets describe with joy how the golden idols will be thrown to the moles (Isa. 2:20); "dung" will be said to them (Isa. 30:22).

They close their eyes to the necessities of national life: for them alliances are nothing but idolatry (e.g., Isa. 7:1–9), and they explain that juvenile craving is the reason for importing horses from Egypt (Isa. 30:16). We have to conclude that today's historians must be cautious about using the prophets' words to describe the circumstances of their time, and especially about using the prophets' judgments.

Just as exaggerated on the other side are the promises of the prophecies of salvation, the moon will shine like the sun, and the sun sevenfold (Isa. 30 : 26); all the heathen will come to worship Yahweh (e.g. Isa. 2:2–4) and to serve Israel (e.g., Isa. 14:1–2). No word is too glorious, no image too exaggerated to express how glorious everything will be! Even the wild animals will lose their evil nature: the lion will lie down with the lamb (Isa. 11:6–9). Indeed, a new heaven and a new earth will appear (Isa. 65:17).

This passion of the prophets erupts in a multitude of plays on words, analogies, allusions, ironic and sarcastic expressions. Their inner emotion is revealed in a constant to and fro, in a flickering unrest (in Hosea and occasionally in Jeremiah); but sometimes also their sentences, with pathos, roll majestically like the mighty waves of the sea (Isaiah).

The prophets especially love depicting in sharp colors the difference between the present and the future: the gluttons and spendthrifts of Jerusalem, the whole boisterous throng, will be swallowed by the gaping mouth of the underworld (Isa. 5:14); the women, now proudly going around in their stylish finery, will then be brought low (Isa. 3:24).The proud ones, who have borne seven sons, have lost everything and now must mourn (Jer. 15:9). The joyful noise of the winepress is stilled, and the din of the battle cry grows loud, (Isa. 16:9–10). The cities of the land are ruins (Isa. 17:9); the palace is desolate, and the noise of the city is stilled (Isa. 32:14).

Or, in contrast: the desert becomes a gorgeous garden (Isa. 41:18–19), mountains and hills will be made low, and every valley exalted (Isa. 40:4); the thirsty will drink water (Isa. 41:17–18); the imprisoned will be set free (Isa. 42:7); the lame will leap like a hart (Isa. 35:6); the worm Jacob will become a sharp threshing sledge and thresh the mountains (Isa. 41:14–16). In such contrasting activities the Hebrew sensitivity, as we see, reconciles the strongest and most baroque elements.

And the prophets often add the impression that the one who is coming will do this at the very outset. Thus they describe the onset of the future:

> Therefore all hands will be feeble,
>   and every man's heart will melt,
>   and they will be dismayed.
> Pangs and agony will seize them;
>   they will be in anguish like a woman in travail.
> They will look aghast at one another;
>   their faces will be aflame.
>
> (Isa. 13:7–8)

Or the rejoicing:

Thou hast multiplied the nation,
  thou hast increased its joy;
they rejoice before thee
  as with joy at the harvest,
  as men rejoice when they divide the spoil.

(Isa. 9:3)

Some prophetic passages are quite full of such images of the mood of the future, for example, extensively described woes (e.g., Isaiah 15—16). A special favorite is to begin with "Cry," "Rejoice," or the like.[17] Here is one of the places where prophecy can make a transition to lyric poetry. In this way, the prophets attempt to draw their people who are living in the present into the mood of the future.

And everywhere at the culmination of their speaking we find the wondrously powerful mythological images that terrify the human heart, or that captivate and thrill it. Fire destroys the universe;[18] a storm breaks out over the earth (Isaiah 2); the earth is broken asunder (Isa. 24:19–20); the heavens roll up like a scroll (Isa. 34:4); the stars fall from heaven (Isa. 34:4); the sun loses its radiance and the moon its shine (Isa. 13:10). And in the proclamations of salvation: Zion will become the highest mountain on earth, the seat of the highest God (Isa. 2:2) and the site of paradise (Isa. 51:3); Jerusalem a fairyland city, its pinnacles of agate, its gates of carbuncles (Isa. 54:11–15)! Such mythological images appear more frequently in the later prophets and the "apocalypticists," where the myth of the conquest of Leviathan appears especially often (Isa. 27:1; Daniel 7; Rev. 13:17; and other places) but are also not unknown in the earlier ones.

XV

We conclude this discussion of the authentically prophetic manner of speaking with something about their "style" of syntax. It is one of the peculiarities of certain genres that they favor particular sentence structures. Characteristic of Hebrew narrative, for example, is the constantly repeated "and then," "and then."[19] Naturally the prophets prophesy in the future tense.[20] In addition, however, they especially like to use a curious perfect tense, ordinarily used to express acts completed in the past. When they use this tense to introduce the future it expresses their total confidence that the prophecy is true; the prophets thus do not see the expected event in front of them, like ordinary people, but behind them: in their eyes it has already occurred.[21]

Moreover, it is noteworthy that they couch their address in the second person. Thus their speeches ordinarily begin with the exhortation "Hear!" This way of speaking is explained by the vocation the prophet has received from Yahweh: as his "messenger," the prophet is to deliver the words he has received from Yahweh to those to whom they apply. He must meet face to face with anyone to whom Yahweh sends him, whether king or prime minister! But when the person is far away, a letter (Jeremiah 29) or a message (Isaiah 18) may suffice. Or when the prophet prophesies against foreign peoples, he turns his face in the direction where they dwell (Ezek. 25:1; cf. 6:2; Jer. 3:12) and he is convinced that they will hear his words, for, after all, these proceed from the mouth of Yahweh. That explains the prophetic practice of summoning and speaking to all people, places, and nations, near and far, even Bethlehem Ephrathah (Micah 5:1), the mountains and hills (Micah 6:2), Nineveh (Nahum 3:5), the Chaldeans (Hab. 2:7–8), indeed, all the peoples (Micah 1:2), and finally heaven and earth (Isa. 1:2).Clearly such language gives the prophet's way of speaking great animation: the prophet places the fate he proclaims squarely before the eyes of the third party, the listener, in the most vivid manner.

In this way, he often speaks in the form of a command; indeed, there are prophetic speeches or passages that consist entirely or predominately of one imperative piled upon another (see esp. Jer. 46:3–4). They are commands of God or of divine beings whom the prophet has heard in his ecstatic state. As an example, one may cite a passage such as Isa. 13:2:

> On a bare hill raise a signal,
>   cry aloud to them;
> wave the hand for them to enter
>   the gates of the nobles.

Or the prophet himself may speak such commands as Yahweh's agent, convinced that in doing so his words will not disappear into thin air. Thus in God's name, Ezekiel in a vision calls upon breath to enter the dry bones and make them alive: "Come from the four winds, O breath, and breathe upon these slain!" And the breath obeys his command (Ezek. 37:9–10). Thus sometimes the prophet, we might say, speaks like a divine stage manager constructing the scenes of world history (Isa. 21:13–14). Or he speaks like a watchman on the battlement who sees what is coming and spreads the warning.[22] Frequently there are admonitions to "weep" or to "rejoice." The prophets especially favor imperatives at the beginning of speeches—a powerful introduction (e.g., Joel 4:9; Zeph. 2:1).

Another stylistic device that, like the imperative, can be explained as something characteristic of the prophets is the use of frequent questions. Questions play a major role in relating visions, whether (Zech. 1:9; 2:2, 4; 4:4; et al.) it is the prophet asking the angel standing beside him for information (What is this that I see?), or whether (Zech. 2:6) he himself speaks to the apparition he sees before him (Who are you? What do you want?), or whether (Amos 7:8; 8:2; Jer. 1:11, 13; Zech. 4:2; 5:2) he hears a divine voice directed to him (What do you see?). The poetic accounts of visions are also laced with questions: the prophet is amazed at what he sees and hears: What is this? How can this be? The prophet sees a sudden rout before his eyes and cries out in surprise,

> Why have I seen it?
> They are dismayed
>   and have turned backward.
> Their warriors are beaten down,
>   and have fled in haste;
> they look not back—
>   terror on every side!
>
> (Jer. 46:5)

Or in the twilight he sees a mighty flood and asks,

> Who is this, rising like the Nile,
>   like rivers whose waters surge?
>
> (Jer. 46:7)

The best example is the fantastic bloody image in Isa. 63:1ff., with its powerful opening:

> Who is this that comes from Edom,
>   in crimsoned garments from Bozrah,
> he that is glorious in his apparel,
>   marching in the greatness of his strength?

Such questions occasionally also begin or interrupt the prophetic words (Micah 4:9; Zeph. 2:15; Jer. 49:1; other examples include Isa. 19:11; 66:8; Jer. 2:10–11, 14; 22:28; 30:6).

All of these characteristics we have mentioned show us how much the prophets' revelations of the future demonstrate an original style that is authentically prophetic.

XVI

This ancient prophetic style never disappeared entirely but rather continued to be nurtured into the later period and into the final age. But, under the hand of the great writers, a great many other genres took their places alongside it. Usually these genres were already in existence, and the writers filled them with their special prophetic content.

In this we may distinguish two different lines of development: the prophets became poets, and they became thinkers.

First, the prophets as poets. Even long before the prophets and those contemporaneous with them there must have been in Israel a richly developed literature with secular and spiritual content. Israel was a people that knew how to sing and enjoyed singing. All festivities were embellished by songs. The singer's voice resounded at victory celebrations; at the royal court the oracles echoed in praise of the ruler, proclaiming victory and praise to him. Having a feast without singing songs was inconceivable. Even at night the watchman sang high up in the tower, and young men returning home perhaps struck up a satirical song about faded beauty. Burials too were accompanied by songs. But singing had its special place in worship. There on festal days hymns to Yahweh echoed in the sanctuary; there when the people were beset by any kind of need they joined in their songs of lament. There were also songs by individuals in Hebrew worship. And even in ancient times it must have been customary to combine different kinds of lyric passages in an impressive "liturgy."

The prophets adopted all of these and some other lyric genres and used them for their purposes: there was no better way for them to bring the voices of the future to the people who were so fond of poetry than to express the future in poems. If they want to depict the anticipated destruction of an enemy before the souls of their contemporaries in an impressive fashion, they sing a victory song flavored with mockery (Isa. 37:22–29; 47). If they want to depict the greatest joy, they recall the "voice of the bridegroom and the voice of the bride," that is, wedding songs (Jer. 33:11). If they want to depict the attitude of blasphemers who have forgotten God, they put a frivolous drinking song in their mouths (Isa. 22:13; 56:12). Another time the prophet uses a deeply sensitive watchman's song, "Watchman, what of the night?" to show the human longing for new light (Isa. 21:11). Indeed, the prophet does not scruple to cite a frivolous song ridiculing a harlot: an unusual contrast, such a serious man and such a tune (Isa. 23:16)! Deutero-

Isaiah, who prophesies Cyrus's triumphal procession, imitates royal oracles for that purpose, something also done in Babylonia, so that these Israelite prophecies correspond quite remarkably with the inscription that the Babylonian priests somewhat later wrote down for Cyrus. But most frequently it is funeral songs that are found in the prophets.[23] Such songs, originally sung at the bier or at the grave and known by heart by everyone, already took on political content in preprophetic poetry: the poet, for instance, sings of a fallen city whose citizens have been deported, as of children robbed of their mother (Lamentations 1). The prophets make use of this type of poetry in order to indicate the inevitability of the destruction they foresee: how powerful and impressive it must have been when they lamented those as already fallen who now were enjoying the best of fortunes! The most famous example of such prophetic funeral songs is the word in Amos 5:2 that pictures Israel as a virgin toppled to the ground.[24] It is customary in funeral songs to sing the praises of the departed, but the prophets insert scorn for their people's fallen opponents. Thus we have bizarre poems in which praise, scorn, lament, and prophecy echo in a confusing mixture.[25] It is especially effective when the prophet, following the custom of the funeral song, ascribes words to the mourners: the poet of Isaiah 14 even summons the cedars of Lebanon, indeed, the underworld and the kings who sit there on their thrones, to mourn at the fall of the world rulers. And here, too, mythological images are employed at the height of the mood: the dejected king is compared to the morning star *hêlēl*, which enthusiastically rose so high and fell so far (Isa. 14:12–15), or with the dragon of the Nile that is caught by the divinity in spite of its vehemence (Ezek. 29:32). Aesthetically, such "eschatological funeral songs" are perhaps the most glorious poems in the prophetic books.

XVII

More common than these secular genres, of course, are the spiritual ones that are found in the prophets. When the prophet wants to make it clear that one day a tremendous joy will echo in the now decaying and silent cities of Judah, he uses the most beautiful tones on earth, the "voice of the bridegroom and the voice of the bride," but at the same time there is the "rejoicing of those who bring thank-offerings into Yahweh's house," and he introduces their song: it is the well-known thank-offering of the Psalms (Psalms 106; 107; 118; 136).

> Give thanks to Yahweh,
>> for he is good,
>> for his steadfast love endures for ever!
>>> (Jer. 33:11)

He clothes the great concept that someday the heathen will turn to Yahweh, in the image of their making a pilgrimage to his sanctuary, and he composes in advance the song they will sing on such a pilgrimage:

> Come, let us go up to the mountain of Yahweh,
>> to the house of the God of Jacob.
>>> (Isa. 2:3)

We shall have to understand these words as an imitation of pilgrimage songs (cf. Ps. 100:2). Likewise, the prophet uses a pilgrimage song to depict the rejoicing of the day when the world empire will collapse before Jerusalem; the joy will be like that of a pilgrim accompanied on a flute:

> To go to the mountain of Yahweh
>> to the Rock of Israel.
>>> (Isa. 30:29)

The wording of the verse above may imitate a pilgrimage song. And how could one better depict the unending joy of the Jerusalem that will one day be free than to give in advance the song that the redeemed will sing when they enter the sanctuary, rejoicing:

> Open the gates,
>> that the righteous nation which keeps faith
>> may enter in.
>>> (Isa. 26:2)

As the funeral songs are significant for the prophets of doom, so are the hymns for the prophets of salvation; this genre appears especially frequently in Deutero-Isaiah. When the soul of the man of God is full of all the glorious things that Yahweh has promised to do, he breaks out in a hymn of joy:

> Sing, O heavens, for Yahweh has done it;
>> shout, O depths of the earth;
> break forth into singing, O mountains,
>> O forest, and every tree in it!
> For Yahweh has redeemed Jacob,
>> and will be glorified in Israel.
>>> (Isa. 44:23)

The forms of these prophetic hymns are well known to us, especially from the Psalms:[26] there the song begins with a summons to rejoice and gives the reason for such rejoicing by adding a "then"; this is the outline of the hymn in the above example.[27] Or God's mighty deeds are recounted in one participial clause after another:

> Who makes a way in the sea,
>   a path in the mighty waters,
> who brings forth chariot and horse,
>   army and warrior,
> they lie down, they cannot rise,
>   they are extinguished, quenched like a wick.
>
>   (Isa. 43:16–17)[28]

Here the prophet so loves to combine this hymnic style with the prophetic style that he prefaces the passage with the prophetic phrase "Thus says Yahweh" and then continues with the hymnic participles.[29] In Isa. 63:17 there is the introduction of a hymn solo: "Yahweh's grace will I praise" (cf. Ps. 89:2). A hymn without such an introduction is the one Isaiah hears the seraphim singing before Yahweh's throne (Isa. 6:3). The song in Isa. 40:12–14 is replete with rhetorical questions that are characteristic of hymns (cf. e.g., Exod. 15:11). Such songs of rejoicing are sung by the people at Yahweh's festivals; the prophet reminds them of hymns at the announcement of "the feast", probably the Passover festival (Isa. 30:29).

In addition, there are the songs of lament, which in various situations of need are performed before the community assembled at the holy places (e.g., Psalms 44; 74; 79; and others). While the prophet ordinarily appears before his people on the side of Yahweh, as is appropriate for Yahweh's representative, in these prayers he stands over against Yahweh as the one who prays and intercedes for Israel. Making intercession had long been the prophet's highest right. Even the most terrifying prophets of doom occasionally break out into short intercessory sighs in the midst of their oracles of doom.[30] Such prayers now occasionally are converted into entire poems in which the prophet voices a song of lament for his poor tormented people (Jer. 14:7–9).[31] Rather different is the Book of Joel, where the prophet summons the people to a general day of repentance during a great plague of locusts and calls upon everyone to lament and wail.

Another variation of the same genre occurs when the prophet sings the future song of repentance. These men who have to fight so bitterly with their stiff-necked people think with deep emotion of the hour when hard hearts will soften and finally, finally the

people will turn to their God. Thus they compose the future song
of repentance with longing in their eyes:

> A voice on the bare heights is heard,
>   the weeping and pleading of Israel's sons,
>
> . . . .
>
> "Behold, we come to thee;
>   for thou Yahweh art our God.
>
> . . . .
>
> Let us lie down in our shame,
>   and let our dishonor cover us;
> for we have sinned against Yahweh our God."[32]

Repentance, along with funeral dirges, marks the mood of the
future festival described in Zech. 12:10–14.

Sometimes the prophet attaches Yahweh's answer to such songs
of lament, whether it is that God inclines his ear to the complaint
of his people or that he turns away in anger. Thus the people pray
in Hosea 14:3,

> Assyria shall not save us,
>   we will not ride upon horses;
> and we will say no more, "Our God,"
>   to the work of our hands.

And then the prophet answers in God's name,

> I will heal their faithlessness;
>   I will love them freely,
>   for my anger has turned from them.
> I will be as the dew to Israel;
>   he shall blossom as the lily.
>
> (Hosea 14:4–5)

Or as the frightening answer comes:

> Though Moses and Samuel stood before me,
>   yet my heart would not turn toward this people.
> Send them out of my sight, and let them go![33]

What results is a unique mixture of poetic and prophetic style.[34]
Elsewhere in the prophets, especially the later ones, we frequently
find passages in which alternating voices speak. In an older epoch,
in order to animate their oracles, they had already introduced the
use of speeches, for example, the boasting speeches of the Israelites
(Isa. 9:8), the Assyrians (Isa. 10:8–11, 13–14; 37:24–25), and the
wise men of Egypt (Isa. 19:11), the expression of despair of the
"inhabitants of this coastland" (Isa. 20:6) and of Moab (Isa. 16:3–
5), and also antiphonal speeches in which sudden changes in the
people speaking (as in German folk songs) are sometimes found

(Isa. 16:3–6). From that it was a short step to constructing an artful form of liturgy that was used in the worship service and that was obviously of very special impressive force. We know such a liturgy from Psalm 15 and Ps. 24:3–6: the lay choir appears at the gates of the sanctuary and asks how one must go about gaining entrance; the priests answer by enumerating the conditions of entrance, and they close with a benediction. This liturgical genre is used in Isa. 33:14–16 in order to represent the conversion of sinners into Zion, which will itself one day be saved. Frightened at the terrifying fall of the power of the heathen that they have just witnessed, they approach the sanctuary and ask, "Who among us can dwell with the devouring fire?" And in place of the priest, the prophet gives the answer: "He who walks righteously and speaks uprightly," and at the conclusion he promises that those who walk thus will enjoy divine protection in this difficult time. Similar but without the benediction is Micah 6:6–8: the contrite sinner recounts in the form of a question all sorts of accomplishments with which he wishes to placate the vengeful God, but the prophet's answer explains the true divine demand to him. The prophets filled such liturgies for worship services with their spirit and enriched them with their manner of speaking. Thus at the conclusion of this development appear extraordinarily rich creations that cannot help but have their effect on us as well insofar as we understand them. One of the most glorious liturgical productions is the passage in Micah 6:2–8, whose second part we have just mentioned: first comes a "speech of judgment" that the prophet addresses to Israel in the name of his God, a speech with a majestic beginning (v. 2) and—in real contrast to that—poignant reproaches (vv. 3–5). Then the second part follows: the man broken by this accusation enumerates the sacrifices he is prepared to offer to placate God, each one greater than the last, until he comes to the most powerful and gruesome one—the offer of his own firstborn son (vv. 6–7).[35] But now it is as if the sun is rising: God proclaims with sublime words that all of this is nothing! No sacrifice, but rather justice, mercy, and humility (v. 8)! Even richer is the liturgy in Isaiah 33. Extended poems of this sort are offered primarily by Trito-Isaiah (Isaiah 59; 61; 63:7—65:25) and the apocryphal Book of Baruch.[36] The appreciation of these liturgies has often been missed previously because the voice that is speaking tends to change without specific notice. To be sure, we must proceed with special caution if we are to identify such "liturgies." Not all those passages in which the same subject is discussed back and forth are to be thought of as a related totality, but rather we must reckon with the possibility that sometimes ordinary individual passages with similar content are written together without any further connection.[37] It will be the task of further investigation to determine which special connections generally appear in the prophetic "liturgies."

XVIII

With most of the prophets, their own personality recedes entirely or almost entirely behind their oracles: even Hosea would not have told about his marriage if it had not been for him an image of a higher event. Not until Isaiah and Jeremiah, who speak much more frequently about themselves than the earlier prophets do, does this change, and consequently we are much better informed about their personal lives. The fact that accounts about Jeremiah, probably from Baruch's hand, are also of a distinctly historical sort and are much more extensive than anything we have about the earlier literary prophets shows us that at this time there must have been general interest in a prophet's personality; people of this time had developed an interest in observing individuals. In the narratives of Genesis we may also observe the same change toward a way of looking at things which is capable of picking out individual details about a certain person. Thus Jeremiah is following the trend of his times as the one prophet who more than any other inserts personal comments among the oracles intended for Israel.[38] Here we become acquainted with his inner self: a man of tender nature, much too soft for his frightful vocation, suffering bitterly in having to do battle with his people, indeed, even with members of his own family, continually vacillating between painful sympathy and raging anger, between merciful intercession and the certainty that here no longer will any prayer be heard, struggling and quarrelling with his God and yet always being overcome by him. So it does not seem strange that he, the most personal of all the prophets, has made a new form his very own; he found it by adopting a genre not previously used by the prophets. We may conclude that such a breakthrough in the compulsory use of genres is this man's contribution. The new genre is the "individual's song of lament."[39] Such songs were sung at that time in the holy place by those who were sick or suffering, doubtless originally to accompany various purification and penance rituals. The prophet adopted this genre because it expressed the lament of and comfort for an individual soul. The heart of the singer of laments is full of anguish and sorrow, as indeed is the prophet's own! The singers lament, above all, over their physical suffering; the prophet's sore spot is that Yahweh's word has still not been fulfilled (Jer. 17:15; 15:18). The singers are surrounded by enemies who doubt their righteousness; how many foes the prophet has because of his prophesying! The singers rise at the end to the certainty that God will hear them and will triumph, sending a terrible fate upon their opponents; to the prophet, God himself announces that he will preserve him and topple his slanderers! Thus it is understandable that Jeremiah formulated his pains and comfort in "lament poems." Anyone who knows the permanence of such genres, however, will not be surprised to see how faithfully he follows the linguistic form of these songs. Earlier scholars, to be sure, assumed just the opposite and regarded Jeremiah as the creator of the entire type of poetry, even calling him the "first psalmist": they did not realize that such genres were not invented by an individual poet but rather developed in a long history, and they overlooked the fact that "lament poems" flourished even in Babylonia and Egypt long before Israel existed.[40] It is just as erroneous to declare, as G. Hölscher has done recently, that these songs of Jeremiah, which so characteristically resemble the Psalms, are not genuine. Instead, as W. Baumgartner has recently shown, their genuineness is guaranteed by the genuinely prophetic element that appears in them along with the common elements of lament songs. Above all, what is of note here is that added to the lament is an oracle of Yahweh that has come to the poet personally,[41] something that does not occur in the individual songs of lament in the Psalter and that is conceivable only with a prophet who hears God's Word.[42]

Deutero-Isaiah announced the experiences of his life, as a prophet in tune with Jeremiah's poems: he speaks about the high goals and the disappointments of his work, and Yahweh announces comforting words to him, entirely in the way that Jeremiah spoke with his God.

All in all, therefore, there is an extraordinarily well developed prophetic poetry, equally sublime both religiously and aesthetically, one of the greatest treasures of the Old Testament.

XIX

But as rich as all this is, in it the prophetic abundance is far from exhausted. For there is now a second line of development by which the prophets became preachers and teachers. The greatest among them were not satisfied with being only prophets. Although their primary concern was always to proclaim what was coming, they were imbued with the certainty that the future they were foretelling was a divine necessity: they demanded it in the name of religion and morality. They knew Yahweh's reasons for his plans. So the prophets of doom—for it is precisely they from whom this development proceeded—began speaking about Israel's sins that draw down Yahweh's wrathful judgment or about the sacrilege of the people whom Yahweh will annihilate.

In the style of the speeches that have been passed down we can still trace how this process slowly took place. In passages of the older style a brief word about the reason for the prophecy is sometimes added to the depiction of the future. Why must Tyre fall? "Yahweh Sabaoth has purposed it, to defile the pride of all glory" (Isa. 23:9). Why do the Persians overthrow the Chaldean empire? In order to punish the world for its evil (Isa. 13:11). Such reasons are often given at the end of the prophecy itself:

> All this is for the transgression of Jacob
>   and for the sins of the house of Israel.
> (Micah 1:5)
> And for all the countless harlotries of the harlot,
>   graceful and of deadly charms,
> who betrays nations with her harlotries,
>   and peoples with her charms.
> (Nahum 3:4)
> This shall be their lot in return for their pride,
>   because they scoffed and boasted
> against the people of Yahweh Sabaoth.
> (Zeph. 2:10; cf. Jer. 13:22; 16:10–13)

The more the moral idea comes to the fore among the prophets, the stronger are the references to the sins that have been committed. Thus "invective" appears alongside threat. Both usually stand so closely together in the same passage that first the doom is announced and then, after a "because," the sins are listed,[43] or the invective is followed by a "therefore" and the threat.[44] If the invective comes first, it is introduced with something like "Ah, you who,"[45] or "Hear, you who" (Amos 4:8; 8:4). Often it also happens that the prophets in their disregard of exact details switch back and forth, from threat to invective and then again to threat.[46]

This listing of sins by the great prophets of doom has now become a major point of their entire activity. They feel they are called to be "testers" (Jer. 6:27) and "watchmen" of their people (Ezek. 3:17); with great elation they distinguish from their own literary activity the pitiful style of the ordinary prophets who speak to people with their mouths (Micah 3:8). Thus a new, really prophetic genre, the independently occurring "invective," comes into existence. Such invectives might begin with the words

> Cry aloud, spare not,
>> life up your voice like a trumpet;
> declare to my people their transgression,
>> to the house of Jacob their sins.
>
> (Isa. 58:1)[47]

It was natural for the prophets to clothe such invective in the form of a "judgment speech" of Yahweh, that is a concrete image congenial to the thinking of ancient Israel and beloved by the prophetic way of speaking:

> Yahweh has taken his place to contend,
>> he stands to judge his people.
> Yahweh enters into judgment
>> with the elders and princes of his people.

And the speech thunders forth:

> It is you who have devoured the vineyard,
>> the spoil of the poor is in your houses.
> What do you mean by crushing my people,
>> by grinding the face of the poor?[48]

Frequently in such a speech of judgment there is an indignant question that makes sense by reference to the specific image of an interrogation, 'What do you mean?' (Isa. 3:15):

> O my people, what have I to do with you?
> In what have I wearied you?
>> Answer me!
>
> (Micah 6:3)
> What wrong did your fathers find in me
>> that they went far from me?
>
> (Jer. 2:5)

The later prophet depicts Yahweh's judgment at the last day as an occasion for assembling all the heathen and then demanding an answer from them for all the injustice they have done to him and to Israel (Joel 4:1-8):

> What are you to me, O Tyre and Sidon,
>> and all the regions of Philistia?

The same genre of eschatological judgment address, but without such questions, is found in the later apocalypses[49] and even in Jesus' amazing and captivating discourses about the last judgment (Matt. 5:31-48).

XX

This essentially describes the style of a man like Amos. But not completely, even for him! For the most austere and frightening person can also have his fill of invective and threat. He would have been no man at all if a "perhaps" did not creep into his soul: perhaps his activity may bring about a conversion and perhaps then Yahweh will show mercy once again (Amos 5:15; Zeph. 2:3; Jer. 26:3)! Driven by this "perhaps" his prophesying slowly turned from threats and invective to warnings. To be sure, threats and invective were always the first word for the prophets of doom, but alongside this they gradually began to use warning speeches, penitential sermons, and in this form they had an opportunity to develop their positive religious and moral demands.

Among the earlier prophets there is little trace of this development. Instead, they were convinced that for such a hardened people as Israel no warning will do any good, no repentance is possible any longer; if the spirit of harlotry once takes hold, it never again releases its grasp (Hosea 4:12)! No, the prophet's own preaching will avail nothing, but it will rather rob the people of the tiny amount of understanding that they still possess and topple them into the abyss (Isa. 6:9–10; 29:9–10)! From this mood then come the frightfully ironic warnings, warnings to do evil!

> Come to Bethel, and transgress;
>   to Gilgal, and multiply transgression.
> (Amos 4:4)
> Add your burnt offerings to your sacrifices,
>   and eat the flesh.
> (Jer. 7:21)

But sometimes the warning does break through even with the early prophets: "Seek me and live" (Amos 5:4–6).

> Hate evil, and love good,
>   and establish justice in the gate;
> It may be that Yahweh Sabaoth
>   will be gracious to the remnant of Joseph.
> (Amos 5:15; cf. Hosea 4:15; 2:4)

In such words we see how minimally the promise itself appears.

The warning appears more clearly in Isaiah who, despite his certainty that his people are marked for destruction, cannot refrain from speaking about weal (Isa. 1:10–14) and from placing a promise, in case they now obey, alongside the threat (Isa. 1:19–20; 7:9; 28:16; 29:5–8; 30:15; et al.); during his lifetime, after all,

Isaiah never tires of giving political advice (Isa. 7:3; 28:12; 30:15).

Even more positive is Jeremiah who, despite continually reinforcing the same fundamental conviction (Jer. 6:10, 27–30; 7:28; 13:23), cannot refrain from warning and admonishing, and in whose activity admonition plays such a major role (Jer. 3:13, 14–15; 4:1, 3–4, 14; 5:20–29; 6:8; 7:1–7; 11:1–5; 13:15–17; 18:11; 21:11–14; 22:3–5; 23:16; 26:13; 27:12) that it may be considered the real content of this message (Jer. 25:5–7), indeed, as it is the content of all prophecy (Jer. 7:23–26; cf. Zech. 1:4). But this change in his own style of speaking is connected with a thorough transformation in his conception of the prophetic vocation: he is convinced that he is proclaiming not an immutable decree of Yahweh but rather a plan that allows God to "repent" if the people repent (Jer. 18:11). Not only does the narrow gate of the "perhaps" stand open for the repentant sinner but the whole gate of divine mercy! And therefore the prophet feels obligated to raise his voice: "Turn back, everyone from his evil way!" (Jer. 18:11). A true prophet has the ultimate goal of "converting" the people from their evil doing (Jer. 23:22)! But in the same way that Jeremiah spoke to the people, Ezekiel spoke to individuals when everything was in ruins: "Cast away from you all the transgressions which you have committed against me. . . . Why will you die?" (Ezek. 18:31). And even among the later prophets, that is, the prophets of salvation, admonishing their hearers to do good is a main element of their activity (cf., e.g., Isa. 55:6–7; 56:1–2; Zech. 1:3–6; 8:9, 16–17; Hag. 1:8).

Such words of admonition, according to the prophets' orientation or the various concrete situations, are connected with promises (cf., e.g., Jer. 3:13, 14–16, 22; 44:1–2) or threats (cf., e.g., Jer. 4:3–4; 7:1–15; 13:15–17; 21:11–12), or with both at the same time (cf. esp. Jeremiah 18; Ezekiel 18; Amos 5:4–6). Then the grammatical connection between the two is something like this: "Listen to my voice, and . . . so shall you be my people" (Jer. 11:4), or "Circumcise yourselves to Yahweh . . . lest my wrath go forth like fire" (Jer. 4:4). In some places it is clear that the prophet regards the oracle that he is proclaiming, as Yahweh's revelation, but the warning that he attaches to it, as his own good counsel (Jer. 26:13; 27:13). The style of these warnings is in part poetry but also—especially in Jeremiah—prose.[50]

As novel as this manner of speaking may be as a whole, it still depends on what is already available. The predecessors of the literary prophets were accustomed to answering questions, a practice that continued into the later period. The practice also had an effect on their style: questions and answers, for example, are sometimes juxtaposed in prophetic speeches (Isa. 21:11–12; 14:32). Frequently people address specific questions to the prophets about what they should do in a certain situation, and to this they receive an answer in the form of a suggestion (cf., e.g., Jeremiah 42). At the same time, however, the priestly torah, that is, "instruction," had an effect on the prophets.

XXI

This priestly torah originated in Israel in the form of oral tradition. It was the chief task of the priests to teach the laity the ordinances of the worship services and also the precepts of law and morality. The torah was usually spoken in prose form—we may think of the Ten Commandments—but also to some extent in the poetic form of torah liturgies that were employed in the worship services and thus that emphatically impressed the demands of God upon the laity.[51] The liturgical and moral torah was usually in the form of "Thou shalt" or "Thou shalt not," [52] or of the conditional statement found especially in the legal codes, "If . . . , thus shall . . .," [53] or of an announcement of what is an "abomination" to Yahweh (cf. Deut. 7:25; 17:1; 18:12; 21:4).

The prophets also appropriated and made use of this genre. They were sharply opposed to one part of the priestly torah insofar as it demanded sacrifices and all sorts of ceremonies (Jer. 8:8), but they thoroughly approved another part, namely, that of the important religious and moral demands (Hosea 4:6; Jer. 11:1–5; 34:12–16; Isa. 2:3; Mal. 2:6). It was natural for them to make use of passages from the law for their purposes (Jer. 3:1; Hag. 2:12–14), or even for them to proclaim the torah themselves, but of course a torah that rejected sacrifices and ceremonies in strident tones (e.g., Amos 5:21–24; other examples include Isa. 1:10–17; Hosea 6:6; Jer. 6:20; 7:21–26; Isa. 58:6–8; 66:3; Zech. 7:4–7). This prophetic torah thus concludes with the third form mentioned above under the priestly torah forms. The prophets also adopted the liturgical torah with questions and answers (Isa. 33:14–16; Micah 6:6–8).

A new tone was introduced into the priestly way of speaking by the "Deuteronomist" and in its revisions and supplements: a peculiarly heartfelt, emotional admonition directed toward the people—style, however, that in its zeal for speaking to the people's heart became widespread. This is the same style of speaking that we find in Jeremiah's prose speeches. In its readily understood prolixity it is sharply different from the concise poetic style the same man is a master of (cf., e.g., Jeremiah 11; 18; 34). Some of this agreement, of course, may result from a subsequent reworking of both texts. Nevertheless, we should not forget that nothing compels us to assume that Jeremiah could have spoken in only one style: for example, the style of Goethe's lyrical poetry in his youthful years and Goethe's mature style in his later narratives are extraordinarily different. We should also not forget that Ezekiel occasionally spoke in the same long-winded torah style (Ezekiel 18). But at whatever time this transition may have occurred, the appropriation of this prolix, quietly flowing torah style is one of the most memorable events in the entire history of the prophetic style.

In these forms of the priestly torah the prophets now either proclaimed God's will or uttered warnings to those who were good. At the same time they found here a form to express their thoughts about the divine rule over nations and men. The basic teaching of Jeremiah about divine retribution, like Ezekiel's, is in the form of legal statutes: if a nation or person whom God threatens turns from its evil he will repent of his evil (Jeremiah 13; Ezekiel 18; cf. Ezek. 14:12–20). The most sublime statement to which the abstract power of prophetic thinking soared, the doctrine—what we should call a "religious philosophy"—of a totally justified retaliation, developed on the foundation of the torah.

No matter how foreign the prophetic and the priestly spirit might be to each other, they did borrow from and mutually enrich each other, something that can be seen in the way the prophets speak. In Ezekiel a priestly style is incorporated in the content of the prophecy. We may especially compare the temple vision at the conclusion of his book (Ezekiel 40—48)—in content a description of the instruments used in worship—with the way the priests later described the tabernacle (Exodus 35—40).

XXII

In order to communicate incisively their abstract thinking, the prophets make use of still another genre, the historical narrative. This too happened by itself. Is there anything more natural for a politician—and to a certain extent that is what the prophets were—than to remind people of the past, namely, the most recent past, in order to create from it a doctrine for the present (Amos 4:6–11; Hosea 5:13; 6:7–10; 7:7, 11; 8:4, 9; 10:9; Isa. 7:17; 10:9–11; 22:5–11; Nahum 3:8–10; Jer. 2:16; Zech. 1:6; et al.)? And again and again the prophets mention the Exodus from Egypt and the entrance into Canaan, for this period is considered the classical age of their religion, and they themselves rightly feel they are related to the figure of Moses in some way (cf., e.g., Amos 2:9–11; 5:25; 9:7; Hosea 9:10; 11:1; 12:14; Jer. 2:1–3; 7:22; et al.). The earliest of them, whose ultimate interest is solely in the present, make very little use of retrospective observations of things long ago. Not until toward the end of the history of Judah and especially in the period of the Exile does this change. Likewise, just as 1870 gave German historiography the task of examining how the unification of Germany came about, and as historians of the future will have to explain the collapse of the German empire and the national revolution in 1918, so did that race have an innate impulse to interpret Judah's fall, as a necessary part of its history writing. During that time, this task lay upon the prophet Ezekiel's soul; he tried to solve it by a series of glimpses into Israel's history.[54] Thus the prophets were attracted to historical philosophy: the powerful idea that history is a unity, a great divine-human activity, is an unforgettable achievement of its spirit. On the other side, to be sure, we should not misunderstand the one-sidedness of this way of looking at history, for its purpose was to give evidence of Israel's sins, which remained significant in all periods. Considering the forcefulness of the prophetic nature and the frightfulness of everything the prophets experienced, this perspective certainly comes as no surprise. That this same consideration was incorporated in the actual writing of history at the same time (cf. Isa. 43:27–28; 47:6; 48:3–5) shows us clearly that it was a necessary effect of the events on the thinking of that time.

What is characteristic is that such observations of history were given by Ezekiel in the form of allegory. This preference for allegory (cf. esp. Hosea 1—3) is perhaps explained by the custom of the prophets of interpreting dreams and visions in an allegorical way.[55]

XXIII

Although we have previously seen how the prophetic style was constantly enriched by adopting nonprophetic genres, we now must look at a drama that shredded this style from within. That process occurs by means of the opposition in which even the greatest of the prophets always stood over against their people. How often did these men who lived in the future set themselves against the natural sensitivity of their contemporaries! In times when their contemporaries rejoiced, they lamented, and they exulted when their contemporaries sorrowed! Thus strife and discord were the watchwords of their lives. In fact, even within the prophetic movement itself parties sometimes formed that fought each other with extreme bitterness.

The strife with their people or with the prophetic opponents had a powerful significance for the prophets and was expressed in their way of speaking. Thus the prophetic disputation came into being.

In order to understand such prophetic "disputations," we may imagine concrete situations in which the prophet meets his opponents. There Amos stands before the priest Amaziah (Amos 7: 10–17), Isaiah before King Ahaz (Isaiah 73), Jeremiah before the prophet Hananiah (Jeremiah 28), just as in the older histories Elijah stood before King Ahab (1 Kings 18:17–18) and the two prophets Micaiah ben Imlah and Zedekiah (1 Kings 22:24–28). The reader should always imagine such disputes when reading the disputations of the prophets.

This necessity of hearing arguments and answering them explains the prophetic practice of citing the words of the people or the opponent and then refuting them, often in a powerful and brilliant way.[56] So the Book of Malachi is almost entirely couched in speeches and replies; much in Haggai is similar.

To be sure, quoted words are often presented in a very subjective manner by the prophets—not in the way they were spoken but rather how they must have sounded to the prophets' ears. "We are hidden in the temple," Jeremiah has the people say, "in order to go on doing all these abominations" (Jer. 7:10); "We have made lies our refuge," the sly politicians say to Isaiah (Isa. 28:15; other cases are Jer. 2:20, 25; Isa. 30:16); it is the prophet's conviction that what his contemporaries are doing is an abomination and that their trust rests on lies, but the people themselves would never have admitted such a thing. After all, the prophets straightforwardly called their opponents "lying prophets," a word that today's scholar certainly should not repeat with them.

A great many of the prophets' ideas are to be understood on the basis of these struggles with their opponents, even those which are not expressly indicated as such. Yahweh will protect us for the sake of the covenant, the people think. No, precisely because of it he will punish you, for precisely because of it can he demand something from you, replies Amos (3:2). Us alone has he brought up, people say; the Syrians and Philistines, too, the prophet adds bitterly (Amos 9:7). When he is called upon to explain why he is prophesying, he makes it clear in an image that he can do nothing else: he has to speak (Amos 3:8). They say, Yahweh's arm is too short to save us. No, he replies, it is your sins; they separate you from him (Isa. 59:1–3)! Even some of the unusual baroque phrases can be explained as products of these vocal or silent confrontations with contemporaries' thought. They praise Canaan as a land that is flowing with milk and honey; so it shall be—says the prophet— namely, when all cultivation of fields ceases and only cattle raising is left (Isa. 7:21–22). To them Israel is Yahweh's glorious grapevine. That it is, the prophet cries, but he adds grimly: And do you not know that grape branches are good for nothing but burning? And that is what will become of you (Ezekiel 15)! "Hear," is the way the popular speaker begins everywhere in the world, thereby hoping that his auditors will be able to hear and understand him. "Hear, as much as you will, you will understand nothing," says the formidable Isaiah (Isa. 6:9). The songs of joy begin: Rejoice, O Israel! But the prophet begins, "Rejoice not, O Israel!" (Hosea 9:1). And the same man named his daughter Not Pitied (Hosea 1:6), whereas other fathers try to give their children beautiful names.

But, above all, the style of the prophets changed most strongly in this constant confrontation. For now they felt themselves obligated to blunt the objections leveled against them, to get the obstinate to feel the magnitude of their sins, to show the secure the necessity of judgment; or contrariwise, to restore the fallen to confidence with comforting words, to display Yahweh's might to the doubters. These are all tasks far removed from the original prophetic genres. Thus the prophets attempted to work through examples and they yearned for parables (Amos 3:3–8; 5:19; Isa. 5:1–7; 28:23–29), or they cited proverbs (Ezek. 12:22; 16:44). They clearly expounded the right of a good cause in the form of "judgment speeches" (Isa. 41:1–13, 21–29; 43:9–13; et al.). In a few prophetic passages this led them away from using the old genres and into developing an excitingly new way of speaking in disputations (examples occur in Jer. 2:14–19 and in Deutero-Isaiah).

XXIV

This prophetic writing then had the most powerful effect on later literature: the genres that the prophets appropriated—filled with their spirit—were reused by their pupils. Thus began a lyricism enriched by the prophets, the writing of Psalms, then a prophetic torah, the "Deuteronomist," and a way of writing history that we meet particularly in the Books of Judges and Kings. Later, these genres, nurtured as they were by the successors of the prophets, had a more profound influence among their people than the prophets themselves had ever had.

XXV

Not until the work described above has been completed and scholarship is acquainted with the prophetic genres and their history will it be possible to depict with complete certainty the literary personalities of the prophets, some of which are distinctive. Here are only a few suggestions about only the most important prophets.

First there is the gloomy Amos, full of wrathful fervor, with his one-sided ruggedness. The genres he employs are primarily threat and invective, and in him those styles are most fully developed. Along with threat and invective are a few very simple visions, and here and there replies to the objections of the people. The units that make up the speeches are usually rather short; as with the earlier prophets, the language is thoroughly poetic, terse and full of images. The book is lacking in organization.

Then there is his contemporary Hosea, a richer nature, vacillating between vehement wrath and fervent love. Alongside frightful threats and invectives he places the attractive promise of total divine mercy and individual lyric elements, indeed, things that are already liturgical in form. Above all, however, the conflict with the people comes to the fore and causes his style to disintegrate. Sometimes it is as if the prophet is addressing his opponents in nervous excitement. Characteristic of him is the lengthy, scintillatingly clever allegory of the first chapter, in the constantly repeated statements of which he may be describing some sleepless nights with groans and tears. The units that make up the speeches are of varying length. Unfortunately the text has been seriously corrupted.

Next comes the sublime, royal Isaiah, not torn apart inwardly like Hosea, but also not as single-minded as Amos. The messages of doom and salvation are amalgamated by him into a total construct, the "counsel" or "work" of Yahweh. His speech, full of power and vitality, rolls majestically forth. Compared with Amos and Hosea, its units have grown significantly; he also understands how to organize these longer passages as a unit. The disjointed and ecstatic elements, which characterize his predecessors, recede in him. He is frightening in his threats and invectives, which for him are also the starting point of his style. He is powerful too when he turns to the proclamation of salvation; and in other genres as well—in the torah, the parable, the funeral song (in a derived sense, Isa. 1:21), the disputation—he is a speaker and poet of the first class. He also has words, along with the "I" discourses of Yahweh, words about Yahweh that express his own prophetic conviction. His masterpiece is the vision of his calling, in the recounting of which he organically weaves together a series of genres: the song of the seraphim that he hears bears the form of a hymn; the words the seraph addresses to him when he is empowered are reminiscent of sacramental priestly words accompanying such actions in the worship service; and then there is a cruel inversion of the introduction of prophetic speech (v. 9), as well as a commission of God to the prophet (v. 10), a terrifying threat (vv. 11–13), and at the conclusion a very secretive, indeed distant, promise.

So much for the first generation of prophets in the Assyrian period. The second generation, which experienced the fall of Jerusalem to the Chaldeans, is, from a literary point of view, distinguished from the first by the fact that now the diversity of styles has increased extraordinarily because of the work of the earlier prophets. By this time there are a multitude of prophetic genres enriched by men like Jeremiah and Ezekiel.

The main genres in Jeremiah: in his prophetic proclamation of the future, as well as in his threats, the basic element of his style, he displays a strongly ecstatic excitement. In the almost passionate, almost melancholy and sensitive, disputations with his people he is comparable to Hosea. In heartfelt, moving warnings he wants to induce Israel to repent. Characteristic is his adoption of the torah genre, in which he, following the prolix prose style of the contemporary "Deuteronomist," presents his people with an "either-or," at the same time, however, expressing the deepest understanding of prophecy. By including personal elements in his speeches to the Deity (*Gottes-Worten*), he dares to describe his own experiences in detail in order to unburden his woes in prayer to his God, by following the rather precise usage of the genre of "individual lament songs." In short visions he follows Amos's style. There are a few symbolic acts.

His younger contemporary Ezekiel, although similar to him in many respects, is in others far different: Jeremiah, cautious by nature and suffering in the depths of his being; Ezekiel, his basic mood poured from the same mold. The former, full of tender sympathy for his miserable people; the latter, without pity, harsh, somber, even cruel, embittered by the struggle, severe even in his prophecies of salvation. The latter, the apex of prophecy in his opposition to all outward "holy things"; the former, following priestly ideas. In invective and threats, as well as in his forceful funeral songs and song of derision, in which he adopts older mythological material of many kinds, Ezekiel, full of untamed ferocity, is more baroque than great. In his visions, which in contrast to Jeremiah's are greatly extended, and in his miraculous acts, he shows himself a thoroughly ecstatic personality. In preaching about God's rule over humanity, in the prose style of the torah he follows Jeremiah. He likewise expresses his philosophy of history, demanded by the events of the time, in prose, in great allegorical historical overviews. The priestly spirit appears prominently in his description of the temple, at the book's conclusion. With Ezekiel one finds, remarkably, extreme, frightful, loudly proclaimed passion standing side by side with wide-ranging, matter-of-fact rational exposition. In his case, the units are often very long. He himself has arranged the whole book chronologically.

At the end of the exile is Deutero-Isaiah, the prophet of salvation. Full of overflowing enthusiasm, he proclaims the liberation of the captives and the radiance of Jerusalem, and breaks out in ecstatic hymns of jubiliation over the greatness of God. With various sorts of observations and proofs he seeks to lead those who are in despair to the heights of his faith. Invective is completely absent; instead of warning, he proclaims trust and comfort. Filled with pain, he speaks personally about his rejection by his people, with a fervent faith that not even the prospect of his death is able to destroy; this builds on Jeremiah's forms of self-expression. The speeches tend to be long. The units are shorter than in Ezekiel. The book is without any further divisions.

In the following age the tones that had sounded, continued, in general without any special originality.

XXVI

The preceding sketch should be taken by the reader not as a "result of scholarship" but as an attempt to master the immense amount of material. The field of a history of prophetic literature is rich indeed; in the future may there be no lack of workers who will understand how to harvest its rich fruit!

Bibliography: H. Gunkel, "Die israelitische Literatur," in *Die Kultur der Gegenwart* (Berlin and Leipzig: B. G. Teubner, 1907–), part 1, sec. 7, pp. 51ff.; idem, "Propheten II," in *Die Religion in Geschichte und Gegenwart*, 2d ed. (Tübingen: J. C. B. Mohr [Paul Siebeck], 1927–30), 4: 1538–54; idem, *Die Propheten* (Göttingen: Vandenhoeck & Ruprecht, 1917), 104ff.; H. Gressman, "Die literarische Analyse Deuterojesaias," *Zeitschrift für alttestamentliche*

Wissenschaft (1914): 34; 254–97; W. Baumgartner, *Die Klagege-dichte des Jeremia* (Giessen: A. Töpelmann, 1917); L. Köhler, *Amos* (Zurich: von Beer, 1917), 33ff.; idem, *Deuterojesaia* (Giessen: A. Töpelmann, 1923); P. Volz, *Der Prophet Jeremia* (Leipzig: A. Deichert, 1927), xxxv ff.

NOTES

1 The same is true for the visions of Amos 7:1–9; 8:1–3, which belong together but have been separated by an account from the life of the prophet in 7:10–17.

2 *mah lāk 'ēpô'*, v. 1; *mah lĕkā pōh*, v. 16.

3 Three sections, each with four double lines.

4 This error is found very frequently in, e.g., the Bible translation by Kautzsch.

5 For such a style, cf. the discourses about Babylon placed together in Jeremiah 50—51.

6 It is completely impossible to contemplate such a large composition, one combining seven long lines each. Hebrew poetry lacks the means for connecting such "stanzas" into a whole.

7 Cf. H. Gunkel, "Mythen und Mythologie in Israel," in *Die Religion in Geschichte und Gegenwart*, 2d ed. (Tübingen, J. C. B. Mohr [Paul Siebeck], 1927–30), 4:38–90.

8 Exceptions, e.g., are the visions in Isaiah 6 and Jeremiah 1, which are delivered in free rhythm.

9 Jer. 4:23–26; Isa. 21:1–10; 63:1–9; cf. also the Balaam oracles.

10 Zech. 1:9–12; 2:2, 4, 6; 4:4–6a; et al. The interpretation of Zech. 4:14 remains unclear.

11 Cf. 1 Sam 2:27–28, and esp. the prophecies of Daniel about the fate of the Seleucids and Ptolemies, Dan. 11:5ff.

12 Num. 24:17. This explains the constantly changing images in the Odes of Solomon.

13 The old name of Jerusalem, Isa. 29:1; 33:7.

14 Isa. 8:3–4. "Before the king of Assyria" certainly should be explained as an addition.

15 Precisely because of this, we should move especially cautiously whenever a name is mentioned; if we remove it by conjecture, the interpretation will be obscured. This applies to Hab. 1:6.

16 On the prophets' use of imperatives and interrogative sentences, see below, sec. 15.

17 Isa. 23:1; Zeph 1:11; Joel 1:5–12; Jer. 22:20; 25:34; Zeph. 3:14; Zech. 2:14; 9:9.

18 Micah 1:4; Zeph. 1:18; 3:8; Deut. 32:22. According to H. Schmidt, the words in Zeph. 1:18 and 3:8 are an addition.

19 *Wāw* consecutive with the imperfect.

20 Hebrew: imperfect and *wāw* consecutive with the perfect.

21 On this *perfectum propheticum*, cf. Gesenius-Kautzsch § 106 n.

22 Jer. 4:5–6; cf. Jer. 6:1, 25; 8:14; 48:6; Hosea 5:8; Zech. 2:10–11.

23 The credit for being the first to discover this genre within the context of other Israelite genres goes to Karl Budde; recently it has been extensively presented and explicated on the basis of many comparable passages from the most varied peoples by Hedwig Jahnow, *Das hebraïsche Leichenfied in Rahmen der Völkerdichtung* (Giessen: A. Töpelmann, 1923).

24 Other examples of the prophetic burial song are Isa. 14:4–20; Jer. 9:16–18; Ezekiel 19; 26:17–18; 27; 28:11–19; 32.

25 The best example is Isaiah 14.

26 Cf. my article in *Theologische Rundschau* 20:265ff.

27 Cf. also Isa. 42:10; 49:13; 52:9; 12; 25:1–5. The same structure of a hymn is already in Miriam's song, Exod. 15:21.

28 Other examples of the participle style are Isa. 40:22–23; 42:5; 44:24–28; 46:10–11; Jer. 31:35; 51:15; Amos 4:13; 5:8; 9:5–6; on this, cf. Ps. 103:3–5.

29 Isa. 43:16–17; likewise Isa. 42:5; 44:24–28; Jer. 31:35.

30 Amos 7:2, 5; Jer. 4:10; Ezek. 9:8; 21:11–12; ironically directed, Hosea 9:14; Isa. 16:9, 11.

31 Other examples are Jer. 14:1–6, 13, 19–22; 15:5–9; Isa. 63:7–9.

32 From Jer. 3:21–25. Other examples include Hosea 6:1–3; 14:3–7.

33 Jer. 15:1; on such rejection of prophetic intercessions, cf. Jer. 7:16–20; 11:14; 14:10–12.

34 Examples of prophetic lament songs of the people with oracles attached are Jer. 3:4, 5a, with the answer in 5b; 3:22–25 with 4:1–2; 14:1–9 with 14:10; 14:19–22 with 15:1–4; Isa. 26:8–14a with 14b, 15; 26:16–18 with 26:19–21; 63:7–64:11 with 65; Hab. 1:12–17 with 2:1–5; Micah 7:7–10 with 7:11–13; 7:14–17 with 7:18–20. Cf. also the oracle in Joel 2:18–27 that follows the summons to repentance and the lament song of Joel 2:17.

35 There is also evidence of such great numbers of applications to the divinity among the Babylonians; cf. H. Zimmern, *Beiträge zur Kenntnis der babylonischen Religion*, 2ff.

36 Bar. 4:5—5:9. Cf. also the beautiful liturgies in Isaiah 25—27 and Micah 7:7–10. The song of Moses in Deuteronomy 32 also belongs here.

37 Cf. Isaiah 40; Jeremiah 30—31. This against P. Volz, *Der Prophet Jeremia* (Leipzig: A. Deichert, 1922), xxxviii.

38 Cf. Jer. 4:10, 19–21; 5:4–5; 6:10–11; 7:16–17, 27–29; 8:6, 18, 21, 23; 9:1; 11:14, 21–23; 13:17; 14:17–18; 15:10; 16:1–13.

39 On this genre, cf. W. Stärck, sec. 3, vol. 1, 2d ed., pp. 157ff. The "lament poems" of Jeremiah are Jer. 11:18–20, 21–23; 12:1–6; 15:10–12, 15–21; 17:12–18; 18:18–23; 20:7–9, 14–18.

40 On Egyptian "lament poems," cf. H. Gunkel, *Reden und Aufsätze*, 145ff.; on Babylonian, cf. W. Stärck, sec. 3, vol. 1, 2d ed., pp. 34*ff.

41 Jer. 11:21–23; 12:5–6; 15:19–21; cf. 15:1; 14:11–12.

42 In addition, the expressions "as my mouth" (15:19) and "stand before Yahweh" (18:20) are genuinely prophetic; likewise the names Anathoth (11:21, 23) and even Jeremiah (18:18 and 15:20–21) agree with 1:18–19.

43 Classic example: Amos 1:3, 6, 9, 11, etc.

44 Amos 4:11; 5:11; 6:7; Isa. 5:13; 10:16; 29:14; Jer. 2:9, 5:6; etc.

45 In Hebrew *hôy* with the participle or something similar; cf. Isa. 1:4–9; 5:8, 11, 18, 20, 21, 22; 29:15; 30:1; Amos 5:18; 6:1; Jer. 22:13–17; et al.

46 A noteworthy example of such movement back and forth is Amos 2:6–16.

47 Other examples of invective are Isa. 1:2–3, 4–9; Jer. 2:10–13.

48 Isa. 3:13–15. This same disguising of invective as judgment address occurs in Isa. 1:18–20; Micah 6:1–5; Jer. 2:4–9; Hosea 2:4–7. Psalm 82 is a replica.

49 The best example is 4 Esd. 7:37–44.

50 The model example is Jer. 7:1–34.

51 Cf. the liturgies mentioned above and in Psalms 15; 24:3–5.

52 As in the Ten Commandments.

53 On the cultic torah, Deut. 12:20–31; 13:2–18; Hag. 2:12–14.

54 Ezekiel 16; 20; 23. An earlier attempt at this is in Jer. 3:6–13.

55 Cf. H. Gunkel, "Allegorie," in *Die Religion in Geschichte und Gegenwart*, 2d ed., 1:219–20.

56 Amos 5:14; Isa. 22:13; 28:9–10, 14–15; 30:16; Zeph. 1:12; Jer. 2:20, 25, 27, 35; 3:4–5; 7:10; Ezek. 11:3, 15; 12:22–23; 18:2; 21:5; Isa. 40:27; 58:1–3; Hag. 1:2; 2:3; et al.

2

Cult and Prophecy*

SIGMUND MOWINCKEL

I *General Matters*

We must now direct our attention to the relationship between the prophetic and the cultic.

If the prophetic elements in the Psalter presuppose a cultic reality, this is an indication that the communication of divine replies must have had a firm place in the cult. That will strike us initially as a bit unusual. We find it natural, to be sure, that the cult and thus also the cult liturgy must have contained a sacramental moment. But the idea which we ordinarily connect with the word "prophecy" apparently does not correspond to the idea we have of cult. After all, we are accustomed to finding in the "prophetic" the antithesis of the "cultic." And at first glance there appears to us to be an unbridgeable gulf between the fixed forms and formulas of the cult and the free inspiration of prophecy.

And yet, in fact, a connection does exist between them. In Israel it appears in that the priest is often at the same time the one who reveals God (see below). The priest can mediate revelation through technical means; thus it was the priest who used the Urim and Thummim. But as officeholder he can also be the one who enjoys a special inspiration that adheres to the officeholder and that is transmitted by succession or initiation into an office: to whom God gives the office, he also gives understanding, in this case inspiration, the prophetic gift. Thus, according to late Jewish belief, the high priest as such has the gift of prophecy (see John 11:51).

In what we have said above about this thesis we have already indicated that we are not using the word "prophetic" in the usual sense of the word in Old Testament history of religion. In itself, the

* First published in *Psalmenstudien III* by S. Mowinckel (1922) 4–29. Translated by James L. Schaaf.

concept "prophetic" is a formal concept. But in theological language it has usually received a very precise content, and the very fact that a formal concept usually, but not always, is used with a precise content, has contributed, I think, to the great amount of squabbling over what is "prophetic" and what is not "prophetic" in Israelite religion,[1] for the different writers use the word in an imprecise manner and are themselves unclear about which meaning they are employing.

In this context I do not, as apparently is usually the case, understand by "prophetic" those trends, persons, and thoughts in Old Testament religion which are also represented, among others, by the so-called "literary prophetics" who emphasize the ethical and the anti-cultic, and in part certainly also the personal side of religion. I am taking the word here precisely in the original, formal sense. I understand a "prophet" here as one who, by appointment of society as well as by the divinity, provides the community with necessary information in religious things directly from a divine source by virtue of an extraordinary supply of power, one who definitely knows about divine things, either because he is inspired or capable of receiving revelations or because technical means are available to him through which he can mediate the will and instructions of the divinity and can convey the same to the community as an answer to a question or to a prayer. In this sense of the word the prophet is altogether not a private person who coincidentally appears. He is an employee of the society, an institutional link between the two members of the covenant, the community and the deity. In this sense the Babylonian-Assyrian religions had their prophets, as did the Greek religions and those of Syria and Asia Minor, and in this sense the primitive religions generally had their prophets, whether called priests, shamans, medicine men, or whatever term might be used.

However, it is obvious that with this word alone nothing is said about the value or lack of value in the different sorts of these manifestations. Rather this question is everywhere dependent on the sort of religious and moral content that the various forms have held. In many places the institution of the prophet did nothing to bring the development of the religion to higher levels. In Israel, by contrast, for reasons which do not interest us here, it became the basis of one of the most significant influences in religious and moral development.

Every cult, as far as its contents are concerned, consists of two elements: the sacrificial and the sacramental, as Christian liturgiologists have often expressed it. In place of these terms, however, we might also say the human and the prophetic. We should not understand this in such a way that the two elements are apportioned purely externally to congregation and to liturgist; the liturgist, the priest, can appear as the one who conveys the sacramental, as well as the sacrificial. Sacrificial elements are actions and words which come from the congregation, from men, and are addressed to the divinity, such as offerings, prayers, laments. Sacramental elements are actions and words in which the divinity speaks to men and deals with them, such as benedictions, answers to prayer, consecrations, sacraments in the strict sense of the word, etc.

Insofar as cult is composed of both these elements and consists of speech and response, action and counteraction, it takes on dramatic characteristics and becomes a drama. And insofar as it is directed toward something and produces something—and this it always does—this drama is a creative act, a real, creative drama.[2]

In some form the sacramental, the prophetic, exists in every cult. And insofar as it appears in the form of words, we must speak about prophetic words in the cult.

Since almost every cult, except perhaps those from certain extreme Protestant movements, begins with the presumption that the transmission of such prophetic words cannot come from just anyone, but rather that certain personal qualifications are necessary, the cult almost always has certain functionaries whose task and privilege it is to be bearers of the cultic word of the prophet. That is, the cult has special cult prophets. It need not always be the case that the cult prophet is a different person from one of the actual liturgists; liturgist and cult prophet can be combined in one person. In other cases, however, the cult under consideration has certain officials who function exclusively or primarily as cult prophets. Then we distinguish between liturgist, that is, the priest in the actual sense, and the cult prophet. In Israel, as we shall see, both cases appear.

The personal qualifications which are associated with the office of cult prophets consist of special equipment, a special gift of power or inspiration which makes them bearers of the prophetic word. This gift of power distinguishes them from the laity, and where the cult prophet is different from the priest, there occasionally his gift of power is also different from that of the priest. Thus in Israel, where the priest emphasizes his serious calling, the cult prophet, as do prophets generally, emphasizes his free inspiration by the spirit.

When the prophetic word appears as part of the cult, we can think of two cases and see them demonstrated. The liturgically fixed elements—for every cult insists on fixed forms of an "agenda" and sees in them a guarantee of its holiness and effectiveness—need only be the matrix of the prophetic appearance; the form and content of the words are left more or less to the genuine momentary inspiration of the individual prophet who appears. Or else the content of the words is also fixed in the agenda; only the style and form of the words that are proclaimed there in the name of the divinity are the product of a free, momentary inspiration. The transition between these two forms is fluid insofar as it frequently may also be true that in the first case the content is also prescribed for the particular prophet delivering the divine announcement; he has to prophesy as the authorities wish (cf. 1 Kings 22:5–13); only the more precise poetic formulation of the words is then left to the prophet.

If the Psalms are really cultic psalms, and if therefore we are examining psalms which are cultic prophecies, it is thus probable from the very outset that we are dealing with words of God of the latter of the two different types mentioned above. For these pronouncements in Yahweh's name through the mouth of a prophet are usually to be considered elements in the agenda of a fixed, frequently repeated liturgy whose content as well as form are prescribed for official reasons. The divine answer is then not "inspired" anew each time, but rather prescribed by the "agenda." Then all that remains for free inspiration in the worship service is the prophetic form.

But here an intermediate form is also conceivable and probable. This or that prophetic psalm may originally have come into existence as the product of a momentary, subjective, genuine inspiration at a time when it was left to the prophet's free inspiration to produce the formulation and in part perhaps also the content of the words, but precisely this kind of oracle was regarded as exemplary and therefore later became associated in the agenda with a certain cultic celebration. This is almost certainly the case with the oracle in Psalm 60 (see below). I also have the impression that this is the way it happened with most of the royal oracles.

Here the pious reader of the Bible may object that this notion that the production of inspired prophecies, yet with prescribed contents, was a responsibility of the cult prophets is certainly a profanation of the Psalms; it would certainly almost lead to a conscious hypocrisy of the authors involved; something like that should not be ascribed to the holy men of the Holy Scriptures.

But the profanation of the Psalms is not nearly as great as the orthodox profanation which lies in suddenly regarding such a burning, fervent cry from the depths as Psalm 22 or Psalm 69 not as a real prayer, but as a "prophecy" of Christ; how for centuries the pious could tolerate and endure this mockery of a prayer life is something I simply cannot comprehend.

But if we think about this a bit more carefully, we shall realize that the interpretation mentioned above of the "prophetic" Psalms in question is not a disparagement of them at all.

First we must observe: if we are correct that men with prophetic gifts and inspiration had their place and calling in the fixed order of the cult, the fact remains that these prophetic Psalms—which unquestionably come from the circles of cultic functionaries—were certainly composed by prophetically gifted men. The initial origin of the psalm may then be an "inspiration"; nevertheless, they were written by men who were filled with the consciousness of their calling and their gift of being able to proclaim the will of God. Whether we share this conviction depends precisely on the impression of personal genuineness which the individual psalms can awaken. Let me note here that, in my opinion, the prophetic Psalms of the Psalter enjoy a pre-eminent position; I sense more of what is genuine and personally experienced in Psalms 73, 122, 123, 126, 130, and 131.

Second, we have to say that we must distinguish between spiritual origin and practical use. The subsequent practical use cannot degrade the origin; on the contrary, the noble origin justifies the subsequent practical use. Thus the Christian *Seelsorger*—whether priest or lay—has an unshakeable right to apply to any Christian who is seeking help the "revelations" of Jesus which promise forgiveness of sins to very specific individuals in his time and thus to claim: in these words God is speaking through me to you. In so doing he will be neither a hypocrite nor a deceiver, and the words of the Lord will not be dragged into the dirt.

II *The Seer and Priest*

As already indicated, cultic prophecies presuppose a firm connection between prophets and holiness, or, if one prefers, between the priestly and prophetic calling and person.

That the priest gave divine replies to certain questions, that is, oracles, is sufficiently known. These oracles are the so-called *tôrôt*, sing. *tôrāh*, the same word that later became the all-encompassing designation of the divine law. The priestly *tôrôt* have their own style.[3]

But now it is noteworthy that it is not this priestly Torah-style, but the nabiistic oracle-style that we encounter in the Psalms. In

Israel the *nābî'* is the real bearer of the divine revelations (cf. Deut. 18:9ff.).

Older than the nabi, however, is the seer *rō'eh* or *ḥōzeh* (see 1 Sam. 9:9), who, however, in the course of time merged with the nabi. The seer's forms of revelation—vision, nocturnal apparition, dream—were taken over by the nabi.[4] The nabi is demonstrably of non-Israelite origin, as is already indicated by the foreign word *nābî'* whose root appears nowhere else in Hebrew, although it does occur in Assyrian;[5] nabiism is a common Canaanite manifestation. But in all probability seerism is genuinely Israelite. The type of the seer is Samuel, and a form of this type is Moses; not until the later tradition are both of them turned into nebiim to correspond to the changed situation at the time.

But it is true of the ancient Israelite seer that he is a priest at the same time. As we said, his type is Samuel. The redactional note in 1 Sam. 3:21 which calls him a nabi is not part of the original content of the tradition. This Samuel belonged to the temple in Shiloh ever since birth. He is a disciple and apprentice of the priest Eli and is his assistant in performing his priestly office: he cares for Yahweh's lamps in the sanctuary. The account of the first revelation to Samuel is now abbreviated for the sake of the later legends which make him into a judge over all of Israel; it is really arranged in order to correspond with the account of Samuel's assumption of the priesthood after the death of the old teacher and the collapse of his godless house.

Samuel's priestly position is also presupposed in the account in 1 Samuel 9. It is closely related to the elevation of the offering, *bāmāh*; no sacrificial meal takes place without him: he first must have "blessed" the sacrificial meal; the cultic blessing, however, is a priestly calling.

Even the later accounts of 1 Sam. 13:7ff. and 15 know Samuel's relationship to the sacrificial worship.

Like Samuel, Moses is also a priest and seer. Num. 12:6–8 places him high above a nabi—Samuel, too, stands higher than the nebiim who are subject and obedient to him (1 Sam. 19:20)—the passages in Deut. 18:15; 34:10, and Hos. 12:13 which make him into a nabi are deuteronomic.

Like Samuel, Moses entered into training for the priesthood, with his father-in-law Jethro (Exod. 18:14ff.). He is the priestly mediator at the establishment of the covenant between Yahweh and Israel (Exod. 24:8). He is the custodian of the holy tent of revelation, the portable sanctuary, and he presents before Yahweh the affairs of the people and of individuals (Exod. 33:7ff.). As a priest he is at the same time a revealer to whom Yahweh conveys his will. In Yahweh's name he makes decisions of legal and cultic nature. And, finally, his descendants become priests after him (Judg. 18:30).

That the priests as such were still mediators of revelation in a later period of history is something we can see elsewhere. They are the bearers of the ephod and, as such, they deliver oracle replies (1 Sam. 14:3, 18–19, 37, 41ff.; 22:18).

We also find that seers were people who were officially appointed. David had his own seers at court (2 Sam. 24:11). But someone officially appointed as a seer has little to do with free inspiration; his activity is of a priestly sort.

In reality, this connection between "priestliness" and "prophetness" is of great antiquity, and, as we have said, very widely attested. We also find other traces of it in the soil of Semitism. In Assyria there was a special class of priests that was called *barû*, that is, seers. It has long been noted that there is a hint of an original connection in the Arabic equivalent of the Hebrew *kōhēn*, *kahīn*, which also means seer.

The connection, or better, the identity, of the two offices rests upon the fact that the seer-priest was originally the one gifted with extraordinary power (*mana*), who because of this also had the discernment to associate with the deity, as well as the gift of "seeing," prophesying, and performing miracles—even in Israel soothsaying and performing miracles go together; Moses the priest is a great miracle worker, who with his miraculous staff (*Wunderstab*)[6] performed the most remarkable miracles (Exod. 4:1ff.; 7:14ff.; 8:12ff.); so were the nebiim (1 Kings 17:7–24; 2 Kings 1:9ff.; 2:8, 14, 19–25; 3:16ff.; 4—8). That the priest is the one who has the power under certain circumstances also to function as seer and soothsayer is indicated by the common Semitic word for priest, *kōmer*, *kûmrā'*, etc., whose basic meaning is "the fervent one," that is, the one with power.[7]

It is precisely the ancient Semitic type of priest whom we meet in the unity of *Heiligtumsmächter*, that is, one who in certain circumstances is also the priest offering sacrifices and the soothsayer (seer, prophet).

In the Israelite evaluation of the monarchy we find the same presupposition that it is the gift of power which equips one to fill the priestly office as well as to soothsay and to prophesy. The king, the chief, was originally the one who had more power than others—a concept that was replaced in historical Israel with the parallel one of his being the one possessed by the spirit of Yahweh. As such he is priest (1 Sam. 13:9–10; 2 Sam. 6:13ff.; 1 Kings 8:5, 14–64; 2 Sam. 7:18; Ps. 110:4) as well as revealer, one who is prophetically gifted (2 Sam. 23:1–7), as was Moses, the chief.

Whether already in pre-Canaanite times there existed this division of the original unity into actual priests, who were more cultic functionaries and manipulators of the technical means of revelation, and the seers, who had a special ecstatic aptitude and whose primary or exclusive calling was that of the mantic, or, in other words, whether at that time there was already a conscious distinction between the general gift of power, knowledge, and skill on the one hand and the specifically ecstatic-visionary ability on the other, is something we do not know.

It is possible that ancient Israel already distinguished between priest and seer; in actuality the name *rō'eh* already speaks in favor of this possibility: a word whose fundamental meaning is perhaps not originally a description of a person whose chief calling was a cultic one; the Arabic *kahīn* first took on this meaning in the course of development. Yet we can also say that the original cultural level of the cult in its specific sense is no everyday occurrence; in everyday life people needed the one with the gift of power, the shaman, etc., more than magicians and people with mantic abilities, more as "seers" than as leaders of the cult; the cultic functionary in the particular sense often developed from the "seer." To this extent it is quite possible that the name *rō'eh* in Israel was an original name for the "seer-priest."

At any rate, the sagas of Moses and Samuel show that it was quite well known at that time that *rō'eh* stood in a precise relationship with the place of the cult.

The original unity of priest and seer had twofold consequences in Israel. First, in certain cases the priest in the later specific sense of the word, that is, the cult priest, always remained the revealer of the divinity. Second, the heirs of the seer, the nebiim, took over many elements from the original connection between cult and priesthood. Thus in later times we also often find priest and nabi united in one person (Ezekiel, Jeremiah).

III *The Priest as Mediator of Revelation*

That the priests performed prophetic functions is frequently attested. Before them were laid serious and difficult situations to which they were to give a divine answer.

Here we can distinguish cultic questions, juridical questions, and questions that relate to the future.

A cultic question was once presented to the priests by Haggai: if one carries holy flesh in the skirt of his garment and the garment accidentally touches something edible, does the food then become holy? The priests answered "No" (Hag. 2:10ff.). In Haggai's time this question had probably become traditional; but in similar situations a direct divine answer would once have had to be obtained.

When it says in Exod. 18:26 that the elders rendered judgment in simple matters while all difficult cases were presented to Moses, the presupposition is that Moses laid the questions before Yahweh and obtained his decision. This priestly pronouncement of oracles in juridical cases ("God's judgments," ordeals) is something we may suppose happened frequently. Especially is this so when it was a matter of revealing a concealed perpetrator of a crime. Compare this to the story in 1 Sam. 14:36ff. Who had provoked Yahweh's wrath, a member of the king's house or one of the people? Through the Urim and Thummim, administered by the priest, the guilty one was discovered.

Saul also attempted to use the same means to obtain an authoritative reply to the practical question: Shall I go after the Philistines or not (1 Sam. 14:36ff.; 1 Sam. 28:6); likewise, David (1 Sam. 23:2ff.; 30:7ff.). These are questions that really pertain to the future: "What will happen, when?" is their content. Thus one inquires what the outcome will be before going to war or engaging in battle: David asks, "Is it true, Yahweh, that Saul will come?" Yahweh answers through the one bearing the ephod, that is, the priest: "Yes." "Will the men of Keilah surrender me and my men into Saul's hand?" Answer: "Yes" (1 Sam. 23:9ff.). Or: "Shall I pursue after this band? Shall I overtake them?" Answer of the priest: "Pursue; for you shall surely overtake them" (1 Sam. 30:7–8. See also 2 Sam. 5:19).

If we observe the form of these questions we see that they are so formulated that a simple Yes or No suffices as an answer. The answers given also correspond to them. Things are no different in 1 Sam. 30:7ff. either. Verse 8 is nothing but a simple Yes to the elaboration in the question.

This agrees with what we know about the priestly means of oracles. Where the revealer is an officially appointed servant of the authorities or of society, then the means of revelation must be purely of a technical sort. The priest must have means in his hands by which he can call forth an answer whenever one is desired. These answers mentioned above were given by the priest bearing the ephod. But the ephod—even in ancient times—is not an image of an idol or of God, but a container or a garment of some sort used in connection with the safekeeping or use of the Urim and Thummim. (See 1 Sam. 14:41–42; LXX, 28:6.) But Urim and Thummim in all these passages are holy lots which are used in delivering oracles. When casting the oracle lots the question can be put in the form of alternatives; the lot will then give the briefest reply possible.

But the example of 1 Sam. 30:7–8 shows that the priest who proclaims the answer is not satisfied with giving a simple Yes or No. He formulates each reply in the style of the question, giving it a richer form. Very probably we have an instructive example of this sort in 2 Sam. 5:23–24. Here, too, analogous to the other uses of oracles, David inquires of the lots, and the answer, looked at carefully, contains nothing more than what the priest can discern by the lots. The question was, in effect: Shall I go after the Philistines or shall I fall upon their rear? The lots replied: You should fall upon their rear. But now the appropriate time for initiating an attack on the rear is at the end of the night, in the morning twilight. But the morning twilight will be signalled by a freshening of the wind before sunrise. The noise of the wind in the treetops will be regarded as the steps of God striding over the heights of the earth. The priest accompanying the troops knew this well. Instead of the simple: "You shall attack them in the rear," the answer gives a richer, more mythological form by giving at the same time the consequences and the self-evident reasons of the divine answer: "You shall not go up; go around to their rear, and come upon them opposite the balsam trees. And when you hear the sound of marching in the tops of the balsam trees, then bestir yourself; for then the Lord has gone out before you to smite the army of the Philistines."

IV *The Nabi as Cultic Functionary*

The ancient Semitic office of the seer and the priest was repressed on Palestinian soil by Syrian-Canaanite nabiism.

That nabiism is not of genuine Israelite origin—if we understand by "Israelite" that which stems from pre-Canaanite times—is not generally acknowledged, to be sure, but it should not be doubted. The office of the enthusiastic-orgiastic prophet—which is the nucleus of the old nabiism—is a common occurrence in Canaan, Syria, and Asia Minor, while we find nothing of the sort on the soil of pure Semitism. Here I refer simply to the material which Gustav Hölscher has collected and examined.[8] The arguments which have been given for an inner-Israelite origin of nabiism are futile. It is claimed that it must have originated as a reaction against what was specifically Canaanite, since the nabi wears the clothing of the wilderness period; but the camelhair coat, as such, as well as the ascetic life style, may not be derived from life in the wilderness and the nomadic ideal; the "magic" coat of the nabi would sooner indicate an orgiastic cult and the initiatory sacrifice associated with it.[9] That the nabiism in Amos 2:11 is regarded as a gift of Yahweh naturally does not serve as proof (contrary to Stade, *Biblische Theologie des Alten Testaments*, p. 67); when the amalgamation of Israelite and Canaanite elements had become a fact, everything of value naturally became regarded as Yahweh's gift and institution. Neither does the co-operation of the nebiim with Jehonadab the son of Rechab (2 Kings 10:15ff.), which Stade also emphasizes, speak in its favor, nor does the general zeal of the nebiim for Yahweh. For whom should the Yahweh nebiim be zealous, if not for the God who inspired them? The most fanatic adherents of Islam are not the Arabs, but the southern Sudanese dervishes. As those possessed by Yahweh, the nebiim naturally were fanatic devotees of Yahweh. People then seek the same thing in any activity inspired by the same fanaticism. But from this we cannot conclude anything about a common origin. The Yahweh cult of the period of the monarchy, just as the people of Israel during the monarchy, arose as a mixture of Israelite and Canaanite elements; nevertheless, the people always felt themselves a unit. The attitude of the later prophets, of whom not a few were really nebiim (cf. Amos 7:14), against Canaanite cultic elements is naturally not proof for its source and original nature; these prophets do not at all represent the genuine and actual nabiism, but they are mostly rejected by the nebiim of their time and thus are involved in continual polemics against them (cf. 1 Kings 22; Jer. 27—28).[10] The common appearance of the nebiim with Jehonadab the son of Rechab thus does not mean that they are reacting to the Canaanite elements as such, but rather that as Yahweh nebiim they are defending themselves against the competition of the Baal nebiim, and that as Yahweh's fervent devotees they are combating the cult of Baal. At that time one could no longer distinguish "the Canaanite as such" from the "genuine Israelite," because at that time both elements had already inseparably amalgamated and had formed the unity of historical Israel. Therefore we also see that everything which was valuable was uncritically represented as Mosaic, even something with such an indubitably "Canaanite" origin as the *mishpatim* of the book of the covenant and the culture that they presuppose. As representatives of the "national religion", the nebiim self-evidently are always "nationalistic" in orientation and in particular circumstances they represent what was considered the ancient legacy of the fathers, as did Samuel against Agag (1 Sam. 15:32ff.); but that nation and that national religion were the Canaanite-Israelite mixed nation and mixed religion. After the mixture had taken place and was no longer recognized as such by those who were alive, its old customs and sanctuaries, from wherever they had come, were venerated and defended with equal zeal by all the elements which had combined in the mixture. The antithesis between Saul and Samuel in 1 Samuel 15 is that between practical, political reason and blind, religious fanaticism, not that between Canaanite and Israelite.[11]

Thus there is also no doubt that it is no coincidence that we first hear of nebiim under Saul; their origin has no connection with the uprising against foreign domination.

In the course of time this nabiism which was taken over from the Canaanites now assumed the nature and functions of the seers. This was especially true of its connection with the temple and cult. We can state it in this way: the old temple "prophetness" always took its character more from the nebiim.

From the very beginning the nebiim were not priests; the Old Testament always distinguishes between priests and prophets. As the priest is the one who bears the *tôrāh* which first of all is connected with the cult, so the nabi is the mediator of the divine *dābār* which is principally regarded as free inspiration (cf. Jer. 18:18). According to the Priestly Code the nebiim were to have no access to the actual temple building; this mirrors the old fact that from the beginning they were not cultic functionaries in the narrow and specific sense of the word, not *měšārětîm*. And thus it is also true, as we shall see below, that not all nebiim as such, who have entered into a firm institutional connection with the cult, stand in the old *rō'îm* and *ḥozîm*; those nebiim of a later time who are active as institutional cult prophets are at the same time viewed as Levites (singers), and perhaps also in most cases they have come out of their ranks.

Since the nature of nabiism is always one of orgiasm,[12] it may be assumed that the nebiim were originally representatives of the community which was captivated by the ecstasy of the orgiastic frenzy of the cultic festival, and were filled by divine power to the point of madness, as the entire community ideally and theoretically really should have been. They, along with the priest-seers, were the real *religiosi* of the community who had come forth from the laity.

And yet—or precisely therefore—they have a close connection with the sanctuaries; in this respect their position is analogous to the *Galli* in Hierapolis.[13] The nebiim are active at festivals and in cultic actions (1 Kings 18:16ff.; Jeremiah 26; 28; 36); the first nabi band which we meet comes from the high place (1 Sam. 10:5). The nabi organizations are based at the cultic sites, in Ramah (1 Sam. 19:19), in Bethel (2 Kings 2:3), in Jericho (2 Kings 2:5), in Gilgal (2 Kings 4:38). Balaam must first build an altar and offer sacrifices before he can prophesy (Num. 23:1ff., 14ff., 29ff.). The nebiim are often mentioned together with the priests (Isa. 28:7; Jer. 4:9; 6:13; 14:18; 18:18; Mic. 3:11; Zech. 7:3).

According to Jer. 29:26 they are under the supervision of one of the priests of the temple. Jeremiah was a priest and a nabi (Jer. 1:1); so was Ezekiel (Ezek. 1:3). We shall not err if we suppose that perhaps most of the later temple prophets came from the circle of the lesser cultic personnel (cf. 2 Chron. 20:14).

This close connection with the priests and the temple rests partially upon the fact that the old cult prophets were replaced by the nebiim or were transformed to accord with that image. The connection of the nebiim with the temple thus became an institutional one.

In Jer. 29:26 we are unquestionably dealing with an institution (*Institut*) of temple prophets. That there was such an organized institution (*Institution*) of temple prophets is proved to us also by the passage in the Chronicler which is either understood incorrectly or, at worst, not understood at all (1 Chron. 15:22, 27). The verses speak about Chenaniah the Levite, the *śar hammassā'* (to be read thus according to the LXX, instead of *ysr bmś'*). Without revealing a trace of doubt, Kittel in the *Handkommentar zum Alten Testament* translates it "the chief bearer," and just as uncritically claims that *maśśa'* can mean "carrying" as well as a "(musical) presentation". Benzinger in the *Kurzer Hand-Commentar zum Alten Testament* also allows carrying, but he quite correctly knows that *maśśā'* has never meant and can never mean a presentation and he has also noted that, in this context, one would hardly expect a notice about carrying or carriers. The wisest is Buhl who in his Danish translation of the Old Testament considers the words untranslatable. And yet the words' sense is very clear. The chapter deals with the preparations for the festival of bringing in the ark, which was celebrated each year with a great procession.[14] Along with sacrifices, singing, and music, the prophetic voices also belong to this festival.[15] As Psalms 132 and 81 show, this prophesying is fixed in both content and form (see below). 1 Chron.

15:22, 27 is to be interpreted in this context. *Maśśā'* here does not mean burden, but oracle. Chenaniah was "the leader of the oracle (affairs)."

The passage shows us that there were also some among the temple functionaries whose calling it was to give divine utterances, *maśśĕ'ôt*; they were organized like the other temple functionaries; at their head was a leader, a *śar*, who "understood" the art of proclaiming oracles (v. 22b). These temple prophets belonged to the Levites, and, according to the context and v. 27b, to the singers (cf. 2 Chron. 20:14). All of this is very natural. Prophetic ecstasy is nurtured by music (1 Sam. 10:5; 2 Kings 3:15); revelations were occasionally accompanied by music (Ps. 49:1–2); and, as we shall see, we have cultic oracles in the form of psalms. Thus we find it completely normal to seek for cult prophets and also authors of prophetic psalms employed among the temple singers. This accords with the circumstances in Babylon. Here a class of priests bore the name *bārû*, that is, seers; here also the *maḫḫû*, the (raving) prophets, were officially organized.

What we see of such temple prophets at a somewhat later time does not have the character of the old seers, but that of nabiism. Or, more precisely, in the main it has the peculiar characteristics of nabiism, but it has been influenced by certain distinctive characteristics of seerism. This accords with the general course of the development of things in Israel: the old Israelite seerism was absorbed and replaced by Canaanite nabiism. Ever since ancient times the seer-priests' most important means of oracles had probably been visions and dreams on the one hand, and on the other hand the purely technical means (oracle lots, etc.), which we have already seen practised. The ability of these people—according to primitive thought—rested on the possession of special power: they were clairvoyants, visionaries, and capable of performing miracles; for example, they had the necessary "soul power" to bless. At that time the vision or dream was probably also stylistically the actual form for revelations.

Later nabiism set the tone. This development is revealed in the following way. In place of the more indefinite gift of power there is inspiration by the divine spirit, the *ruaḥ Yahweh*. This means, however, that the enthusiastic form of the prophetic office has supplanted the visionary-ecstatic one. The visionary, the ecstatic person, is "outside himself"; his soul, his "heart" sometimes departs from him, seeks faraway places, and sees secret things (cf. 2 Kings 5:26); he is whisked away and his alter ego looks on tranquilly in the heavenly councils (cf. Zechariah's nocturnal vision), or his soul wanders to some distant place (cf. Ezek. 8:1–3; 11:1ff., 24–25). Meanwhile the seer's body lies absorbed and as if dead in its usual place (cf. Num. 24:4); while Ezekiel's soul is in ecstasy in Jerusalem his seemingly lifeless body lies in Chaldea "before the elders of Judah" (cf. the account in Ezek. 3:12–15).

In contrast, an alien power has entered the one possessed by the spirit, has taken control of him; he has been "divinized"; the spirit of Yahweh speaks through his mouth. The nabi also performs miracles; this he does because the spirit is in him. Because the spirit, who knows everything, is the divine word "in him," he utters true prophecies. The form of revelation that is characteristic of the nabi is therefore the word spoken rhythmically by the spirit or by Yahweh, the word in which Yahweh speaks in the first person. Here, therefore, the purely technical means of revelation, such as oracle lots and the like, recede; the nabi always appears as one observing the form of free, momentary inspiration, even when, upon request or as his duty, he is proclaiming the word expected and required of him. Such things appear as indirect means of revelation which, according to experience, encourage the enthusiastic-orgiastic situations: music and dance (1 Sam. 10:5–6, 10ff.; 2 Kings 3:15), loud, repeated shouts, self-inflicted wounds (1 Kings 18:26–29), hand clapping and wild movements (Ezek. 6:11; 21:19, 22), etc. While the seer by the nature of his gifts and his priestly office was usually, if not always, a man who stood by himself, the first nebiim always appear in bands and communally seek even greater excesses of orgiastic ecstasy (1 Sam. 10:5; 19:20; 1 Kings 18; 22:6; 2 Kings 2; 6:1ff.; on this, see the expression referring to organization and communal life, *běnê hanněbî'îm*, 1 Kings 20:25; 2 Kings 2:3; 4:1, 38; 5:22; 6:1; Amos 7:14; the expression *něwāyōt*, 1 Sam. 19:18ff., probably goes back to a communal dwelling, a type of cenobium.) Thus in later times the name *rō'eh* also disappeared; from now on someone who conveys divine revelations is instead always called a *nābî'*, even when he belongs to the real nebiim (Amos 7:14).

This does not mean that the older forms of revelation have disappeared. It is well known that visions and revelations in dreams were forms which the nebiim also favored highly. In reality there is no psychological distinction between ecstasy and enthusiasm; in large measure the actual psychic concerns of the seer and the nabi were the same. In ancient Israel, too, the conceptual demarcations were fluid. Thus Ezekiel says that his transferral in a vision from Chaldea to Jerusalem was done by (Yahweh's) spirit (Ezek. 3:12, 14; 8:3; 11:1, 24); this spirit is depicted in part as a being that grasps him from without (Ezek. 8:2–3), and in part it is thought of as a spirit that has entered into the prophet (Ezek. 2:2; 3:24).

Alongside what in theory is the free inspiration of the nabi, certain of the purely technical means of revelation also remained in existence, the sacred lots, for example. But it appears that in later times these were restricted to those who were priests in the strict sense of the word; this was the case, at any rate, with the Urim and Thummim. But the revelations of the nebiim, insofar as they are subjectively genuine, are always psychologically transmitted. The nabi is viewed as someone permanently endowed with the spirit. As such, when speaking ex professo, he always speaks at Yahweh's commission. This explains the cult prophet's bona fides and inspired manner of speech both when speaking in the line of duty and to some degree when speaking the precisely prescribed words of the cultic liturgy. In many cases this consciousness would have evoked certain psychic conditions in him which he would have interpreted as being possessed by the spirit and which would have allowed him to appear as bona fide.

That these temple prophets were obligated at certain cultic ceremonies to give an oracle with a content appropriate for the ceremony and one that agreed with the faith and expectations of the majority of the community or its authorities is something that we can conclude from numerous accounts. For example, the four hundred prophets of Ahab came together at a day of prayer before the campaign in order to deliver a prophecy about the outcome; naturally they prophesy in the same way as most clergy in warring states now preach; in this regard the Old Testament prophets are no better and no more perfect than the Catholic, Lutheran, Anglican, or Methodist priests and preachers; they even expected a favorable oracle from Micaiah and declared it treason when he did not give one (1 Kings 22).

The same thing is found in Jeremiah 28. Here, too, all the people have assembled to pray in the temple. The event is the planned revolt against Nebuchadnezzar: Will it succeed or not? "Give us good fortune, Yahweh, O let it succeed, Yahweh!" Then Hananiah the son of Azzur steps forward; he knows his "state churchly" duty and responsibility. "Thus says the Lord of hosts, the God of Israel: I have broken the yoke of the king of Babylon."

The account in 2 Chronicles 20 is typical. The enemies of Judah are about to attack. King Jehoshaphat appoints a great day of repentance and celebration, and the whole community comes together in the temple. The king as the priest and the people's intercessor calls upon Yahweh for help. It is obvious that this is not something without form, but that it is taking place according to a fixed ritual. And, in accordance with the analogies above, it is also part of the ritual, the "agenda," that the Levite—a singer, see below—Jahaziel the son of Zechariah falls into an ecstatic rapture; as we learn in 2 Kings 3:15, 1 Kings 18:28, and 1 Sam. 10:5, the nebiim knew of technical means that could induce rapture. Its form is naturally a free, unsought, momentary inspiration; therefore the Chronicler also says: the spirit of the Lord came upon him (2 Chron. 20:14). The enthusiastic singer now promises in Yahweh's name the complete destruction of the enemy. Thereupon all in the community fall upon their faces to honor Yahweh; the festival closes with an (anticipated) hymn of thanksgiving.

Both in this account as in the above mentioned passage in 1 Chron. 15:22, 27 the cult prophets involved were numbered among the Levites, more specifically among the singers. Indeed, we certainly must conclude from the latter passage that if the leader of the oracle givers belonged to the singers, the same must have been true for the entire organization of institutional cult prophets. This accords with the view of the later, postexilic period which permitted no non-Levite among the temple officials; even the Gibeonite hewers of wood and bearers of water are made into Levites in P and Chr. Nevertheless, we must conclude that the postexilic period had taken the cult prophets into the ranks of the Levites (singers) in order thereby to legitimatize them. From then on they are primarily singers, secondarily prophetically gifted men. To the same degree that the cultic prophecies they presented were bound to the agenda (see above) and yet came to be regarded in line with the other cultic psalms, the distinction between cult prophets and ordinary singers was obscured, until finally the sense that the cultic giving of oracles had once been a special cultic task of a special order was lost. Thus to the Chronicler the above mentioned Jahaziel the son of Zechariah is scarcely more than an ordinary singer-Levite who was grasped by the spirit in a coincidental way at this special occasion and who thus could proclaim Yahweh's answer. Perhaps the Chronicler thought this was a special display of Yahweh's grace toward the pious King Jehoshaphat.

Thus the institution (*Institut*) of cultic prophecy gradually died out. It was gradually and almost imperceptibly replaced by a precentor singing certain, long-fixed prophetic psalms. The entire music of the temple became more or less the work of a very pallid divine inspiration indeed (1 Chron. 25:1–3), within which the precentorial presentation of oracle psalms was nothing out of the ordinary.

How early or late this happened is something we cannot say. The old institution (*Institut*) of cultic prophecy, whose nature and form were free, was surely alive until the exile; this is shown by Jer. 29:26 (cf. Jer. 20:1–2), as well as by the circumstance that at that time so many of the completely free nebiim came from the ranks of the priests (Jeremiah, Ezekiel).

But even after the exile we meet prophets who are totally temple prophets: primarily Haggai and Zechariah. Especially with Zechariah is it apparent that virtually his entire imagery and general worldview come from the cult: the candelabra, the temple oil, the cultic cursing, the purification rites (symbolically expelling the impurity by swinging birds; cf. birds in the purifications in Lev. 14:6–7), the days of fasting, etc. It was his chief aim to see the temple completed and the cult re-established; besides that, he is extremely interested in reconciling the two rival temple authorities, the governor and the high priest. Zechariah, too, is very probably of priestly descent.[16]

Joel is very probably also a cult prophet (see below). And even under Nehemiah we meet nebiim who reside in the temple and appear in the religious and political controversies as supporters of the concerns of the priestly party, and who are subject to the authority of the priests, as are the temple nebiim in Jeremiah's time (Neh. 6:10–14); that these temple nebiim were also active in some way in the official cult is a very natural assumption.

At the time of the Maccabees, in contrast, there apparently was no institutional cultic prophecy, just as there no longer was institutional prophecy at all (see 1 Macc. 14:41)—unless Psalm 110 is regarded as "Maccabean," a claim which I reject, among other reasons because it can not be reconciled with the aforementioned passage.

V *Form and Technique of the Cultic Oracle*

At any rate, the means by which the priest or prophet learned the divinity's answer to a question or request originally presented to him were certainly also of a technical nature.[17] This is clearly seen in the obtaining of oracles by using the Urim and Thummim, the sacred lots, and the ephod mentioned above. Other legitimate means of oracles also appear to have been known. Thus it is possible that the superscription *'al šošannîm, 'al šûšan 'ēdût* in the psalms (Pss. 45:1; 60:1; 69:1) refers to a particular method of obtaining cultic oracles (see *Psalmenstudien IV*).

Many analogies support the assumption that obtaining oracles in Israel was somehow related to sacrifices; compare the Babylonian-Assyrian inspection of livers and the Etruscan-Roman auguries and haruspices. Balaam's sacrifice (Num. 23:1ff.) points to a relationship between sacrificing and prophesying; compare the account about King Zakar-Baal's sacrificial festival in Byblos in the Golenischeff papyrus.[18] The sacrificial auguries consisted of taking certain characteristics of the entrails (e.g. the liver) of the animals sacrificed, or the circumstances surrounding the sacrificial acts, such as the rising of the smoke or the like, and regarding these as "signs" and interpreting them as the divinity's will. Gen. 4:4–5 indicates that such auguries were also practised in Israel. There are many of these signs, to be sure, and not all of them need be interpreted in the context of auguries. In Ps. 74:9 the people complain that they no longer "see our signs," that is, oracles that are favorable to them (the same expression in Assyrian); on the contrary, they say, the prophets are silent. When Ps. 86:17, a typical psalm of lament,[19] says, "Show me a sign of thy favor," it is certainly to be interpreted in the light of the petitions which frequently appear in the Babylonian-Assyrian psalms: "Give me a good sign," and it is very probably a reference to the sign of an augury.[20] Finally, mantic signs could have been part of the prophet's everyday experience.[21]

Dreams must also be considered as sources of cultic oracles and signs. It is well known that the dream is a means frequently used by the nabi.[22] "Give me a good dream (i.e., one that promises well-being)," appears frequently in the Babylonian-Assyrian psalms.

A special sort of dream oracle which must have been employed by the cult prophets is incubation. We see in 1 Sam. 21:8 and 1 Kings 3:5 that this form was known in Israel. Perhaps the psalms of lament refer to it a few times.[23]

The account in 2 Chron. 20:14ff. as well as the prophetic psalm of Hab. 3 (see v. 16) show, however, that in the course of time the cult prophets adopted the forms and expressions of nabiism which were free and based on inspiration of the spirit. The difference between the technical and the more psychologically based revelations of the nebiim is not a sharp one; technical means can evoke psychic effects which the one involved regards as signs of divine inspiration. This happens, for example, when ecstasy is evoked by external means such as music and dance; the ecstasy then produces mysterious situations of the soul in which faces are seen and voices heard, and the prophet's normal or subconscious experiences of consciousness are objectified as divine inspirations. Hence the oracle forms merge together; everything is derived from the "spirit."

Thus the claim will be made that even the professional priest-prophets are possessed by the spirit and therefore they receive the gift of prophecy as part of their office. We have seen above that this belief was still alive in the Gospel of John.

VI *Cultic Prophecy and the Writing of Psalms*

The examples which we have mentioned above deal mostly with public days of fasting and repentance and with cultic inquiry about wars and battles. In addition the cultic oracle appears at a great religious-national festival (1 Chronicles 15). The prophetic psalms must now be set in this context.

We may regard it as already proved that on certain occasions the direct divine speech by the mouth of an official and authorized mediator of revelation had a place within the liturgy for prescribed days in the ancient Israelite cult. That the liturgy, at least in part, must have had poetic and musical forms is something we know from the many cultic psalms; in fact, many psalms are cultic liturgies. And from the very beginning the word of divine revelation in Israel had a poetic, rhythmical-metrical form. The same thing must have applied to the words of revelation in the liturgies.

A cultic liturgy in which different voices (such as lament, trust, prayers of the congregation) echo with the cult prophet's answer given in the name of the divinity, and which concludes with a hymnic psalm of thanksgiving—this is a psalm in both the broad sense and in the Old Testament sense of the word. Truly, the psalms of the Psalter are not always unified creations in the sense that they speak with but one voice and one sentiment; many of them are cultic liturgical compositions which express several voices and sentiments.

From this point of view we must now examine the traditional psalms which also contain prophetic voices. It will be our task to identify cultic oracle psalms among the traditional "prophetic psalms" and in certain cases to demonstrate that they are such.

Here a few words may also be said about the author of the psalm. It is in the nature of the case that the responsibility of composing cultic psalms should fall to the cultic officials; they also would be the ones with an interest in having many such psalms available. In addition, the activity of so doing would undoubtedly cause many of the temple officials to have a desire and aptitude for such work.

Among the cultic officials there is one order that we may assume had a special interest in the writing of psalms. That is the order of the temple singers. They were responsible for the temple music, and we know that at that time singing and music always belonged together. At any rate, the songs that were sung in the name of the congregation, the people, were undoubtedly sung by the official singers. And we shall hardly err in assuming that the cultic songs of an individual, such as the songs of lament to be sung at the rites of purification, were not sung by the sick person, but by the singers. There certainly were not many of the common people who understood the artistically correct way of rendering the psalms that accorded with the tradition and all of the ritual details. All analogies indicate that the songs were not sung from the "printed page," but from memory. And that could not have been expected of the laity. Every ancient cult put great store on correctly performing all the prescribed details with precision.

But we also shall not err in assuming that most, if not all, of the ancient cultic songs were composed by men who belonged to the order of temple singers. For that was the order which had to deal with cultic songs.

Moreover we now know from the ancient orient that writing at that time derived from special inspiration. The writer was a divinely inspired man who had received a "supernatural" gift.

We know from many indications that ancient Israel also shared this belief. At that time the writer and the prophet were very closely related. The nabi is always a writer at the same time; in ancient time his oracles always have the rhythmical-metric form (cf. the words of Balaam and the benedictions of Jacob and Moses). The ancient hymn of victory in Judges 5 was ascribed to the prophetess Deborah; only someone gifted with prophecy—so they thought—could have composed such a song. Just as the prophet "whose eye is closed" can see even distant and future things (Num. 24:3) so that his closed eye is in reality the only truly "uncovered" one (Num. 24:4), and just as with his open ears he can hear the secret divine and heavenly voices (1 Sam. 9:15; Isa. 22:14), so does the writer of Ps. 19:1–4a receive the hymn of heaven "which cannot be heard (by human ears) without speech and without word." Just as the prophet is transported by music into the state of inspiration (see above), so also is the writer (Ps. 49:2–5); his ear becomes sensitive so that he can receive the secret wisdom that comes from the divinity (*ḥokmāh, māšāl, ḥîdôt*) and transmit it to humankind; at the sound of the lyre he shares his secret tidings; it is precisely the prophetic consciousness which speaks in the introductory words of this psalm. A *maśkîl* is a cultic song, originating from such an extraordinary giftedness, "ability," and knowledge, which also explains its real efficacy.[24] This is how we also understand it when the Chronicler uses the word *nibbā'* (1 Chron. 25:1, 2, 3) to describe the cultic functions of the singer, or even calls the singers *nĕbî'îm* (ibid., kethib[25]): the singers are prophetically gifted and exercise their art in the strength of prophetic inspiration.

If this is so, we must also suppose that the liturgies, which evidence a prophetic consciousness in the specific sense of the word and in which direct divine revelations are imparted, also originated among the temple singers. But this means, to turn things around, that it was also exceptional singers who appeared in the cult as inspired cult prophets, or perhaps more correctly, whose duty it was to appear as such at certain occasions. For as such they had the gift of singing and writing, that is, the gift of inspiration, of being possessed by the spirit, of prophecy. This was just as obvious to ancient Israel as it was to Mohammed: anyone who can write is inspired, and can, if need be, also prophesy.

Our hypothesis is also confirmed in the sources. The cult prophet Jahaziel the son of Zechariah mentioned above is, according to 2 Chron. 20:14, a descendant of Asaph, that is, he belongs to the temple singers.

And even the fact that we have so many prophetic psalms among the temple songs, as we shall see below, confirms the close connection that existed between writing psalms and temple prophecy.

In addition, we have another source that confirms the connection between prophecy and temple singers and psalm writers, namely the book of Habakkuk.

Here I place less weight upon the fact that Habakkuk apparently is a man well acquainted with the cultic writing of psalms and their form. I note that the first two chapters of his book not only adopt individual motifs of psalm composition, but that they take precisely the form of a liturgy for a day of lament and prayer, with a lament ("O Lord, how long?" 1:2), a description of need (1:3–4), the praise motif (1:12–13), the conviction that one is heard (2:5–20), and a divine answer (2:1–4), so that one might be tempted to say that the two chapters are to be regarded not as a prophecy with lament motifs, but, on the contrary, as a liturgy for a day of prayer that is strongly influenced by the prophets' style and conceptual world and written by one prophet. It is more important in this context, however, that ch. 3 is a genuine psalm, so strongly influenced by the prophetic nature, that it was certainly written by a nabi (cf. 3:16). And that this psalm was employed in the cult and also that it was probably written for cultic use is shown in the cultic-liturgical notes in v. 1 and v. 19b (on this, see also vv. 3, 9, 13).

The genre of the psalm is to be regarded as a mixture of prophecy and of a psalm of trust.

It begins as a psalm of trust (v. 2); the author's trust rests as much on Yahweh's earlier great deeds (v. 2b) as especially on the fact that he has received a revelation (v. 16). The content of this revelation is transmitted in vv. 3–15. From this we also conclude that the psalm does not intend to be a psalm of trust in general; the ascription of trust is based on a special circumstance of need in which the people and the king, the whole "congregation," find themselves (vv. 12–14); the plea for help in being delivered from the need is clearly audible in the confidence expressed, for the psalm intends to be a petition offered in trust, a *tĕpillāh* (v. 1). Here the revelation received is not conveyed directly to the congregation as a response to its petition, but instead the author expresses his grateful "assurance of being heard" in the form of describing Yahweh's coming. The description begins with Yahweh speaking in the third person, then changes in v. 8 to the second person, thus increasing the impression that the description is intended to function as an "assurance of being heard." All Yahweh's great salvific deeds in ancient times and in the present, and those yet to be expected, merge here into a single one, so that one really dare not pose the question of whether here the prophet is describing past or future events; the author wants to say: Thou who always doest such things wilt also this time save thy people and thy anointed.

Here Yahweh's intervention is depicted in terms of the enthronement myth: appearance in order to do battle, battle of the primeval sea, new creation (the present time of need is a time of chaos, *tōhû wābōhû*, v. 17), "war of the peoples" myth, deliverance from need (see *Psalmenstudien II*, Part 1, chapter II, 1).

The psalm ends with an explicit statement of the assurance of being heard and with the anticipated thanksgiving (vv. 18–19), as the lament psalms and liturgies of the days of prayer often do (e.g., Ps. 60).

The author of this psalm is given as the nabi Habakkuk, the same man whose prophecies in chapters 1—2 were so strongly influenced by the style of the psalms, and there is absolutely no reason to doubt the accuracy of this ascription. The psalm must be pre-exilic at any rate, for it presupposes an anointed one, a king of Israel (v. 13).

The plight of which the author is thinking is the foreign rule of the Assyrians, and in the advancing Chaldeans he sees the signs of the approaching great day of Yahweh,[26] the day of judgment and of the enthronement of the God of Israel. We must assume that the people, the "righteous"—Habakkuk is a nationalistic prophet of salvation, certainly standing in the line of the Deuteronomic school of thought—who were encouraged by the signs of the time, took some opportunity to organize a day of prayer to plead for an end to the Assyrian foreign rule which had become especially hated after Josiah's reform; perhaps there may also have been special political reasons for it. On this occasion the temple prophet and psalmist Habakkuk, who perhaps was one of the singers, composed the psalms (or one of them) that were to be sung and therein promised Yahweh's help to his people. The psalm was sung at one of the cultic rites as a psalm of petition with the intention of "getting Yahweh to be gracious" (*lmnsh*, literally: "to make [Yahweh's countenance] shine," see *Psalmenstudien I V*).

And if there is anyone who wishes to dispute the accuracy of the tradition in v. 1, it will have to be said that the verse is still evidence in support of our main thesis. It shows at any rate that it was considered quite natural to look for the author of a prophetic cultic psalm among the nebiim; however, this would hardly be the case if such a thing did not in reality occur frequently.

The book of Joel also points in this direction. Here, too, is the same mixture of psalm style and prophetic style.

Gunkel certainly is correct that the book's first two chapters contain "a liturgy depicting a great plague of locusts" (*RGG*, 2d ed., s.v. "Psalmen, 4").

NOTES

1 This leads to the question, for example, of whether this religion was originally "prophetic" or not.

2 See *Psalmenstudien II*, Part 1, ch. 1, 4, b.

3 S. Mowinckel, *Ezra den skriftlærde* (Kristiania, 1916), 98, 102, 111.

4 S. Mowinckel, "Om nebiisme og profeti," *NTT* (1909), 192ff.

5 *nb'*, to speak, to proclaim. From it comes the name of God, *Nabi'u, Nabû*.

6 One should not say magic wand (*Zauberstab*); cf. *Psalmenstudien I*, 59ff.

7 See Mowinckel, *ZAW* (1916), 238–39.

8 A. Alt, et al., *Alttestamentliche Studien, Rudolf Kittel zum 60. Geburtstag dargebracht*, Vol. 13 of Beiträge zur Wissenschaft vom Alten Testament (Leipzig: J. C. Hinrichs, 1913), 88–100. In "Om nebissme og profeti," *NTT* (1909), 217–24, 358–60, I have already examined much of the material presented by Hölscher and have drawn the same conclusions as Hölscher does.

9 See *NTT* (1909), 203–4, 227–37. It is still customary among present-day

dervishes to make the dervish's emblems of office out of the sheep's wool which is brought by the novice and used as the initiation sacrifice; see ibid.

10   In a youthful work, which is somewhat exaggerated, I emphasized the distinction between the nebiim and the "literary prophets" and dealt with the most important passages; see "Profeternes forhold til nebiismen," *NTT* (1910), 126–38.

11   In opposition to H. Schmidt, *RGG*, 2d ed., s.v. "Prophetentum, ältestes." One should not build too much on the Ahijah legend in 1 Kings 11:29ff. The account is deuteronomic; we know nothing about Ahijah's actual motives. At any rate, this or that nabi could be secured for any revolutionary or political act. An Israelite nationalism against Judean rule may perhaps have been at work in Ahijah.

12   Cf. Mowinckel, "Om nebiisme og profeti," *NTT* (1909), 224ff.

13   Mowinckel, *NTT* (1909), 220–21; 224–25.

14   See *Psalmenstudien II*, Part 1, ch. II, 3, c.

15   See *Psalmenstudien II*, 117 and passim.

16   This is the solution for the apparent contradiction between Zech. 1:1 and Ezra 5:1; 6:14; Iddo is not the prophet's personal grandfather, but the family from which he comes, identical with Iddo in Neh. 12:4.

17   Cf. Paul Volz, *Biblische Altertümer* (Stuttgart: Calwer, 1914), 162ff.

18   Hugo Gressmann (with Hermann Ranke), *Altorientalische Texte und Bilder zum Alten Testamente*, vol. 1 (Tübingen: J. C. B. Mohr [Paul Siebeck], 1909), 226, last paragraph.

19   *Psalmenstudien I*, 72, 145.

20   Ibid., 145.

21   Cf. the "images" of Amos (the basket of fruit) and of Jeremiah (the almond tree).

22   Cf. *RGG*, 2d ed., s.v. "Traum."

23   *Psalmenstudien I*, 154–57.

24   See *Psalmenstudien IV*.

25   There is no need here to alter the position of the kethib.

26   I agree completely with Budde in his interpretation of the book of Habakkuk.

3

*The Prophet**

MAX WEBER

What is a prophet, from the perspective of sociology?

We shall forego here any consideration of the general question regarding the "bringer of salvation" (*Heilbringer*) as raised by Breysig. Not every anthropomorphic god is a deified bringer of salvation, whether external or internal salvation. And certainly not every provider of salvation became a god or even a savior, although such phenomena were widespread.

We shall understand "prophet' to mean a purely individual bearer of charisma, who by virtue of his mission proclaims a religious doctrine or divine commandment. No radical distinction will be drawn between a "renewer of religion" who preaches an older revelation, actual or supposititious, and a "founder of religion" who claims to bring completely new deliverances. The two types merge into one another. In any case, the formation of a new religious community need not be the result of doctrinal preaching by prophets, since it may be produced by the activities of non-prophetic reformers. Nor shall we be concerned in this context with the question whether the followers of a prophet are more attracted to his person, as in the cases of Zoroaster, Jesus, and Muhammad, or to his doctrine, as in the cases of Buddha and the prophets of Israel.

For our purposes here, the personal call is the decisive element distinguishing the prophet from the priest. The latter lays claim to authority by virtue of his service in a sacred tradition, while the prophet's claim is based on personal revelation and charisma. It is no accident that almost no prophets have emerged from the priestly class. As a rule, the Indian teachers of salvation were not Brahmins, nor were the Israelite prophets priests. Zoroaster's case is excep-

* First published in English in *The Sociology of Religion* (1963) 46–59; German original (1922).

tional in that there exists a possibility that he may have descended from the hieratic nobility. The priest, in clear contrast, dispenses salvation by virtue of his office. Even in cases in which personal charisma may be involved, it is the hierarchical office that confers legitimate authority upon the priest as a member of a corporate enterprise of salvation.

But the prophet, like the magician, exerts his power simply by virtue of his personal gifts. Unlike the magician, however, the prophet claims definite revelations, and the core of his mission is doctrine or commandment, not magic. Outwardly, at least, the distinction is fluid, for the magician is frequently a knowledgeable expert in divination, and sometimes in this alone. At this stage, revelation functions continuously as oracle or dream interpretation. Without prior consultation with the magician, no innovations in communal relations could be adopted in primitive times. To this day, in parts of Australia, it is the dream revelations of magicians that are set before the councils of clan heads for adoption, and it is a mark of secularization that this practice is receding.

On the other hand, it was only under very unusual circumstances that a prophet succeeded in establishing his authority without charismatic authentication, which in practice meant magic. At least the bearers of new doctrine practically always needed such validation. It must not be forgotten for an instant that the entire basis of Jesus' own legitimation, as well as his claim that he and only he knew the Father and that the way to God led through faith in him alone, was the magical charisma he felt within himself. It was doubtless this consciousness of power, more than anything else, that enabled him to traverse the road of the prophets. During the apostolic period of early Christianity and thereafter the figure of the wandering prophet was a constant phenomenon. There was always required of such prophets a proof of their possession of particular gifts of the spirit, of special magical or ecstatic abilities.

Prophets very often practised divination as well as magical healing and counseling. This was true, for example, of the prophets (*nābî, nĕbî'îm*) so frequently mentioned in the Old Testament, especially in the prophetic books and Chronicles. But what distinguishes the prophet, in the sense that we are employing the term, from the types just described is an economic factor, that is, that his prophecy is unremunerated. Thus, Amos indignantly rejected the appellation of *nābî'*. This criterion of gratuitous service also distinguishes the prophet from the priest. The typical prophet propagates ideas for their own sake and not for fees, at least in any obvious or regulated form. The provisions enjoining the nonremunerative character of prophetic propaganda have taken various forms. Thus developed the carefully cultivated postulate that the apostle, prophet, or teacher of ancient Christianity must not professionalize his religious proclamations. Also, limitations were set upon the length of the time he could enjoy the hospitality of his friends. The Christian prophet was enjoined to live by the labor of his own hands or, as among the Buddhists, only from alms which he had not specifically solicited. These injunctions were repeatedly emphasized in the Pauline epistles, and in another form, in the Buddhist monastic regulations. The dictum "whosoever will not work, shall not eat" applied to missionaries, and it constitutes one of the chief mysteries of the success of prohetic propaganda itself.

The period of the older Israelitic prophecy at about the time of Elijah was an epoch of strong prophetic propaganda throughout the Near East and Greece. It is likely that prophecy in all its forms arose, especially in the Near East, in connection with the growth of great world empires in Asia, and the resumption and intensification of international commerce after a long interruption. At that time Greece was exposed to the invasion of the Thracian cult of Dionysos, as well as to the most diverse types of prophecies. In addition to the semiprophetic social reformers, certain purely religious movements now broke into the magical and cultic lore of the Homeric priests. Emotional cults, emotional prophecy based on "speaking with tongues," and highly valued intoxicating ecstasy vied with the evolving theological rationalism (Hesiod); the incipient cosmogonic and philosophic speculation was intersected by philosophical mystery doctrines and salvation religions. The growth of these emotional cults paralleled both overseas colonization and, above all, the formation of cities and the transformation of the *polis* which resulted from the development of a citizen army.

It is not necessary to detail here these developments of the eighth and seventh centuries, so brilliantly analyzed by Rohde, some of which reached into the sixth and even the fifth century. They were contemporary with Jewish, Persian, and Hindu prophetic movements, and probably also with the achievements of Chinese ethics in the pre-Confucian period, although we have only scant knowledge of the latter. These Greek "prophets" differed widely among themselves in regard to the economic criterion of professionalism, and in regard to the possession of a "doctrine." The Greeks also made a distinction between professional teaching and unremunerated propagandizing of ideas, as we see from the example of Socrates. In Greece, furthermore, there existed a clear differentiation between the only real congregational type of religion, namely Orphism with its doctirne of salvation, and every other type of prophecy and technique of salvation, especially those of the mysteries. The basis of this distinction was the presence in Orphism of a genuine doctrine of salvation.

Our primary task is to differentiate the various types of prophets from the sundry purveyors of salvation, religious or otherwise. Even in historical times the transition from the prophet to the legislator is fluid, if one understands the latter to mean a personage who in any given case has been assigned the responsibility of codifying a law systematically or of reconstituting it, as was the case notably with the Greek *aisymnetes* (e.g., Solon, Charondas, etc.). In no case did such a legislator or his labor fail to receive divine approval, at least subsequently.

A legislator is quite different from the Italian *podesta*, who is summoned from outside the group, not for the purpose of creating a new social order, but to provide a detached, impartial arbitrator, especially for cases in which the adversaries are of the same social status. On the other hand, legislators were generally, though not always, called to their offices when social tensions were in evidence. This was apt to occur with special frequency in the one situation which commonly provided the earliest stimulus to a planned social policy. One of the conditions fostering the need for a new planned policy was the economic development of a warrior class as a result of growing monetary wealth and the debt enslavement of another stratum; an additional factor was the dissatisfaction arising from the unrealized political aspirations of a rising commercial class which, having acquired wealth through economic activity, was now challenging the old warrior nobility. It was the function of the *aisymnetes* to resolve the conflicts between classes and to produce a new sacred law of eternal validity, for which he had to secure divine approbation.

It is very likely that Moses was a historical figure, in which case he would be classified functionally as an *aisymnetes*. For the prescriptions of the oldest sacred legislation of the Hebrews presuppose a money economy and hence sharp conflicts of class interests, whether impending or already existing, within the confederacy. It was Moses' great achievement to find a compromise solution of, or prophylactic for, these class conflicts (e.g., the *seisachtheia* of the year of release) and to organize the Israelite confederacy by means of an integral national god. In essence, his work stands midway between the functioning of an ancient *aisymnetes* and that of Muhammad. The reception of the law formulated by Moses stimulated a period of expansion of the newly unified people in much the same way that the leveling of classes stimulated expansion in so many other cases, particularly in Athens and Rome. The scriptural dictum that "after Moses there arose not in Israel any prophet like unto him" means that the Jews never had another *aisymnetes*.

Not only were none of the prophets *aisymnetae* in this sense, but in general what normally passes for prophecy does not belong to this category. To be sure, even the later prophets of Israel were concerned with social reform. They hurled their "woe be unto you" against those who oppressed and enslaved the poor, those who joined field to field, and those who deflected justice by bribes. These were the typical actions leading to class stratification everywhere in the ancient world, and were everywhere intensified by the development of the city-state (*polis*). Jerusalem too had been organized into a city-state by the time of these later prophets. A distinctive concern with social reform is characteristic of Israelite prophets. This concern is all the more notable, because such a trait is lacking in Hindu prophecy of the same period, although the conditions in India at the time of the Buddha have been described as relatively similar to those in Greece during the sixth century.

An explanation for Hebrew prophecy's unique concern for social reform is to be sought in religious grounds, which we shall set forth subsequently. But it must not be forgotten that in the motivation of the Israelite prophets these social reforms were only means to an end. Their primary concern was with foreign politics, chiefly because it constituted the theater of their god's activity. The Israelite prophets were concerned with social and other types of injustice as a violation of the Mosaic code primarily in order to explain God's wrath, and not in order to institute a program of social reform. It is noteworthy that the real theoretician of social reform, Ezekiel, was a priestly theorist who can scarcely be categorized as a prophet at all. Finally, Jesus was not at all interested in social reform as such.

Zoroaster shared with his cattle-raising people a hatred of the despoiling nomads, but the heart of his message was essentially religious. His central concerns were his faith in his own divine mission and his struggle against the magical cult of ecstasy. A similar primary focus upon religion appeared very clearly in the case of Muhammad, whose program of social action, which Umar carried through consistently, was oriented almost entirely to the goal of the psychological preparation of the faithful for battle in order to maintain a maximum number of warriors for the faith.

It is characteristic of the prophets that they do not receive their mission from any human agency, but seize it, as it were. To be sure, usurpation also characterized the assumption of power by tyrants in the Greek *polis*. These Greek tyrants remind one of the legal *aisymnetae* in their general functioning, and they frequently pursued their own characteristic religious policies, for example, supporting the emotional cult of Dionysos, which was popular with the masses rather than with the nobility. But the aforementioned assumption of power by the prophets came about as a consequence of divine revelation, essentially for religious purposes. Furthermore, their characteristic religious message and their struggle against ecstatic cults tended to move in an opposite direction from that taken by the typical religious policy of the Greek tyrants. The religion of Muhammad, which is fundamentally political in its orientation, and his position in Medina, which was in between that of an Italian *podesta* and that of Calvin at Geneva, grew primarily out of his purely prophetic mission. A merchant, he was first a leader of pietistic conventicles in Mecca, until he realized more and more clearly that the organization of the interests of warrior clans in the acquisition of booty was the external basis provided for his missionizing.

On the other hand, there are various transitional phases linking the prophet to the teacher of ethics, especially the teacher of social ethics. Such a teacher, full of a new or recovered understanding of ancient wisdom, gathers disciples about him, counsels private individuals in personal matters and nobles in questions relating to public affairs, and purports to mold ethical ways of life, with the ultimate goal of influencing the crystallization of ethical regulations. The bond between the teacher of religious or philosophical wisdom and his disciple is uncommonly strong and is regulated in an authoritarian fashion, particularly in the sacred laws of Asia. Everywhere the disciple-master relationship is classified among those involving reverence. Generally, the doctrine of magic, like that of heroism, is so regulated that the novice is assigned to a particularly experienced master or is required to seek him out. This is comparable to the relationship in German fraternities, in which the junior member (the *Leibbursche*) is attached by a kind of personal piety to the senior member (the *Leibfuchs*), who watches over his training. All the Greek poetry of pederasty derives from such a relationship of respect, and similar phenomena are to be found among Buddhists and Confucianists, indeed in all monastic education.

The most complete expression of this disciple-master relationship is to be found in the position of the *guru* in Hindu sacred law.

Every young man belonging to polite society was unconditionally required to devote himself for many years to the instruction and direction of life provided by such a Brahminic teacher. The obligation of obedience to the *guru*, who had absolute power over his charges, a relationship comparable to that of the occidental *famulus* to his *magister*, took precedence over loyalty to family, even as the position of the court Brahmin (*purohita*) was officially regulated so as to raise his position far above that of the most powerful father confessor in the Occident. Yet the *guru* is, after all, only a teacher who transmits acquired, not revealed, knowledge, and this by virtue of a commission and not on his own authority.

The philosophical ethicist and the social reformer are not prophets in our sense of the word, no matter how closely they may seem to resemble prophets. Actually, the oldest Greek sages, who like Empedocles are wreathed in legend, and other Greek sages such as Pythagoras stand closer to the prophets. They have left at least some legacy of a distinctive doctrine of salvation and conduct of life, and they laid some claim to the status of savior. Such intellectual teachers of salvation have parallels in India, but the Greek teachers fell far short of the Hindu teachers in consistently focusing both life and doctrine on salvation.

Even less can the founders and heads of actual "schools of philosophy" be regarded as prophets in our sense, no matter how closely they may approach this category in some respects. From Confucius, in whose temple even the emperor made obeisance, graded transitions lead to Plato. But both of them were simply academic teaching philosophers, who differed chiefly in that Confucius was centrally concerned and Plato only occasionally concerned to influence princes in the direction of particular social reforms.

What primarily differentiates such figures from the prophets is their lack of that vital emotional preaching which is distinctive of prophecy, regardless of whether this is disseminated by the spoken word, the pamphlet, or any other type of literary composition (e.g., the *suras* of Muhammad). The enterprise of the prophet is closer to that of the popular orator (*demagogue*) or political publicist than to that of the teacher. On the other hand, the activity of a Socrates, who also felt himself opposed to the professional teaching enterprise of the Sophists, must be distinguished in theory from the activities of a prophet, by the absence of a directly revealed religious mission in the case of Socrates. Socrates' daemon (*daimonion*) reacted only to concrete situations, and then only to dissuade and admonish. For Socrates, this was the outer limit of his ethical and strongly utilitarian rationalism, which occupied for him the position that magical divination assumed for Confucius. For this reason, Socrates' daemon cannot be compared at all to the conscience of a genuine religious ethic; much less can it be regarded as the instrument of prophecy.

Such a divergence from the characteristic traits of the Hebrew prophets holds true of all philosophers and their schools as they were known in China, India, ancient Hellas, and in the medieval period among Jews, Arabs, and Christians alike. All such philosophies had the same sociological form. But philosophic teaching, as in the case of the Cynics, might take the form of an exemplary prophecy of salvation (in the sense presently to be explained) by virtue of practising the pattern of life achieved and propagated by a particular school. These prophets and their schools might, as in the case of the Cynics, who protested against the sacramental grace of the mysteries, show certain outer and inner affinities to Hindu and Oriental ascetic sects. But the prophet, in our special sense, is never to be found where the proclamation of a religious truth of salvation through personal revelation is lacking. In our view, this qualification must be regarded as the decisive hallmark of prophecy.

Finally, the Hindu reformers of religion such as Shankara and Ramanuja and their occidental counterparts like Luther, Zwingli, Calvin, and Wesley are to be distinguished from the category of prophets by virtue of the fact that they do not claim to be offering a substantively new revelation or to be speaking in the name of a special divine injunction. This is what characterized the founder of the Mormon church, who resembled, even in matters of detail, Muhammad and above all the Jewish prophets. The prophetic type is also manifest in Montanus and Novitianus, and in such figures as Mani and Manus, whose message had a more rational doctrinal content than did that of George Fox, a prophet type with emotional nuances.

When we have separated out from the category of prophet all the aforementioned types, which sometimes abut very closely, various others still remain. The first is that of the mystagogue. He performs sacraments, that is, magical actions that contain the boons of salvation. Throughout the entire world there have been saviors of this type whose difference from the average magician is only one of degree, the extent of which is determined by the formation of a special congregation around him. Very frequently dynasties of mystagogues developed on the basis of a sacramental charisma which was regarded as hereditary. These dynasties maintained their prestige for centuries, investing their disciples with great authority and thus developing a kind of hierarchical position. This was especially true in India, where the title of *guru* was also used to designate distributors of salvation and their plenipotentiaries. It was likewise the case in China, where the hierarch of the Taoists and the heads of certain secret sects played just such hereditary roles. Finally, one type of exemplary prophet to be discussed presently was also generally transformed into a mystagogue in the second generation.

The mystagogues were also very widely distributed throughout the Near East, and they entered Greece in the prophetic age to which reference was made earlier. Yet the far more ancient noble families, who were the hereditary incumbents of the Eleusinian mysteries, also represented at least another marginal manifestation of the simple hereditary priestly families. Ethical doctrine was lacking in the mystagogue, who distributed magical salvation, or at least doctrine played only a very subordinate role in his work. Instead, his primary gift was hereditarily transmitted magical art. Moreover, he normally made a living from his art, for which there was a great demand. Consequently we must exclude him too from the conception of prophet, even though he sometimes revealed new ways of salvation.

Thus, there remain only two kinds of prophets in our sense, one represented most clearly by the Buddha, the other with especial clarity by Zoroaster and Muhammad. The prophet may be primarily, as in the cases just noted, an instrument for the proclamation of a god and his will, be this a concrete command or an abstract norm. Preaching as one who has received a commission from god, he demands obedience as an ethical duty. This type we shall term the "ethical prophet." On the other hand, the prophet may be an exemplary man who, by his personal example, demonstrates to others the way to religious salvation, as in the case of the Buddha. The preaching of this type of prophet says nothing about a divine mission or an ethical duty of obedience, but rather directs itself to the self-interest of those who crave salvation, recommending to them the same path as he himself traversed. Our designation for this second type of prophecy is "exemplary."

The exemplary type is particularly characteristic of prophecy in India, although there have been a few manifestations of it in China (e.g. Lao Tzu) and the Near East. On the other hand, the ethical type is confined to the Near East, regardless of racial differences there. For neither the Vedas nor the classical books of the Chinese—the oldest portions of which in both cases consist of songs of praise and thanksgiving by sacred singers, and of magical rites and ceremonies—make it appear at all probable that prophecy of the ethical type, such as developed in the Near East or Iran, could ever have arisen in India or China. The decisive reason for this is the absence of a personal, transcendental, and ethical god. In India this concept was found only in a sacramental and magical form, and then only in the later and popular faiths. But in the religions of those social classes within which the decisive prophetic conceptions of Mahavira and Buddha were developed, ethical prophecy appeared only intermittently and was constantly subjected to reinterpretations in the direction of pantheism. In China the notion of ethical prophecy was altogether lacking in the ethics of the class that exercised the greatest influence in the society. To what degree this may presumably be associated with the intellectual distinctiveness of such classes which was of course determined by various social factors, will be discussed later.

As far as purely religious factors are concerned, it was decisive for both India and China that the conception of a rationally regulated world had its point of origin in the ceremonial order of sacrifices, on the unalterable sequence of which everything depended. In this regard, crucial importance was attached to the indispensable regularity of meteorological processes, which were thought of in animistic terms. What was involved here was the normal activity or inactivity of the spirits and demons. According to both classical and heterodox Chinese views, these processes were held to be insured by the ethically proper conduct of government, that followed the correct path of virtue, the Tao; without this everything would fail, even according to Vedic doctrine. Thus, in India and China, rita and Tao respectively represented similar superdivine, impersonal forces.

On the other hand, the personal, transcendental and ethical god is a Near-Eastern concept. It corresponds so closely to that of an all-powerful mundane king with his rational bureaucratic regime that a causal connection can scarcely be overlooked. Throughout the world the magician is in the first instance a rainmaker, for the harvest depends on timely and sufficient rain, though not in excessive quantity. Until the present time the pontifical Chinese emperor has remained a rainmaker, for in northern China, at least, the uncertainty of the weather renders dubious the operation of irrigation procedures, no matter how extensive they are. Of greater significance was the construction of dams and internal canals, which become the real source of the imperial bureaucracy. The emperor sought to avert meteorological disturbances through sacrifices, public atonement, and various virtuous practices, for example, the termination of abuses in the administration, or the organization of a raid on unpunished malefactors. For it was always assumed that the reason for the excitation of the spirits and the disturbances of the cosmic order had to be sought either in the personal derelictions of the monarch or in some manifestation of social disorganization. Again, rain was one of the rewards promised by Yahweh to his devotees, who were at that time primarily agriculturists, as is clearly apparent in the older portions of the tradition. God promised neither too scanty rain nor yet excessive precipitation or deluge.

Throughout Mesopotamia and Arabia, however, it was not rain that was the creator of the harvest, but artificial irrigation alone. In Mesopotamia, irrigation was the sole source of the absolute power of the monarch, who derived his income by compelling his conquered subjects to build canals and cities adjoining them, just as the regulation of the Nile was the source of the Egyptian monarch's strength. In the desert and semiarid regions of the Near East this control of irrigation waters was indeed one source of the conception of a god who had created the earth and man out of nothing and not merely fashioned them, as was believed elsewhere. A riparian economy of this kind actually did produce a harvest out of nothing, from the desert sands. The monarch even created law by legislation and rationalization, a development the world experienced for the first time in Mesopotamia. It seems quite reasonable, therefore, that as a result of such experiences the ordering of the world should be conceived as the law of a freely acting, transcendental and personal god.

Another, and negative, factor accounting for the development in the Near East of a world order that reflected the operation of a personal god was the relative absence of those distinctive classes who were the bearers of the Hindu and Chinese ethics, and who created the godless religious ethics found in those countries. But even in Egypt, where originally Pharaoh himself was a god, the attempt of Ikhnaton to produce an astral monotheism foundered because of the power of the priesthood, which had by then systematized popular animism and become invincible. In Mesopotamia the development of monotheism and demagogic prophecy was opposed by the ancient pantheon, which was politically organized and had been systematized by the priests, and was further opposed and limited by the rigid development of the state.

The kingdom of the Pharaohs and of Mesopotamia made an even more powerful impression upon the Israelites than the great Persian monarch, the *basileus kat' exochen*, made upon the Greeks (the strong impact of Cyrus upon the Greeks is mirrored in the eulogistic account of him formulated in the pedagogical treatise, the *Cyropaidia*, despite the defeat of this monarch). The Israelites had gained their freedom from the "house of bondage" of the earthly Pharaoh only because a divine king had come to their assistance. Indeed, their subsequent establishment of a worldly monarchy was expressly declared to be a declension from Yahweh, the real ruler of the people. Hebrew prophecy was completely oriented to a relationship with the great political powers of the time, the great kings, who as the rods of God's wrath first destroy Israel and then, as a consequence of divine intervention, permit Israelites to return from the Exile to their own land. In the case of Zoroaster too it can be asserted that the range of his vision was also oriented to the views of the civilized lands of the West.

Thus, the distinctive character of the earliest prophecy, in both its dualistic and monotheistic forms, seems to have been determined decisively—aside from the operation of certain other concrete historical influences—by the pressure of relatively contiguous great centers of rigid social organization upon less developed neighboring peoples. The latter tended to see in their own continuous peril from the pitiless bellicosity of terrible nations the anger and grace of a heavenly king.

Regardless of whether a particular religious prophet is predominantly of the ethical or predominantly of the exemplary type, prophetic revelation involves for both the prophet himself and for his followers—and this is the element common to both varieties—a unified view of the world derived from a consciously integrated and meaningful attitude toward life. To the prophet, both the life of man and the world, both social and cosmic events, have a certain systematic and coherent meaning. To this meaning the conduct of mankind must be oriented if it is to bring salvation, for only in relation to this meaning does life obtain a unified and significant pattern. Now the structure of this meaning may take varied forms, and it may weld together into a unity motives that are logically quite heterogeneous. The whole conception is dominated, not by logical consistency, but by practical valuations. Yet it always denotes, regardless of any variations in scope and in measure of success, an effort to systematize all the manifestations of life; that is, to organize practical behavior into a direction of life, regardless of the form it may assume in any individual case. Moreover, it always contains the important religious conception of the world as a cosmos which is challenged to produce somehow a "meaningful," ordered totality, the particular manifestations of which are to be measured and evaluated according to this requirement.

The conflict between empirical reality and this conception of the world as a meaningful totality, which is based on a religious postulate, produces the strongest tensions in man's inner life as well as in his external relationship to the world. To be sure, this problem is by no means dealt with by prophecy alone. Both priestly wisdom and all completely nonsacerdotal philosophy, the intellectualist as well as the popular varieties, are somehow concerned with it. The ultimate question of all metaphysics has always been something like this: if the world as a whole and life in particular were to have a meaning, what might it be, and how would the world have to look in order to correspond to it? The religious problem-complex of prophets and priests is the womb from which nonsacerdotal philosophy emanated, wherever it developed. Subsequently, nonsacerdotal philosophy was bound to take issue with the antecedent thought of the religious functionaries; and the strugle between them provided one of the very important components of religious evolution. Hence, we must now examine more closely the mutual relationships of priests, prophets, and non-priests.

4

*The Prophet as Yahweh's Messenger**

JAMES F. ROSS

If one may be permitted to anticipate the verdict of those who will write the history of biblical studies in the twentieth century, the contribution of James Muilenburg seems to be clear. Both in the classroom and on the printed page he has done much to advance our understanding of and appreciation for the depth and breadth of Hebrew literary form. His articles on the subject [1] give evidence of his sensitivity not only to the sequence of the words but also to the theological significance of a given *Gattung*. To date his most extensive effort is the masterly introduction to and commentary upon Isaiah 40—66. [2]

This article stems from a reference in one of Muilenburg's most recent studies of literary forms. [3] Commenting on Exod. 19: 3b, he notes that we have "the characteristic speech of the messenger, the rôle which Moses is to assume here." [4] The questions arise: What are the characteristics of the messenger speech? What is the relationship of the messenger to the sender, and the locus of his authority? Finally, what is the task and responsibility of the messenger; what does he actually say and do? Let us examine these questions in terms of their bearing upon the form and content of Old Testament prophecy.

I

Ludwig Köhler was among the first to demonstrate the existence of the prophetic *Botenspruch*. [5] In his classic analysis of the stylistic elements in Deutero-Isaiah he isolated numerous passages where the prophet assumes the role of a messenger and couches his oracles in the standard messenger style; we have not only the usual opening,

---

* First published in *Israel's Prophetic Heritage* (1962) 98–107.

Kô 'āmar yhwh, followed by qualifying titles, but also the standard conclusion, *nᵉ'um yhwh*.[6] Köhler finds no less than sixty-one examples, more or less completely preserved, and concludes that Deutero-Isaiah uses the *Botenspruch* much more freely than his predecessors.[7]

It is surprising that so few scholars have made use of Köhler's suggestions.[8] For the comparative material is not confined to these opening and closing phrases alone. It is obvious that the verb ordinarily used to describe the sending of a messenger, *šālaḥ*, is common both in the accounts of the prophets' inaugural visions and in the introductions to subsequent oracles.[9] Other features of the messenger narratives may also be discerned. For example, when Jacob sends messengers to Esau, he commands them, "Thus shall you say to my lord, to Esau: 'Thus says your servant, Jacob . . .'" (Gen. 32:4–5—EVV 32:3–4).[10] Almost exactly the same language is used in the introductions to many of the prophetic oracles. The word of Yahweh comes to Nathan, "Go and say to my servant David, 'Thus says Yahweh'" (2 Sam. 7:4–5,8); Yahweh says to Ezekiel, "The people also are impudent and stubborn: I send you to them; and you shall say to them, 'Thus says Adonai Yahweh'" (Ezek. 2:4; cf. 3:11).[11] Or a messenger may begin, "Hear the word of [the sender] . . . ," and continue, "Thus says [the sender] . . ."(2 Kings 18:28–29); this form is particularly characteristic of Jeremiah (7:2–3; 17:20–21; 22:2–3). There are exceptions to this pattern, however; the expression *nᵉ'um yhwh*, which so frequently concludes the prophetic *Botenspruch*, is found only once in this meaning outside the prophetic books or narratives: as a parenthesis in a message of the *mal'ak yhwh* (Gen. 22:18).

A comparison of prophetic *Botensprüche* with those found in extra-biblical sources may also be of interest here. The most striking example is to be found in the Mari texts.[12] In one of these a man has a dream in which Dagan tells him, "Now go! I send you to Zimri-lim [the king of Mari]: [to him] you yourself shall say: Send me thy messenger. . . ."[13] Two other letters have been discovered in which a "man of the god Dagan" (*awîlum mu-uḫ-ḫu-um ša ᵈDagan*) says that the god has sent (*šaparu*) him to say, "Send speedily to the king" (or, "thy Lord").[14] Noth comments that we have here not only the phenomenon of a messenger of God, but also a remarkable similarity in wording to the prophetic oracle; he cites in this connection the well-known narrative of Wen-Amon, where we find a reference to a messenger of Amon.[15]

The Ras Shamra texts also contain material parallel to the Old Testament message form. Ugaritic letters commonly begin, "To *NN* [sometimes qualified by adjectives or titles], say: 'Message of NN [similarly qualified] ....'"[16] The Hebrew equivalent is 'ᵃᵉmōr lᵉ NN *kô 'āmar.* Similarly messenger narratives in the mythological texts usually begin, "Say [rgm] to NN; message [*thm*] of NN [variously qualified]";[17] occasionally *thm* is paralleled by *hwt*, "word."[18]

We may conclude that the form of the prophetic oracle was often derived from that of the typical ancient Near Eastern *Botenspruch* as found both in biblical narratives and in the literature of Israel's neighbors.

II

It would seem that the question of the messenger's authority could be answered simply: it is that of the one who sends him. Thus a messenger is to be treated as if he were his master. Rahab is rewarded for her reception of Joshua's messengers (Josh. 6:17, 25); Abigail washes the feet of the messengers sent by David to take her to him as his wife (2 Samuel 25:40–41); conversely, the disgraceful treatment of the messengers sent by David to the king of Ammon results in warfare between the two countries (2 Samuel 10).[19] The existence of this close relationship between master and servant may also account for the occasional confusion between Yahweh and his *mal'āk.* The *mal'ak yhwh* appears and speaks to Hagar, but she thinks she has seen God himself (Gen. 16:7–13); the narrative in Genesis 18 oscillates between Yahweh and the three men; Jacob, in blessing Joseph, apparently makes no distinction between 'ᵃᵉlōhîm and his *mal'āk* (Gen. 48:15–16); it is the *mal'ak yhwh* who appears in the burning bush, but it is Yahweh himself who sees that Moses has taken notice (Exod. 3:2–4).[20]

Passages such as these, however, merely illustrate the way in which the messenger was received. For the real source of his authority we must step behind the scenes, so to speak, into the divine council itself. For just as a human group can and does commission messengers,[21] so also Yahweh is conceived as acting in concert with his council of "holy ones" (*qᵉdōšîm*) when sending his emissaries.

This council is sometimes call a *qāhāl* or an *'ēdâ* (Ps. 89:6—EVV 89:5 and 82:1 respectively), but the more precise term is *sôd.*[22] A *sôd* was a small, intimate group of close friends; the psalmist laments the treachery of his companion with whom he walked *sôd* (used adverbially), and Job complains that all the men of his *sôd* turn away from him in disgust.[23] Jeremiah says, somewhat wistfully, that he did not join the *sôd* of the merrymakers; rather, he "sat alone" (Jer. 15:17). But a council was not merely a chance collection of individuals. It had a purpose; in it decisions were made and plans laid after mutual discussion.[24] And although we have no reference to the sending of messengers from a human *sôd*, we may assume that this was a common practice. For the word *sôd* came to mean not only the council itself but also a decision ("secret") emanating from it;[25] this decision was probably transmitted by a messenger.

The divine council was of the same order.[26] Its members were the "holy ones," the "sons of God," or simply "the gods."[27] It has been thought that its meetings were held only once a year, on New Year's Day;[28] the language in Job 1:6 and 2:1 (literally, "And it was the day, and the sons of God came . . .") would at least seem to point to some regularity. Like the human *sôd*, the divine council also made decisions. The first person plural pronouns in Gen. 1:26 ("Let us make man in our image, after our likeness . . ."); 3:22 ("the man has become like one of us . . ."); and 11:7 ("Come, let us go down, and there confuse their language . . .") probably have the divine council as their antecedent.[29] As in human affairs, the word *sôd* can thus be used for the "counsel" proceeding from the "council"; this is the meaning of the term in Amos 3:7. And we may assume that messengers were again used to carry out the "counsels"; this may be the significance of the *mal'ākîm*, who ascend and descend the ladder between heaven and earth (Gen. 28:12). Certainly a "spirit" can be sent from the council ("to entice Ahab"—1 Kings 22:20–22); similarly Satan proceeds from a meeting of the "sons of God" to test Job (Job 1:12; 2:7). So also the Mesopotamian "assembly of the gods" imposes the death sentence on a rebellious god, decrees the flood, decides to destroy a city, and in general "fashions" or "proclaims" destinies.[30] Furthermore the assembly sends forth agents to carry out its decisions; various gods participate in the creation of the primeval flood.[31]

Thus it is probable that the ultimate source of the messenger's authority was in a council, and that he is to be regarded as the means by which the deliberations of that body are made effective. When we turn to the Old Testament prophets, we find a similar phenomenon. The inaugural visions of Isaiah of Jerusalem and Deutero-Isaiah are to be interpreted against the background of the *sôd yhwh*: Yahweh says, "Whom shall I send, and who will go for *us*?" (6:3), and uses the plural imperative in ch. 40.[32] The most instructive example, however, is to be found in Jer. 23:18, 22. In the course of his diatribe against the false prophets Jeremiah asks,

For who among them has stood in the council of Yahweh [*bᵉsôd yhwh*]

to perceive and to hear his word,
or who has given heed to his word and listened?[33]
and concludes,

But if they had stood in my council [$b^e s\hat{o}d\hat{\imath}$]
then they would have proclaimed my words to my people,
and they would have turned them from their evil way,
and from the evil of their doings.[34]

It is interesting to note that the latter verse is preceded by the statement that Yahweh has neither sent (*šālaḥ*) nor spoken (*dibbēr*) to these prophets.[35] Clearly Jeremiah claims that his ultimate authority as God's messenger is to be found at the highest level, in the divine council itself. He has heard words and has seen visions; he is under constraint to make the people hearken, to carry out the decision of the *sôd*. And while the term *sôd* is used only here in connection with the prophet's authority,[36] it is probable that the *idea* of the divine council is to be seen as the background of the prophetic *Botensprüche* as a whole.

III

A comparison of the actual content of the nonprophetic *Botenspruch* with that of the prophets themselves shows that the former is usually a promise or a blessing. The divine *mal'āk* or *'îš* *ʷelōhîm* announces the forthcoming birth of a child (Genesis 18; Judges 13); he rescues those in distress (Gen. 16:7–12); he goes before or accompanies someone on a dangerous journey (Gen. 24:7, 40; Exod. 23:20; 33:2); he fights against the people's enemies (Ps. 35:5–6; cf. Josh. 5:13–14; 2 Kings 19:37). The function of the human messenger is similar. He, too, announces births (Jer. 20:15); he carries back the news of victory on the battlefield (1 Sam. 31:9; 2 Sam. 18:19–33; cf. Ps. 68: 12–13—EVV 68:11–12); he consoles the bereaved (2 Sam. 10:2). The "herald of good tidings" (*mebaśśēr,-éret*) of Isa. 40:9; 41:27; and 52:7 announces the advent of Yahweh, the rise of Israel's deliverer, and the reign of God. Only rarely does a messenger convey bad news or proclaim judgment. A messenger of God calls for the curse of Meroz and threatens to destroy Jerusalem (Judg. 5:23; 2 Sam. 24:16); on one occasion a *m'baśśēr* reports military defeat and the capture of the Ark (1 Sam. 4:17); the news of various disasters is brought to Job by messengers (1:14, 16, 17, 18).

The prophetic "message" is, of course, similar in many respects. The prophet also announces a birth (Isa. 7:14), predicts victory (the

400 prophets of Yahweh in 1 Kings 22:6, 11), consoles (Isa. 40:1; where Deutero-Isaiah is to be conceived as standing in the *sôd yhwh*), and tells of Yahweh's coming (Habakkuk 3). Many other parallels will occur to the reader. Nevertheless, there is a difference of emphasis. Whereas the ordinary messenger and the divine *mal'āk* usually bring good tidings, and only rarely news of defeat or a threat of judgment, just the reverse is the case with Israel's prophets. While we should not make the common error of assuming that the earlier prophets preached "woe" while their successors promised "weal", we must admit that the relative emphasis upon doom and mercy changes with the times.

Perhaps this emphasis upon Yahweh's coming judgment in the pre-exilic prophets accounts for the fact that they never use the actual *word* "messenger' in describing themselves or their task. As noted above, the ordinary message is one of peace. It often begins with *šālôm* (1 Sam. 25:5–6; 2 Sam. 18:28; cf. Judg. 21:13; Deut. 2:26).[37] But the pre-exilic prophets denounced those who cried, "'Peace, peace,' when there [was] no peace" (Jer. 6:14; 8:11; Ezek. 13:10). Just as they avoided the term *rûₐh* because of its association with the more violent forms of "ecstasy,"[38] so also they hesitated to call themselves *mᵉl'ākîm* because of the ordinary connotations of the title. It is also significant that only one of these prophets refers to the *mal'ak yhwh* (Hos. 12:5—EVV 12:4).

The situation changes in the exilic and post-exilic periods, however, when the message *is* "peace." Israel, as the servant of Yahweh, is called "my messenger whom I send."[39] And the prophets them- selves are said to be Yahweh's messengers (Isa. 44:26); similarly the author of Isa. 61:1 seems to refer to himself, at least in part, when he says

> The Spirit of Adonai Yahweh is upon me,
>   because the Lord has anointed me
> to bring good tidings to the afflicted;
>   he has sent me to bind up the brokenhearted,
> to proclaim liberty to the captives,
>   and the opening of the prison to those who are bound. . . .

Other specific references to the prophets as messengers are in the third person: "Then Haggai, the messenger of Yahweh, spoke to the people with Yahweh's message . . ."; "Yahweh . . . sent per- sistently to them by his messengers . . . , but they kept mocking the messengers of God, despising his words, and scoffing at his prophets . . . (Hag. 1:13; 2 Chron. 36:15–16). Finally, the editor of an anonymous collection of late prophetic oracles does not hesitate to provide it with the title *mal'ākî*.[40]

Thus the prophets, although they seldom called themselves "messengers," used the form of the *Botenspruch* and claimed that their authority was that of one sent by Yahweh or from his council. They did not identify themselves with the one who sent them; there is no "mystic union" with the divine.[41] Nevertheless, they did not "prophesy the deceit of their own heart" (Jer. 23:26), for they had "stood in the council" of Yahweh. The line is not easy to draw: does a messenger speak only the words of his lord, or are they in some sense his own? Perhaps we say more than we know when we refer to "the message of the prophets."

NOTES

1 J. Muilenburg, "The Literary Character of Isaiah 34," *JBL* 59 (1940) 339–65; idem, "Psalm 47," *JBL* 63 (1944) 235–56; idem, "A Study in Hebrew Rhetoric: Repetition and Style," VTSup (*Congress Volume, 1953*) 97–111.

2 J. Muilenburg, *IB* 5 (1956) 381–773.

3 J. Muilenburg, "The Form and Structure of the Covenantal Formulations," *VT* 9 (1959) 347–65.

4 Ibid., 354 n. 2.

5 L. Köhler, *Deuterojesaja (Jesaja 40—55) stilkritisch untersucht*, BZAW 37 (1923) 102–9.

6 This is the full form, best preserved in 45:11–13, *"ein formstrenger Botenspruch,"* (ibid., 195).

7 Ibid., 109.

8 See, however, V. Maag, *Text, Wortschatz und Begriffswelt des Buches Amos* (1951), where passages such as Amos 1:3—3:2; 3:12a; 5:3; 5:4–6; 5:16–17; and 8:3 are called *Botensprüche*; cf. also E. Jacob, *Theology of the Old Testament* (New York: Harper & Row; London: Hodder & Stoughton, 1958) 130–31; and R. Rendtorff, "prophētēs ktl," *TDNT* 6 (1968) 796–812. See now C. Westermann, *Grundformen prophetischer Rede* (5th ed., 1978 [1960]; ET: *Basic Forms of Prophetic Speech* [Philadelphia: Westminster Press, 1967]).

9 Yahweh sends (*šālaḥ*) a divine messenger ("angel"): Gen. 24:7, 40; Exod. 23:20; 33:2; Num. 20:16; Judges 13:8; etc.; a man sends (*šālaḥ*) a man: Gen. 32:4, 6—EVV 32:3, 5; 37:13–14; 42:16; 46:28; Num. 20:14; 21:21; 22:5; Josh. 2:1; 7:22; Judges 6:35; 7:24; 9:31; 11:12, 14, 17, 19; etc.; Yahweh sends (*šālaḥ*) a prophet: Exod. 3:10, 13–15; 4:28; 5:22; 7:16; Num. 16:28; Deut. 34:11; Josh. 24:5; 1 Sam. 12:8; Micah 6:4; Ps. 105:26 (all Moses); 1 Sam. 15:1; 16:1 (Samuel); 2 Sam. 12:1, 25 (Nathan); 24:13 (Gad); Isa. 6:8; 61:1; Jer. 1:7; 7:25; 19:14; *et passim* Jeremiah; Ezek. 2:3–4; Hag. 1:12; Zech, 2:12, 13, 15—EVV 2:8, 9, 12; 4:9; *et passim* Zechariah; Mal. 3:23.

10 Cf. also Gen. 45:9 (Joseph to Jacob); 1 Kings 14:7 (Ahijah to Jeroboam); 22:27 (Ahab to his officials concerning the imprisonment of Micaiah); 2 Kings 1:6 (Elijah to Amaziah); 18:19 (Rabshakeh to Hezekiah); 19:6 (Isaiah

to Hezekiah). All of these accounts have the form, "Say to ... 'Thus says...'"

11 Other examples may be found in Isa. 7:3–4; Jer. 8:4; 11:3; 13:12; 15:2; *et passim* Jeremiah, Ezek. 6:3; 11:15; 12:10; 14:6; *et passim* Ezekiel; Hag. 2:2–6; Zech. 1:3; 6:12.

12 Martin Noth, "History and the Word of God in the Old Testament," *BJRL* 32 (1949–50) 194–206; cf. also H. H. Rowley, "Ritual and the Hebrew Prophets," *JSS* 1 (1956) 340 n. 5, where further references are given.

13 Noth, "History and the Word of God," 197.

14 Ibid., 197–98. The second of these passages is imperfectly preserved.

15 Ibid., 198–99.

16 E.g., Gordon 89:1–5; 1. *mlkt adty rgm thm. tlmyn bdk;* cf. also texts 18, 21, 95, 117, and *PRU*, II, p. 30, no. 14. In 54, 138, and *PRU*, II, p. 31, no. 15, we have *thm* (sender), *rgm* (addressee). Note also the Akkadian form *a-na* NN (often qualified) *qi-bi-ma-um-ma* NN ..., "To NN, my lord my son, etc., say: Thus NN ..."; Amarna letters *passim*; *PRU*, III, texts, 16.112, 15.178, 10.046, 16.116, and, with the transposition of *um-ma* and *a-na*, 13.7, 15.77, 8.333, etc. Cf. Köhler, *Deuterojesaja*, 102.

17 E.g., 137 (III A B B): 16–17, 33: Krt (KRT A): 248–49; cf. also Krt 125, 268, and 305.

18 49 (I A B): IV:34; 51 (II A B): VIII:32–34; 67 (I* A B): I:12–13; III:10–11, 17–18.

19 Cf. also 1 Sam. 8:7, where Yahweh (the sender) tells Samuel (the messenger) that the people "have not rejected you, but they have rejected me from being king over them." A broken passage in Ras Shamra 137 (III A B B): 38–42 may be relevant here. El has granted the request of Yamm, brought by his messengers, that Baal be surrendered to him; Baal is angry and seizes weapons, but is restrained by Ashtoreth (and Anath or Asherah?). They apparently ask how he can presume to strike a messenger, for "a messenger has upon his shoulders the word of his lord" (*mlak . bm . ktpm . rgm . b'lh;* cf. Isa. 9:5—EVV 9:6). This reconstruction of the text by Gordon (*Ugaritic Manual* [Analecta Orientalia 35; 1955] 168) is followed by H. L. Ginsberg (*ANET* 130). Cf., however, G. R. Driver, *Canaanite Myths and Legends, Old Testament Studies III* (1956) 80–81, where a radically different restoration and translation is proposed. Note also Ereshkigal's wrath when her messenger, Namtar, is not shown due respect (*ANET* 103–4).

20 See also the theophanies in Judges 6 and 20, and for a general discussion, Johannes Pedersen, *Israel: Its Life and Culture III–IV* (1940) 497; Jacob, *Theology of the Old Testament,* 76.

21 Gen. 42:16; Num. 21:21; Deut. 1:22; 19:12; Josh. 6:17; 10:6; Judges 11:17, 19; 20:12; 21:13; etc.

22 Jer. 23:18, 22; Pss. 25:14; 89:8—EVV 89:7; Job 15:8. Cf. also Job 29:4, where, however, the text should probably read *besôk* (see *Biblia Hebraica*, 3d ed., n. b). On Amos 3:7 see below, p. 115.

23 Ps. 55:15—EVV 55:14; Job 19:19; cf. Pedersen, *Israel I–II* (1926) 307.

24 Pedersen, *Israel I–II*, 130; Ludwig Köhler, *Hebrew Man* (1956) 87–88; cf. also

H. Wheeler Robinson, *Inspiration and Revelation in the Old Testament* (1946) 170 n. 4.

25 Prov. 11:13; 20:19; 25:9. We read that "without counsel [*sód*] plans go wrong" (Prov. 15:22). On the dual meaning see S. R. Driver and G. B. Gray, *A Critical and Exegetical Commentary on the Book of Job* (ICC; Edinburgh: T. & T. Clark, 1921), 2:95.

26 For a general description see Robinson, *Inspiration and Revelation*, 167–69; idem, "The Council of Yahweh," *JTS* 45 (1944) 151–57; G. E. Wright, "The Faith of Israel," *IB* 1 (1952) 360–61; idem, *The Old Testament Against Its Environment* (SBT 2; London: SCM Press, 1950) 30–41.

27 See also Deut. 33:2, where Yahweh comes from "the ten thousands of holy ones." For a discussion of the possibility that the heavens, the earth, and the mountains were members of the council, see H. B. Huffmon, "The Covenant Lawsuit in the Prophets," *JBL* 78 (1959) 290–91.

28 J. Morgenstern, "The Book of the Covenant," *HUCA* 5 (1928) 48–50.

29 See, among others, Robinson, "The Council of Yahweh," 154–55.

30 *ANET* 68, 94, 458, and 70 respectively. Cf. T. Jacobsen, "Primitive Democracy in Mesopotamia," *JNES* 11 (1943) 159–72.

31 *ANET* 94.

32 See Muilenburg, *IB* 5 (1956) 422–23; Robinson, "The Council of Yahweh," 155; P. A. H. DeBoer, *Second Isaiah's Message, Oudtestamentische Studien* 11 (1956) 40; and esp. F. M. Cross, Jr., "The Council of Yahweh in Second Isaiah," *JNES* 12 (1953) 274–77, where other passages are listed.

33 Strictly speaking, the Hebrew seems to imply that *no one* has ever stood in the council; since this contradicts v. 22, many add *mehem* after *mi* (e.g., Rudolph; thus the RSV), while others (e.g., Volz) regard the verse as an addition based upon Job 15:7–8, where Eliphaz asks Job, "Are you the Urmensch? . . . Have you listened in the council of God (*beˢód ˀᵉlóah*)?"

34 Cf. Ezek. 13:9, where it is said that the false prophets will not be in the council (*sód*) of Yahweh's people.

35 Cf. the parallelism between "send" and "go for us" in Isa. 6:8, as has been quoted.

36 Cf., however, Amos 3:7.

37 The same word or a cognate is often used in the introductions or conclusions to ancient Near Eastern letters; cf. Lachish letters II.2; III.3; VI.2; IX.2; and probably V.2. For similar formulas see *ANET*, 482–83, 491–92; cf. also the beginnings of Ugaritic letters 18, 21, 54, 95, 101, 117, and 138 (Gordon's numbering).

38 S. Mowinckel, "'The Spirit' and 'The Word' in the Pre-Exilic Reforming Prophets," *JBL* 53 (1934) 199–227.

39 Isa. 42:19. Perhaps *meˢullām* (RSV "dedicated one"), the parallel to *mal'āk* in this passage, should be interpreted as "the one whose message is perfected, completed," on the basis of *ˁᵃṣat māl'ākāw yaślim* ("performs the counsel of his messengers") in 44:26. This would bring out the chiastic structure of the verse (a-b-b-a: servant–messenger–faithful envoy–servant of Yahweh). For a convenient list of the various interpretations of *meˢullām* see Muilenburg, *IB* 5 (1956) 476.

40 It is generally held that the title was taken from Mal. 3:1, where Yahweh promises that he will send "my messenger" and/or "the messenger of the covenant" to prepare the way before him; later this messenger was identified with Elijah (3:23—EVV 4:5).

41 Cf. Pedersen, *Israel III–IV*, 493–94.

5

*Assyrian Statecraft and the Prophets of Israel**

JOHN S. HOLLADAY, Jr.

The explosive emergence of the so-called "writing prophets" in the history of Israel is one of the great historical mysteries of Old Testament scholarship. The first, and in some ways one of the greatest of these figures, Amos of Tekoah, can hardly be dated much before 750 B.C., and the beginnings of the prophetic careers of Hosea ben Beeri, Isaiah of Jerusalem, and Micah of Moresheth all fall within the following decade and a half. From this time forward, with the single exception of the dark and bloody reign of Manasseh, there is a steady succession of prophetic literature, ending somewhere around the mid-fifth century B.C. Once initiated, this succession moves in what seems to the historian, operating with the full confidence of hindsight, to be an entirely logical and reasonably consistent fashion. Yet its origins are wholly obscure. Like Melchizedek, Amos seems to have been born without benefit of ancestors. (And it goes without saying that such an [apparently] "uncaused happening" in the historical sphere is as troubling to the modern historian as the thought of an ancestorless Jebusite king would be to the historian's colleague in the biology department.) But what sort of events would be deemed to constitute "sufficient historical causation" for the rise of the classical prophets of Israel?

The answer to this question clearly hinges upon the answer we are able to give to the logically antecedent question: what was the rôle of the prophet in Israel?[1] That is, what is it that he thought he was doing? How did he construe his position in Israelite society? On what secular institution, if any, did he model his activities? And how did his contemporaries regard him? Recent investigations have greatly clarified this aspect of the problem.

* First published in *HTR* (1970) 29–51. Composed to honor Professor R. B. Y. Scott on the occasion of his retirement from Princeton University.

The Prophetic Office

For all the prophets from Samuel on, that is, from the first "individual" prophet on,[2] there is but one answer to this question of the rôle of the prophet. He was the messenger of Yahweh, God of Israel.[3] He was "called" by Yahweh—the Hebrew נביא being exactly cognate with the Akkadian *nabī'um*, "the called one," found already in its feminine form in the Code of Hammurabi.[4] In other words, he is an officer of the heavenly court.[5] He was "sent" by Yahweh to "tell Saul/ David/ this people." He typically delivered his message in the form כה אמר יהוה, "Thus says Yahweh"—that is, in the typical letter form of his day.[6] And, although the evidence is not incontrovertible, he seems to take pains to distinguish his own words, his own interpretations from those of his divine master.[7] Although the term מלאך, "messenger," only rarely appears in the books of the pre-exilic prophets, and never (unless Isa. 33:7 is an exception) with the intended meaning "heavenly messenger,"[8] it is hardly a chance matter that the last prophet in the Hebrew canon styled himself (or was named (Malachi, "my messenger."

But we must be careful not to allow our own somewhat limited conception of "messenger" to color our understanding of the messenger in the ancient Near East. The messenger was an official representative of the sender himself.[9] The royal messenger stood in the court of the Great King,[10] participated in the deliberative processes of the court, received the declaration of the king's wishes from the king's own mouth, and then carried the tablet or sealed roll of papyrus to its destination—in the case of imperial state administration, to the court of the vassal king. Here, received in the manner befitting a representative of the Great King, he would break the seals, hold up the letter, and proclaim: "To PN_1, thus (says) PN_2: I am well, may your heart be at peace.[11] Now concerning the matter of..."[12]

As is well known, it was precisely in this manner that the day-to-day business of the great empires of the ancient Near East was carried on, and the occasional finds of great caches of diplomatic correspondence testify to the energy and care given to this essential function of the suzerain's rule. The third of the eighth-century Aramaic treaty inscriptions found near Sefire—a typical suzerainty treaty of this period—is illuminating in this regard:

> Now (in the case of) all the kings of my vicinity or any one who is
> well-disposed toward me and (when) I send [ואשלח] my ambassador
> [מלאכי][13] to him for peace or for any of my business or (when) he

sends his ambassador to me, the road shall be open to me; you shall not (try to) dominate me[14] on it nor assert your authority over me concerning (it). (And) if you do not do so, you will be false to this treaty.[15]

From this perspective a chronically misunderstood passage in Jeremiah snaps sharply into focus. In his condemnation of the שלום prophets (Jer. 23:9ff.) the prophet proclaims:

> Thus says Yahweh of hosts concerning the prophets . . . Who among them has stood in the council of Yahweh[16] to perceive and to hear his word, or who has given heed to his word and listened? . . . I did not send [לא־שלחתי] the prophets, yet they ran [i.e., ran as couriers]. I did not speak to them, yet they prophesied. But if they had stood in my council, then they would have proclaimed my words to my people, and they would have turned them from their evil way, and from the evil of their doings. (23:15ff.)

If then, as Ross has demonstrated,[17] the function of the prophet, that is, as messenger of the heavenly court, remains remarkably constant from at least the eleventh century through the first part of the sixth century B.C.,[18] our problem seems to become more, rather than less, difficult of solution. What *is* the watershed between the classical prophets of the eighth century and their lesser-known forebears? Before we are in a position to answer this question, we must turn to a closer analysis of the "politics" of divine rule in ancient Israel.

The "Politics" of Divine Rule

If the prophet is understood to be a messenger/ambassador of the heavenly Lord, what is the conceptual model in terms of which the heavenly lordship of Yahweh was understood? For the period of the twelve-tribe league, it appears that Yahweh, in terms of his governing function, was conceived under the rubric "king of Israel,"[19] a concept which plays so important a rôle in the struggle which accompanied the elevation of Saul to the kingship. His living rule of Israel was exercised through the charismatic office of the Judge—a figure strangely combining qualities of king, judge, prophet, and warlord.[20] This time-to-time rule sufficed for a time. "But when the people of Israel cried to Yahweh, Yahweh raised up a deliverer for the people of Israel, who delivered them" (Judg. 3:9, similar passages *passim*). The secular model here is that of the far-off suzerain sending a commander and contingent of troops to the succor of a beleaguered vassal.[21] Many of the Amarna letters—letters of Canaanite kings to their Egyptian suzerain during the first part of the fourteenth century B.C.—illustrate this situation perfectly.[22] But what of the relation of Israel to her Suzerain after the establishment of the monarchy? How could Yahweh's free charismatic rule be exercised in the new situation of hereditary leadership? It is hardly a coincidence that prophecy arose simultaneously with the kingship. While we cannot take the full time here to make the demonstration, it is becoming increasingly clear that the prophet's primary function vis-à-vis the government of early Israel was to serve as the continuing agent of God's rule in Israel.[23]

With the adoption of the monarchy, Israel moved to vassal-kingdom status in the divine world order.[24] Far too much has been made of the unequivocal nature of the Davidic Covenant. From the outset it is clear that the individual king, even David himself, ruled only at the pleasure of Yahweh and at his direction. What has gone largely unrecognized, however, in this pattern of rule by the divine Suzerain is the official character of the prophetic messenger. Far from being a peripheral figure serving as a constant reminder of the old time religion of the twelve-tribe league, the prophet is the vital and essential living element in the divine government of the Kingdom of Israel.[25] He, and he alone, represents Yahweh's day-to-day interests in the governance of his vassal kingdom. Exactly as the envoy of the Pharaoh or the king of Assyria brought the word of the Great King to his vassal rulers in the city-states bordering his empire, so also the prophet was "sent" with the message of the Lord of Israel—couched in exactly the same form as a written communication from an earthly king: "To PN_1 say: thus says PN_2 . . ." or, more simply, the "address" is omitted and the prophet announces "Thus says Yahweh."[26]

The significance of this for the understanding of the difference between the pre-classical prophets and the "writing" prophets becomes clear when we ponder the implications of the often made observation that the pre-classical prophets were primarily "court-prophets," while the classical prophets were primarily "popular prophets." As a matter of fact, with the lone exception of the most legendary sections of the Elijah-Elisha cycles, there is not one single indication of a prophetic oracle being delivered to anyone outside of the royal court[27] prior to the time of Amos. Nor is there any indication that any of the pre-classical prophets uttered even one oracle against the whole nation or individual non-royal groups within the nation. Even in the Mount Carmel confrontation, where we would expect such a proclamation of the Word of Yahweh, the prophet conspicuously speaks only his own words—and Yahweh answers, not by word, but by fiery deed.

Here, then, is the point of difference between the prophets of the ninth and tenth centuries and those of the seventh and eighth centuries. Stripped to its simplest terms, this mutation involves a dramatic shift of the primary *object* of the prophetic address *away* from the ruling houses of the twin kingdoms and *to* the people of Israel as a whole. In this respect Isaiah alone among the eighth-century prophets retains a close relationship with the ruling house— a circumstance undoubtedly reflecting both his conservative Judaean background and his deep rootage in the Jerusalem cultus. Thus we are afforded an indirect witness to older patterns of prophetic conduct.

Now the question of the historian again intrudes: "What sort of circumstances would tend to bring about such a shift?" From the evidence at hand, it seems impossible to separate this sudden mutation in the rôle of the messenger of the Divine Council from the only slightly earlier shift in rôle of his secular counterpart—the imperial messenger. That is, we cannot separate this sudden rupture in the prophetic tradition from the dramatic shift in Assyrian imperial policy affecting Israel at precisely this time.[28]

The Assyrian Crisis

During the preceding centuries of imperial rule in the ancient Near East, outlying territories were often ruled through vassal kings— appointed by the suzerain (cf. Samuel's anointing first of Saul, then of David; Nathan's rôle in assuring the succession of Solomon, etc.)—and dismissed by the suzerain (cf. Samuel's message of Yahweh's rejection of Saul, Ahijah's condemnation of the House of Jeroboam, etc.). International communications were, naturally, between kings—between the Great King and his vassals.

From the ninth century forward, Assyria was the greatest military power in the fertile crescent, ruling through an intricate system of vassal-treaties with local kings, a highly developed messenger-ambassadorial service, regular military shows of strength through the subject lands, and a systematic campaign of extermination with regard to the mountain tribesmen who constantly threatened her northern flank. Rebellion was commonplace, and at first seems to have been treated simply and directly, continuing the earlier Egyptian and Hittite traditions.[29] The vassal king rebelled: the vassal king was eliminated. And either a compliant relative was placed on the throne or the entire house was eliminated and a new dynasty established, with, in either case, a substantial boost in the annual exactions of tribute. The parallels between the diplomacy appropriate to this pattern and the pattern of prophetic activity in the ninth, tenth, and eleventh centuries are obvious. Toward the end of the ninth century, however, and culminating in the reign of Tiglath-pileser III, the peoples of Syria-Palestine were suddenly. confronted with a radically new mode of dealing with subject peoples.

This much of the Assyrian state policy during the middle decades of the eighth century is common knowledge: the terroristic activities of Assyrian soldiers, the gloating reliefs depicting siege, torture, and deportation scenes decorating the audience chambers of Assyrian kings; the wholesale deportations of entire population groups, of which the depopulation of Samaria in the eighth century and Judah in the sixth century (by the successors to the Assyrian technique) are only two of many. Thus, the whole terror psychology of Assyrian statecraft swung its focus of attention from master to slave, prince to peasant, king to citizen.[30] No longer was only the king and his court butchered or led into captivity. Now whole *countries* went into exile.[31]

But what of the day-to-day statecraft which accompanied this new mode of imperial rule; how did it differ from the older models, and, in particular, what possible effect could it have had upon Israelite prophetic traditions? We must present the material, which is massive, only in summary fashion. For present purposes, it will suffice to explore two major categories: (1) international treaty provisions; and (2) royal letters.

1. *Treaties* which from the fifteenth century B.C. on (at a minimum) have been made between the great king and his house and the vassal king and his house are no longer simply agreements between royal houses. Starting with the treaty of Shamshi-Adad V of Babylon (ca. 823 B.C.),[32] the treaty is consummated between the great king and the vassal king *and all of his people.*[33] Only a fragmentary section of the treaty-curses remains to this document, but the new dimension in some of these curses is readily apparent if we place them side by side with the older curse formulae. For example, a typical "blanket-curse" from a Hittite treaty of the late second millenium reads:

> May the gods of the oath destroy Duppi-Tessub together with his person, his wife, his son, his grandson, his house, his land and together with everything that he owns.[34]

Contrast the Shamshi-Adad formulation:

> [May Marduk the great lord] ... bring sickness upon you and dissolution for your people ... through disease and famine may he overwhelm your people.[35]

This universal applicability of the treaty document is even more concretely illustrated in the Aramaic treaty inscriptions from Sefire (ca. 750 B.C.) recently republished by Fitzmyer,[36] the first of which begins:

> The treaty of Bir-Ga'yah, king of KTK, with Matî'el, the son of 'Attarsamak, the king [of Arpad; and the trea]ty of the sons of Bir-Ga'yah with the sons of Matî'el; and the treaty of the grandsons of Bir-Ga'ya[h and] his [offspring] with the offspring of Matî'el, the son of 'Attarsamak, the king of Arpad; and the treaty of KTK with [the treaty of] Arpad; and the treaty of the citizens of KTK with the treaty of the citizens of Arpad ...[37]

And the strikingly new note in Amos' prophecy, the threat of national exile, finds a nearly contemporary expression in the treaty-curses of the Ashurnirari V treaty with Mati''el of Arpad:

> Just as this ram is [taken] away from his fold, will not return to his fold, will [no longer stand] before his fold, so may ... Mati'ilu, with his sons, [his nobles], the people of his land [be taken away] from his land, not return to his land, he shall [no longer] stand at the head of his land.[38]

In this connection it is worthy of note that the major documents analyzed by J. Harvey in his article "Le 'Rîb-pattern,' réquisitoire prophétique ...,"[39] the "Milavata letter,"[40] the "Indictment of Madduwattaš,"[41] the closely similar document concerning Mita of Paḫḫuwa,[42] and the Tukulti-Ninurta letter,[43] all represent indictments of *individual* rulers in contrast to the *rib-Gattung* in the classical prophets, which is pre-eminently a blanket condemnation of all Israel. On the other hand, the parallel between these "indictments" of rebellious vassal rulers and the heavenly *rîb* in 1 Kings 22:17–22, in which *King Ahab* is condemned, can hardly be accidental.[44] Nor does it seem to be coincidental that, at about the time that Mati''el takes upon himself and his people—at the Assyrian behest—a treaty-curse involving wholesale exile from the land of Arpad, Amos should threaten the *people* of Syria and Israel with exile from their lands, Micah and Hosea should declare that "Yahweh has a controversy with his people" (Mic. 6:2; Hos. 4:1; 12:3[2]), and Amos, Micah, and Isaiah should all three use the characteristic *rîb-Gattung* "call to witnesses" to testify against "the house of Jacob" (Amos 3:9ff.) and against "my people ... Israel" (Isa. 1:2ff., cf. Mic. 6:1ff.).[45]

2. *State Letters and Royal Proclamations*: Here our resources are again limited by the chances of discovery to the Late Bronze Age and to the eighth and seventh centuries B.C. and later. They thus bracket the period under discussion. Yet the contrasts are striking and strongly corroborate the pattern of development witnessed by factors previously considered.

In the correspondence unearthed at El-Amarna and similar materials excavated at individual Palestinian sites,[46] we have an invaluable collection of over three hundred and fifty letters—mostly either from the Egyptian king to his vassal kings or from these vassals to their overlord. The latter are in the great majority. Two letters of this large collection represent petitions from the citizens of a city-state to the Pharaoh.[47] Two others come from a vassal ruler and his city.[48] There are no letters from the king of Egypt to population groups.

In the some sixty royal letters or proclamations[49] from the archives of King Esarhaddon[50] (the archive as a whole ranges from ca. 722 B.C. to 609 B.C.), there are fifteen letters either to cities, countries, population groups or to one of these groups of people together with their vassal ruler or governor. There are probably four letters to the kings of Elam (on a parity basis with Assyria) and some forty-plus letters to various officers of the king. One of the most colorful of the letters to a population group, "To the non-Babylonians," well illustrates the manner in which population groups are now held to be directly responsible to the suzerain, and, incidentally, illustrates the equally blunt and direct manner in which these population groups were confronted with this responsibility:

> An order of the king (Esarhaddon) to the "Non-Babylonian" inhabitants of Babylon: I am fine. There is a proverb often used by people: "The potter's dog, once he crawls into the (warm) potter's shop, barks at the potter." There you are, pretending—against the commands of the god—to be Babylonians, and what unspeakable things you and your master have devised against my subjects! There is another proverb often cited by people: "What the adulteress says at the door of the judge's house carries more weight than the words of her husband." Should you ask yourselves after I sent back to you, with seals intact, your letters full of empty and insolent(?) words which you had dispatched: "Why did he return the letters to us?" I am telling you that I would have opened and read whatever message my loyal and loving Babylonians had sent me but . . . [end broken].[51]

By its very nature, such direct appeal to population groups as a whole brought about a change in the function of the imperial messenger. No longer was it sufficient for the letter to be read only to the vassal king and his court. As the Rabshakeh showed himself well aware (2 Kings 18:26ff.), such a procedure would have been tantamount to addressing the letter to the Dead Letter Office. Thus, alongside the older system of *private* official communications to vassals,[52] the Neo-Assyrian period witnessed the spectacular rise to prominence of the royal herald as an essential instrument of imperial government.[53] So pervasive was this practice, it would seem, that even the style of the introductory formula of the royal letters was conformed to the proclamation-formula: *"Amāt šarri* (or the Assyrian *abīt šarri) ana PN,"*—"Word/proclamation/edict of the king to PN."[54] Thus, the *"amāt šarri"* can be "fixed in [a man's] mouth."[55] It is proclaimed simultaneously before rulers and "before the people of the land" (*RCA* no. 174; cf. 2 Kings 18:17ff. and the nearly identical scene in the first of the Nimrud Letters,[56] dating only thirty years before the Rabshakeh's speech). It is spoken against rebellious cities (*RCA* no. 246); to rebellious army units (*RCA* no. 251); "to the Sealanders" (*RCA* no. 289); "in the assembly of the people (*RCA* no. 344), etc., as well as to individual rebellious vassal kings or governors (*RCA* no. 282).[57]

Again, it can hardly be coincidental that this change in the conduct of the office of the royal Assyrian messenger is paralleled by a similar functional shift in the office of the messenger of the heavenly court in Judah-Israel. Nor are the reasons for this shift far to seek. The radical changes in the conduct of "secular" imperial government to which Israel was exposed in the later part of the ninth century and early part of the eighth century *necessarily* brought about tensions in Israelite thinking about the modalities of *divine* rule—tensions which were all the more quickly resolved in favor of the new model since this "democratization" of responsibility already had deep-seated parallels in the institutions of the twelve-tribe league.

Once indicated, the parallels between the rôle of the prophet in eighth-century Israel and the rôle of the royal herald in Neo-Assyrian statecraft are unmistakable. Since obedience is now demanded not only of the ruling house but of the entire people as well—the *nation* being held responsible for the action of its rulers—that which originally was of importance only to the royal court now was of life-and-death importance to the welfare of every man in the nation. Those things which formerly had been spoken only in private court-circles (the oracles of the court-prophets) and preserved, if at all, only in court-archives and in chronicles of the kings (hence the rise of popular stories *about* the prophets) now *must* be spoken publicly (hence the preservation of the prophetic *logia*).[58] The new image of the prophet, that is to say, the new "secular model" from which he took his cue, is most strikingly preserved in the accounts of the Assyrian siege of Jerusalem in 701 B.C. (2 Kings 18:17ff.), where we encounter for the first time in *recorded* Israelite history the "new" form of messenger-speech. Brevard Childs' comments on this passage, although intended for another purpose, are highly appropriate to our present analysis:

> The first speech of the Rabshakeh is interrupted by the protest of the Judaean emissaries. They urge him to speak in the diplomatic language of Aramaic instead of Hebrew, which was being overhead and understood by the people on the wall. The biblical account reflects with remarkable accuracy elements of a scene which could hardly have arisen apart from genuine historical tradition. The crude answer of the Assyrian fits exactly into the setting of the disputation which has been sketched above. By their consternation, the emissaries only play into the hands of the experienced Assyrian negotiator. His role is not merely to communicate a message, but rather to persuade and agitate. He reacts immediately to the new situation, and far from complying to the request, appeals directly to the populace in an attempt to arouse support against Hezekiah's position.[59]

While Childs is describing *only* the Rabshakeh's activity—and it should be noted that the essential authenticity of both the Rabshakeh's mission and speech is vindicated by exceedingly close cuneiform parallels[60]—the description of the Rabshakeh's rôle is identical to that which one would ordinarily give of the classical prophets. That is, it "is not merely to communicate a message, but to persuade and agitate." As Amaziah reported to Jeroboam: "Amos has conspired against you in the midst of the house of Israel; the land is not able to bear all his words" (Amos 7:10b). Functionally, no distinction can be made between the Rabshakeh's proclamation of the "word of the king" at the great gate of the city and the seventh- and eighth-century prophets' proclamation of "the word of Yahweh" to a stubborn and rebellious people. Ironically, even the abortive efforts at silencing the messenger are parallel.[61]

One measure of the distance we are here removed from the sphere of *pre*-classical prophecy may be seen in the mere juxtaposition of two statements regarding the commissioning of two prophets—one of the tenth century and the other from the end of the seventh century:

1. And Yahweh sent Nathan to David. . . . (2 Sam. 12:1a)
2. The word of Yahweh came to [Jeremiah], saying, "Go and proclaim in the hearing of Jerusalem, Thus says Yahweh. . . ." (Jer. 2:1–2a)[62]

The Indirect Evidence for the Rise of Popular Prophecy

In addition to the rather general observations made in connection with our analysis of the prophetic office, at least one other piece of internal evidence has already been mentioned. This is the ambivalent rôle of Isaiah. So far as we can tell, he alone of the classical prophets actively sought the ear of the king and spoke to him regarding both personal affairs and matters of state (Isaiah 7; 37— 39). There are extremely close parallels here to the activity of the pre-classical prophets. Yet the burden of Isaiah's prophecy was, as the editorial heading to the Isaiah Book rightly notes: "Concerning Judah and Jerusalem" (1:1b). He is commissioned to "go, and say to this people. . . ." (6:9), to proclaim Yahweh's *rîb* against his sons (1:2ff.) "until cities lie waste without inhabitant and houses without men, and the land is utterly desolate, and Yahweh removes men far away" (6:11b–12a). There can be little question that in Isaiah we see a truly transitional figure—still clinging to the old patterns (much as one would expect of a prophet of his generation active in the Jerusalem temple)—yet forced by the winds of change into new and ill-charted modes of prophet behavior.

Another indication that the eighth-century prophets represent a radical break with their past is afforded us by Amaziah's (unavoidable) misinterpretation of Amos's oracles against Israel: "Amos has conspired against *you* in the midst of the house of Israel" (7:10b, emphasis ours). By the time of Jeremiah, no such misunderstanding of the prophetic message was possible. He is rightly accused not of *lèse majesté*, but of simple treason: "This man deserves the sentence of death, because he has prophesied against this city, as you have heard with your own ears" (Jer. 26:11b).

Thus, from two quite different types of "boundary-phenomena" we may quite properly, it seems to me, infer that Amos and Isaiah of Jerusalem each stand very close to the point of origination of "classical" prophecy, that is, prophecy "against the whole house of Israel." It yet remains for the deuteronomic historian to tell us *how* close.

The objection might well be raised against our interpretation of the pre-classical prophets as "court prophets" that such an interpretation merely derives from the nature of the source material for the history of this period. That is, if the deuteronomic historian's materials derive largely from "court histories," royal chronicles, propagandistic outpourings of the Solomonic court and the like, what else would one expect? Such sources would not be particularly interested in accounts of "popular" prophecy. This argument could be very strong. Yet indications are not lacking in the Book of Kings that the editor is quite aware of the impact of popular prophecy. In particular, two little-noted editorial passages may be taken to be indications that the historian, despite his apparent silence regarding Amos, Micah, and Hosea, has a strong tradition concerning the origination of the prophetic speech against the nation.

1. In the account of Jeroboam II's reconquest of the original Davidic limits of the Northern Kingdom "according to the word . . . which [Yahweh] spoke by his servant Jonah ben Amittai, the prophet . . . from Gath-hepher," the reason given for Yahweh's support of an obviously unworthy ruler is that "Yahweh [had seen] that the affliction of Israel [by the Aramaeans] was very bitter, for there was none left, bond or free, and there was none to help Israel. *But Yahweh had not said that he would blot out the name of Israel from under heaven*, so he saved them by the hand of Jeroboam ben Joash" (2 Kings 14:25b–27, emphasis added). Here the editor seems to show himself aware of a tradition which maintained that, through the time of Jeroboam II, no blanket condemnation of Israel had yet been made by the prophets of Israel.

2. In the account of the apostasy of Israel during the reign of Hoshea and his immediate predecessors in the third quarter of the eighth century, the first summarizing statement of *general* prophetic condemnation of Israel and Judah occurs: "Yet Yahweh warned Israel and Judah by every prophet and seer, saying, 'Turn from your evil ways and keep my commandments and my statutes, in accordance with all the law which I commanded your fathers, and which I sent to you by my servants the prophets.'"[63] (2 Kings 17:13; cf. also vv. 14–18). This summary obviously must also be attributed to the deuteronomic editor, yet not only is it poles apart from his earlier notice relative to the reign of Jeroboam II, but, from this point in the narrative on, similar summarizing statements or allusions to total destruction appear with monotonous regularity: 2 Kings 17:22–23; 18:12; 19:25ff.; 20:16ff.; 21:10ff.; 22:15ff.; 23:27; 24:2.

Thus, in a sense, the deuteronomic historian has presented us with *termini ante quem* and *ad quem* for his traditions concerning the rise of what we now call "classical" prophecy. "Yahweh had not said," prior to the great victories of Jeroboam II, "that he would blot out the name of Israel from under heaven." While the military record of Jeroboam II is unfortunately too obscure to furnish us with any firm dates, a date of ca. 750 B.C. for the peak of Israel's resurgence cannot be far wrong.[64] And yet, by the time of

Hoshea's ascension to the throne (ca. 732 B.C.) "Yahweh [had] warned Israel and Judah by every prophet...." One feels inclined to insert: "By Amos of Tekoa, by Isaiah ben Amoz, by Hosea ben Beeri, and by Micah of Moresheth."

Summary

The institution of the suzerain, or "great king," as it classically flourished in the ancient Near East, furnished an ideal theological model for Israel's understanding both of the sovereignty of God and of her peculiar relationship to him. As studies of covenant theology, royal theology, prophetic oracle-forms, etc., progress, it is increasingly clear just how far-reaching the implications of this mode of conceptualization actually were. In this study I have attempted to investigate some of the ramifications of this understanding as they illuminate the changing nature of the prophetic office in pre-exilic Israel.

1. Prior to the expansion of the neo-Assyrian empire during the latter part of the ninth and first portions of the eighth century, imperial rule in the area of Syria-Palestine normatively was exercised through the agency of vassal or client kingship, each vassal being directly responsible to the suzerain for that area under his control. The vital link between suzerain and vassal was the royal messenger. Indeed, it could be argued that the viability and strength of the empire was in large measure directly proportional to the efficiency of its courier/ambassadorial system. During the period of the pre-classical prophets the theory of imperial government might be diagrammed as follows:

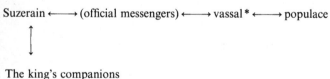

Suzerain ⟷ (official messengers) ⟷ vassal * ⟷ populace

The king's companions
("Those who see the king's face")

* = the party directly eliminated in case of rebellion.

With the substitution of Yahweh for suzerain, the *sôd YHWH* for the inner circle of courtiers, and the court-prophets for the messengers, this diagram could equally well represent the theology of divine rule in ninth- and tenth-century Judah and Israel.

2. The genius of the neo-Assyrian modification of the above

scheme was that it placed the populace on a par with the vassal king, making the entire community responsible for its actions—and therefore the king's actions—vis-à-vis the central government. Messengers continued to go from king to king, but a new dimension was added to their activity. Now, as heralds, they also proclaimed the will of the suzerain to the people of the land. The double speech of the Rabshakeh outside the gate of Jerusalem may be taken as paradigmatic. By this democratization of responsibility, Assyria decisively undercut the potential for unilateral action on the part of the vassal king. Simultaneously, by imposing frightful and well-publicized penalties for rebellion—coupled with promises of soft treatment for populations refusing to join their ruler in rebellion—the Assyrian overlords so quelled the spirit of the populace at large that rebellion became a progressively less attractive option for either party. The new form of Assyrian rule may be diagrammed thus:

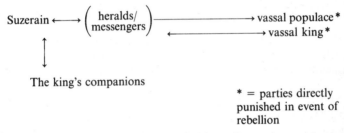

The king's companions

* = parties directly punished in event of rebellion

The earliest certain application of this policy seems to be in the treaty of Shamshi-Adad V with Marduk-zakir-shum I of Babylon, ca. 823 B.C. By the time of the rise of popular prophecy in Israel ca. 750 B.C., it was well-established practice in the Syro-Palestinian corridor, as is witnessed by the various treaties of Mati''el, king of Arpad.

Given the historical priority of the change in Assyrian statecraft and the appropriateness of the new model of imperial rule as descriptive of the rule of God in normative Israelite theology during the seventh and last half of the eighth centuries B.C., there can hardly be any question of the causative factors involved in the transition from pre-classical (court) prophecy to classical (popular) prophecy. As the implications of the new secular order became apparent in early eighth-century Israel, a corresponding shift in Israel's understanding of the demands of divine obedience was made possible. Additional warrants for this evolution surely were provided by anti-monarchical sentiments still current among the populace. By the middle of the eighth century, the days of the pre-classical "court" prophet were at an end. Like the Rabshakeh standing at the entrance of the city proclaiming "'the word of the great king, the king of Assyria,' . . . to the men sitting on the wall . . .," so also Amos proclaims: "Hear this word that Yahweh has spoken, O people of Israel. . . ."[65]

NOTES

1 For both this point and important elements of the following analysis I am indebted to the observations of G. E. Wright, "The Lawsuit of God," in *Israel's Prophetic Heritage* (ed. B. W. Anderson and W. Harrelson; New York: Harper & Row, 1962) 63–64.

2 Cf. Wright's analysis of the origins of the prophetic office (ibid.) and the brief notice in "The Nations in Hebrew Prophecy," *Encounter* 26 (1965) 229ff.

3 Cf. the survey of previous discussion in C. Westermann, *Basic Forms of Prophetic Speech* (Philadelphia: Westminster Press, 1967) 13ff.; and the essay of J. F. Ross, "The Prophet as Yahweh's Messenger," in *Israel's Prophetic Heritage* (= chap. 3 in this I R T vol.).

4 W. F. Albright, *From the Stone Age to Christianity* (2d ed.; New York: Doubleday & Co., 1957) 303. Note also the use of קרא in Exod. 31:1; Isa. 43:1; 45:3, 4 (all exilic), and the parallel use of *nabû(m)* in similar contexts— i.e., the appointing to a divinely ordained task—common in Akkadian royal inscriptions from the time of Sargon I on. Cf. W. von Soden, *Akkadisches Handwörterbuch* (1959–); and M. J. Seux, *Epithètes royales Akkadiennes et Sumériens* (Paris, 1967) 175–79.

5 Cf. the citations in n. 2 and the discussion and references in Ross, "The Prophet," chap. 4 of this vol. Additionally, cf. nn. 10 and 63.

6 Cf. J. Lindblom, "Die prophetische Orakelformel," in *Die literarische Gattung der prophetischen Literatur* (U U Å; 1924:1; Uppsala) 97ff. More convenient, if less detailed, is his *Prophecy in Ancient Israel* (Philadelphia: Fortress Press, 1962) 103–4. Westermann's position (*Basic Forms*, 98ff.) fails to take seriously enough the long usage of this formula as a literary cliché precisely in the Syro-Palestinian area. After something like a millennium and a half of constant use as an epistolary introductory formula (taking the usage in the fertile crescent as a whole into account) it is simply academic to say, "One can see that the oral procedure for sending a message still lives in these formulas centuries after the first technicalization of the message through writing was accomplished" (ibid., 104).

7 Cf. Jer. 23:25ff.; 28:6ff. Compare H. M. Gevaryahu's analysis, "The Speech of Rab-Shakeh to the People on the Wall of Jerusalem" (Hebrew), in *Studies in the Bible Presented to M. H. Segal* (Jerusalem, 1964) 96–97. (I owe the reference to B. Childs's citation, *Isaiah and the Assyrian Crisis* (S B T 2d Ser., No. 3 [London: S C M Press, 1967] 79 n. 27).

8 The "historical" reference in Hosea 12:5(4) is, of course, quite another matter.

9 E.g., 2 Sam. 10:1–5 (cf. *A B L* 1260 in L. Waterman, *Royal Correspondence of the Assyrian Empire* [henceforth Waterman's translations of *A B L* will be cited as *R C A* no. 000], part 2 [Ann Arbor, Mich., 1930] 376–77); 1 Sam. 25:39ff.; and 2 Kings 20:12ff. Further, cf. Ross, "The Prophet," in this vol., and Lindblom, *Prophecy*, 296–97.

10 In the royal Assyrian epistolary literature, for especially serious matters, the messenger of the king may be either a member of the king's bodyguard (*lúmutîr pûti*) or, exceptionally, one of the king's "personal companions" (*lúmanzaz pâni*). Cf. E. Klauber, *Assyrisches Beamtentum* (Leipzig, 1910) 23ff., 100–101, 105ff.; and *RCA*, part 4, 22–23. *RS* 17.137 likewise demonstrates that *Teḥitešub* and *Tilitešub*, messengers of "the Sun," were highly placed members of the court, since their seals are placed on an international pact witnessed by, among others, the *Qardabbu* official of "the Sun" and the chamberlain of the king of Ugarit. Cf. J. Nougayrol, *Le Palais Royal d'Ugarit IV*, Mission de Ras Shamra IX (Paris, 1956) 107–8. Further, cf. n. 63, below.

11 This phrase, characteristic of "friendly" correspondence, is lacking in threatening letters, e.g., *ABL* 403, "To the Non-Babylonians," below.

12 Although the letter involved seems to have been a captured document, the description of the reading of such a document in the presence of a group of courtiers in *ND*. 2603 is illustrative of the practice. Cf. H. W. F. Saggs, "The Nimrud Letters, 1952– I," *Iraq* 17 (1955) 32–33.

13 The ubiquitous Northwest Semitic term for messenger, courier, ambassador in this context is equivalent to the ordinary Akkadian term *lúmā šipri*, "messenger."

14 The messenger as alter-ego of the suzerain.

15 J. Fitzmyer, "The Aramaic Suzerainty Treaty from Sefire in the Museum of Beirut," *CBQ* 20 (1958) 450.

16 The סוד יהוה, or Divine Council, was the royal court of heaven assembled in its deliberative function—a function vividly described in the vision of Micaiah ben Imlah in 1 Kings 22. Cf. the discussions cited in n. 5.

17 Ross, "The Prophet."

18 The separation of the נביאים, under the rubric "salvation prophets," from the "judgment prophets" (so, e.g., Würthwein, quoted with approval by Westermann, *Basic Forms,* 77, 80) must be regarded as one of the curious byproducts of recent research. If the "judgment prophets" are not נביאים, what *are* they? Certainly such a distinction seems to be unknown either to the editor of the "B" material in Jeremiah (cf. esp. chaps. 28—29) or to the writer of the Books of Kings (e.g., 2 Kings 17:13 [Isa. 37:2]; 17:23; 19:2; 20:1 [Isa. 38:1], 14 [Isa. 39:3]; 21:10; 22:14ff.; 24:2).

19 Only so can one explain the adoption of the "Suzerainty Treaty" form as the model for Israel's covenant with Yahweh. Cf. G. E. Wright, "Reflections Concerning Old Testament Theology," in *Studia Biblica et Semitica*—Th. C. Vriezen dedicata (Wageningen, the Netherlands, 1966) 386.

20 For an introduction to the historical reconstruction developed here, see W. F. Albright, *Samuel and the Beginnings of the Prophetic Movement* (Cincinnati: Hebrew Union College, The Goldenson Lecture for 1961); Wright, "The Lawsuit of God," 63ff.; and idem, "The Nations in Hebrew Prophecy," 225ff.

21 Note the presence of heavenly troops in the holy-war traditions. Cf. particularly the remarkable tradition concerning the "commander of the army of Yahweh" (שר־צבא־יהוה) in Joshua 5:13ff., the participation of the stars in the conflict (Judges 5:20) with the forces of Sisera, the "sound of marching in the tops of the balsam trees" (2 Sam. 5:24), and the wonder-story concerning the heavenly army (commanded by Elisha?) in the Elisha cycle (2 Kings 6:11ff.).

22 E.g., *EA* no. 244: ". . . Let the king know that ever since the archers returned (to Egypt?) Lab'ayu has carried on hostilities against me, and we are not able to pluck the wool, and we are not able to go outside the gate in the presence of Lab'ayu, since he learned that thou hast not given archers; and now his face is set to take Megiddo, but let the king protect his city. . . . Let the king give one hundred garrison troops to guard the city lest Lab'ayu seize it." *ANET*² 485a.

23 Cf. Wright, "The Lawsuit of God," 63.

24 For the vassal status of the Davidic king, cf. R. de Vaux, "Le roi d'Israël, vassal de Yahvé," in the *Tisserant Festschrift, Studi e Testi* 231 (Vatican City, 1964) 119–33. For a précis of the study, cf. D. J. McCarthy, "Covenant in the Old Testament: The Present State of Inquiry," *CBQ* 27 (1965) 237–38.

25 Cf. Wright, "The Lawsuit of God," 63 n. 68.

26 As one might expect, the "address" has been stripped off in most contexts, being preserved mainly in narrative passages, e.g., 1 Kings 12:23–24; 2 Kings 20:5 (cf. Isa. 38:5); Jer. 2:2 (LXX omits), 28:13 (reflexes of this formula *passim*); Amos 7:15–16.

27 This category would, of course, cover "kings-designate" (e.g., 1 Kings 11:29ff.). If 1 Samuel 3 is insisted upon, it remains that the "House of Eli" is the ruling house of Israel at this time.

28 Wright ("The Lawsuit of God," 64) sees this movement from "court" to "popular" prophecy developing as a Northern Israelite theological reaction to the civil wars ensuing from the division of the kingdom and the events attendant upon the rise of the Omri dynasty. This almost certainly was a contributing factor to the acceptance of the new theology. Yet there is no compelling reason why this distress could not just as easily have been laid at the king's door. That is, God is punishing the people because of the *king's* sin (cf. the account of David's census in 2 Samuel 24, esp. v. 17). This was, in fact, the Chronicler's general point of view (Wright, ibid., n. 69). That the people should be punished for their *own* sins would have been incomprehensible to a "true" monarchist. It remained for the new Assyrian techniques of world domination to provide a model by which God's righteous acts of judgment could be viewed in a new light.

29 While it seems to the present writer that this reconstruction is probable, it should freely be admitted that our present knowledge of the details of Assyrian history during the early years of the first millennium B.C. is extremely thin. Certain indications can, in fact, be cited in support of the argument that the innovations commonly associated with the Neo-Assyrian Empire (see below) had their roots in much earlier times. The question is, however, academic as far as the Israelite experience goes. Cf. n. 33.

30 *ABL* 310 furnishes a fascinating glimpse into some of the reasoning behind this policy. Sharruemuranni, in the course of a letter dealing with the acquisition of horses for the king, writes his master, Sargon, as follows: ". . . When the sheep did not come unto us, I sent the servants of the king my lord to the city of Kibatki. The people were terrified; (some) were put to the sword. When the city of Kibatki had been terrified, they continued to fear, (so that) they may be expected to send (tribute)" (*RCA* no. 310, rev. ll. 3–14). Further, cf. the carefully reasoned arguments of H. W. F. Saggs ("Assyrian Warfare in the Sargonid Period," *Iraq* 25 [1963] 145–54), to the effect that such "atrocities" were part of

a carefully planned propaganda campaign of "high military value, and did not spring from some sadistic element peculiar to the Assyrian character" (p. 154).

31 The impact of this policy upon Judah-Israel is readily apparent in the Book of Amos. Exile, or the threat of exile, hangs heavy not only over Israel (4:1ff.; 5:5, 27; 6:7; 7:11, 17; 9:4, 9) but over the surrounding nations as well (cf. esp. 1:5, but the emphasis upon exile throughout the oracles against the foreign nations [vv. 6, 9, 15] can hardly be disassociated from the same general Zeitgeist).

32 Cf. E. F. Weidner, "Der Staatsvertrag Assurniraris VI mit Mati'ilu von Bit-Agusi," *AfO* 8 (1932–33) 27–29.

33 It is not impossible, as was suggested in n. 29, that we are here dealing with a characteristically Assyrian practice of somewhat greater antiquity. Note already the (partial?) blinding of 14,400 prisoners by Shalmaneser I (1274–1245 B.C.), the mass deportation of the Babylonians to Assyria by Tukulti-Ninurta I shortly after 1235 B.C., and the (claimed) deportation of 28,800 Hittites by the same ruler (most recently, see J. M. Munn-Rankin in *The Cambridge Ancient History,* vol. 2, chap. 25. [fasc. 49] [rev. ed.; Cambridge: Cambridge Univ. Press, 1967] 10, 15–16, 20; the dates given are those of Munn-Rankin). However, this may be, such practices are clearly new in the Syro-Palestinian corridor, which, up to this time, has been dominated by Egyptian and Hittite patterns of rule. For the tenth through the early ninth centuries note, inter alia, the characteristic Assyrian name for Syria-Palestine (^{kur} Ḫatti, "Hittite-land") and the Egyptianizing courts of David and Solomon (cf. esp. R. de Vaux, "Titres et fonctionnaires égyptiens à la cour de David et de Salomon," *RB* 48 [1939] 403–5). Israel's international relations during this period have to do principally with Egypt, Tyre, and Damascus. Certainly there is nothing in the inscriptions of Shalmanezer III (859–825 B.C.) to suggest that he is imposing unusual treaty obligations upon his rebellious "Syro-Hittite" vassals, which included Jehu *mār Ḫu-um-ri-i,* "son of Omri." In fact, it may be suggested that it is just this strong and continued resistance to Shalmanezer III's attempts to establish his suzerainty over this area, with its long traditions of city-state and small kingdom independence, which led to modifications of the traditional modus operandi.

34 Treaty of Mursilis with Duppi-Tessub of Amurru (l. 20**), cf. *ANET*², 205.

35 Weidner, *Der Staatsvertrag,* 29 (ll. 16–17, 19).

36 J. Fitzmyer, "The Aramaic Inscriptions of Sefire I and II," *JAOS* 81 (1961) 178–222; idem, "The Aramaic Suzerainty Treaty from Sefire in the Museum of Beirut," *CBQ* 20 (1958) 444–76.

37 Fitzmyer, "The Aramaic Inscriptions," 179ff. (I–A, ll. 1–4. Cf. also ll. 24ff., 30ff., 35ff.; I–B, ll. 1–6, 21, etc.). Compare the equally comprehensive introductory formula of the treaty between Ashurnirari V of Assyria and this same Mati''el of Arpad (754 B.C.): ". . . Mat[i'lu . . . seine Söhne], seine Töchter, [seine] G[rossen, die Leute seines Landes], soveil . . . [gap] sein [and], soveil . . ." (cf. Weidner, *Der Staatsvertrag,* 17ff.; the restorations are certain: cf. ll. 6ff.). Cf. also the introduction to the somewhat later (672 B.C.) treaty of Esarhaddon ". . . with Ramataia, city ruler (EN.URU) of Urakazabanu, with his sons, his grandsons, with all the Urakazabaneans young and old, as many as there may be . . ." (D. J. Wiseman, *The Vassal Treaties of Esarhaddon* [London, 1958] 29–30, col. i, ll. 3–5).

38 *Obv.,* 1:16–20 (trans. W. G. Lambert in Delbert R. Hillers's *Treaty-Curses and*

the Old Testament Prophets, Biblica et Orientalia 16 [Rome: Pontifical Biblical Institute, 1964] 34). Cf. esp. Amos 7:11, 17. From the context, it is clear that the references to the possible exile of the "Hurrian Men" and their families in the Late Bronze Age Hittite treaty K. Bo. I,1 (and duplicates—cf. *ANET*[2] 205–6) refer only to those two "Hurrian Men" (governors?) taking the oath with Mattiwaza, who went up to Hattiland with "only three chariots, two 'men of Harri' and two men-at-arms. . . ." This text, therefore, does not constitute a parallel to the Mati"el treaties, nor does it constitute an exception to the pattern of Late Bronze Age treaties outlined above.

39   J. Harvey, "Le 'Rîb-pattern,' réquisitoire prohétique . . . ," *Biblica* 43 (1962) 172–96.

40   Ibid., 186.

41   A. Götze, *Madduwattaš* MVAG XXXI, 1 (Leipzig, 1928).

42   *KUB* XXIII, no. 72. Cf. O. R. Gurney, "Mita of Pahhuwa," *The Annals of Archaeology and Anthropology* (Liverpool) 28 (1948) 32ff.

43   Cf. references in Harvey, "Le 'Rib-pattern,'" 180–81.

44   Cf. Wright, "The Lawsuit of God," 64. In this connection cf. also Wright's analysis of the non-*rib* (in terms of his definition) character of Nathan's indictment of David: "The prophet stands in relation to the king, instead of to the whole people: the Mosaic covenant is not in view" (ibid., 62 n. 66). In the light of Harvey's analysis, it seems clear that we are here dealing not with two *different* concepts (a "true" vs. a "false" *rib* category) but with *one* legal procedure that has undergone a historically conditioned shift in the ultimately responsible party/parties of the covenant (treaty) arrangement. To use a currently fashionable term, we are witnessing the "democratization" of responsibility for the fulfillment of treaty obligations.

45   Ibid., 41ff.; esp. 44ff.

46   For the principal corpus, cf. J. A. Knudtzon et al., *Die El-Amarna-Tafeln,* VAB, vol. 2 (Leipzig, 1907–15), and O. Schroeder, *Die Tontafeln von El-Amarna* (Leipzig, 1915). For further bibliography, cf. W. F. Albright, "The Amarna Letters from Palestine," *Cambridge Ancient History,* vol. 2, chap. 20 (fasc. 51) (rev. ed.; Cambridge: Cambridge Univ. Press, 1966).

47   *EA* nos. 59, 100.

48   *EA* nos. 139, 140 (from *Ilirabiḫ* and the city Gubla [Byblos] to the king).

49   Cf. n. 54 below.

50   The Harper corpus, comprising 1471 documents, is most readily accessible in Leroy Waterman's *Royal Correspondence of the Assyrian Empire,* vols. 1–4 (Ann Arbor, Mich., 1930–36).

51   *ABL* 403 as translated in A. Leo Oppenheim, *Letters from Mesopotamia* (Chicago, 1967) 116. Cf. also B. Meissner, *AfO* 10 : 242ff., and for the historical situation, Oppenheim in *JAOS* 61:266. The rhetorical effect of proverbial material, frequently encountered in epistolary literature of the ancient Near East, is sufficient reason for its use. Without going further into the problem at present, it may be suggested that similar elements of "wisdom" traditions in the prophetic literature—given the suasive and proclamatory character of that literature—are only what we would expect. By no means do they call for a systematic attempt to trace all roots of Israelite law and ethical concern back to

some supposed *Sitz im Leben* in proto-Hebrew tribal or family wisdom traditions. Cf. the remarks of R. B. Y. Scott, *Proverbs and Ecclesiastes,* Anchor Bible (New York: Doubleday & Co., 1965), xxvii–xviii.

52 Cf. *RCA* no. 282, ll. 15ff.

53 This by no means implies that the "royal messenger" and the "royal herald," as the terms are employed in this essay, are different individuals. This is determined by the nature of the communication. In delivering his first speech (2 Kings 18:19ff.) to the king's representatives, the Rabshakeh is acting in one capacity. The people on the wall are "accidental" eavesdroppers with respect to the reading of the royal message. But with the opening provided by the overwrought delegation, the Rabshakeh turns and makes proclamation of the suzerain's message to the men on the wall (vv. 28ff. using precisely a Hebrew translation of the *"amāt šarri"* edict-formula (see below).

54 This formula, despite the indications of R. H. Pfeiffer ("Assyrian Epistolatory Formulae," *J A O S* 43 [1923] 26ff.), is almost invariable in letters of the king to his subjects (letters 273 [?], 543, 914, 926, and 1121 seem to be the only exceptions in the Harper corpus). Here Lindblom's instincts (*Die Literarische Gattung,* 102ff.) as to the diversity of roots—principally letter-openings and proclamation formulae—displayed in the formulae introductory to prophetic oracles is clearly to be preferred to Westermann's all-encompassing rubric "messenger-formula" (*Basic Forms,* 109–10 [the curious statement with regard to the Cyrus-edict should furnish historians of modern tradition-shifts with an interesting illustration of the perils of compounding an inaccurate citation by inaccurate translation]). That *amāt šarri* is an especially authoritative, compelling mode of address (equivalent to "edict of the king") is shown: (a) By the fact that it appears as an introductory formula only in the king's letters. *RCA* no. 308, an overbearing message from a royal princess presumably aping the royal style, is the only exception. Even the crown prince utilizes the standard introductory formulae: *"ana šarri beli-ia arduka P N* (etc.)" (cf. *RCA* 196–99 [Sennacherib to Sargon], 1001 [Ashurbanipal to Esarhaddon], or *"duppu P N,"* "tablet of P N" [*RCA* no. 430]); (b) By the fact that, when the king addresses his letters to presumed equals (i.e., the kings of Elam), he invariably uses the introduction normally reserved for more personal or familial communication: *"Duppu P N"* (e.g., *RCA* no. 1151: "Tablet of Ashurbanipal the king, king of Assyria, to Indabigash, king of Elam, his brother . . ."). Cf. *RCA* nos. 214 (to a brother), 219 (to the writer's father), 896 (to the writer's mother), 1385 ("to the king, my brother . . ."). Cf. the insolent letter of Urzana, king of Muṣaṣir, to the palace overseer (*RCA* no. 409), where the introductory formula (*"Tuppa P N"*) and the independent stance of the writer are wholly in accord with each other—and in clear variance to the expected deportment of a petty king with respect to a "great king."

55 *RCA* no. 282.

56 H. W. F. Saggs, "The Nimrud Letters, 1952—Part I," *Iraq* 17 (1955) 23ff.

57 In addition to the obviously proclamatory letters to population groups, other pertinent letters from the Harper corpus would include nos. 101, 194, 208, 516, 544, 571, 608, 615, 645, 685, 846, 890, 965, 1043, 1044, 1046, 1050, 1063, 1114.

58 In at least a few cases, and quite possibly in a great number, something more than simple oral tradition or loyal disciples seems to be involved. I hope to deal

with this aspect of the problem in some detail in a forthcoming study, "Prophetic *Sēper* as Prophetic Act."

59 Childs, *Isaiah and the Assyrian Crisis*, 86.

60 For the first Nimrud Letter see the citation in n. 56 (a convenient extract is given in Childs, *Isaiah and the Assyrian Crisis*, 80ff.). Cf. also *RCA* no. 685 (rev.): "Unto the fortress of Mushezib, *of which* the king my lord has written, we went thither *together with* Belsharusur, the bodyguard. I summoned *the body*guard official of the city. *He took his stand* (and) Belsharusur drew near (and) *conferred with him.* We have caused Mushezib to go forth unto the king our lord. . . ." Even the dual object of the address—to the king and to the common people—is attested. Cf. *RCA* no. 174, ll. 5–18: "*In regard to* the news of the land of Nagiu, *of which the king* spoke, saying, '*Send word,*' a messenger has spoken to [ᵐ] Kibakkashshe *and* to [ᵐ] Dasukku as follows, 'The king has given the land of Ellipa to me and the land of Shungibutu to [ᵐ] Marduk-sharusur. It is established. Your cities are taken away. [If you want to make war, make war! Or let it be! I have nothing to do with it' (in the sense that 'It makes no difference to me').] After this manner he spoke before the people of the land." (Bracketed ll. 14–17 translated with G. Meier, *Lexikalische Bemerkungen*, *Orientalia* N.S. 8:305. Cf. also A. L. Oppenheim, *JAOS* 64:191.)

61 E.g., Jer. 38:4; Hosea 9:8; Amos 7:10ff.; Micah 2:6.

62 This bit of "autobiography" is missing in LXX. Cf., however, the essentially identical command given to Isaiah (6:9), Ezekiel (3:4–11), and Amos (7:15–16).

63 We should parenthetically note here that the designation "my servants" designates the bearer of the title as a high-ranking officer of a royal court, as the frequently found seals "PN, servant of the king" testify. Cf. the observations in n. 10 above.

64 Cf. John Bright, *A History of Israel* (Philadelphia: Westminster Press, 1959), 238ff.

65 Two colleagues, R. B. Y. Scott of Princeton University and A. K. Grayson of the University of Toronto, have read this study in various drafts and have offered many valuable criticisms. The final draft but one was also generously read and criticized by G. E. Wright. Any mistakes or failings in the present article are, of course, the writer's responsibility.

ADDITIONAL NOTE: The bibliography relative to the study of prophetic speech forms and the rôle of the prophet has expanded considerably in the interval between the initial submission of this study and the present. Two contributions in particular may be singled out for brief comment. James Limburg's, "The Root רִיב and the Prophetic Lawsuit Speeches" (*JBL* 88 [1969] 291ff.) underscores the point made in sections A and B of the present study with a fresh and, to me, wholly convincing study of the key legal terminology involved in the *rîb-Gattung.* I find, however, that I simply cannot agree with the major conclusions reached by Klaus Baltzar in his stimulating "Considerations Regarding the Office and Calling of the Prophet" (*HTR* 61 [1968] 567ff.). Specifically, it seems to me that the source of a very serious misunderstanding arises from his downgrading of the rôle of the messenger: "[It is] . . . clear also that one should not go down too far in the hierarchy of offices. To point to the office of messenger hardly explains the claims which men like Isaiah, Jeremiah, Ezekiel made with respect to the rank of their office" (p. 570). With the office of messenger thus eliminated, it becomes necesssary to cast around for another appointive office on which the rôle of the prophet was modeled. Suffice it to say that no royal messenger was that lacking in authority (cf. the discussion of this point above and the additional references cited by Limburg, 304 n. 41). Even in terms of relative ranking in the Egyptian court, the King's Messenger (*lpwty-nśw*) was a very high ranking official indeed, as his titulary and the description of his duties indicate. Cf. the forthcoming study that Professor D. B. Redford and I hope to have ready in the relatively near future.

6

*Justice: Perspectives from the Prophetic Tradition**

JAMES L. MAYS

One way in which the Old Testament can be useful as Scripture is to inform our consciousness and conscience about the importance and meaning of justice for faith and life. It is urgent business for the church to be sensitized and instructed about justice. Today, and in the coming years, we are going to do our believing and deciding in the midst of a new phase in the continuing struggle over economic rights in the nation and the world. The struggle may shape our society more decisively than the struggle over civil rights.

One place in the Bible where justice is very much the subject of the texts is the message of the prophets. When the theme of justice in their sayings is described and clarified it takes on resonance with the actualities of our society.The following study attempts to uncover the relation between some features of the prophetic stance and the kinds of issues inherent in thinking about justice. Certainly, the question of what the prophetic view of justice implies for those who take such issues seriously is controversial. For instance, there are theologians of liberation who are reading the Bible with a Marxian hermeneutic and claiming the prophets as authority for the abolition of private property, capital, profit, inherited wealth, and for the creation of a socialist society. Whatever reservations one must have about the method and reasoning in a work like José Miranda's *Marx and the Bible*, it is an interpretation of the prophets for the Latin American context of such authentic passion and involvement that to ignore its challenge is to involve oneself in a kind of betrayal of the prophetic tradition. Surely it raises the question for all who attribute some authority to the prophetic tradition of the Old Testament:"How do we understand the prophets in our social context," a question which is hardly without its own grave and threatening problems.

* First published in *Int* (1983) 5–17.

In concentrating on the theme of justice, one is being quite selective within the materials. However important the theme is, it does not nearly exhaust the agenda of the prophetic vocation. Their persistent attack on apostasy and idolatry, to name only one other item, is thus set aside when its relevance to idolatrous faith in economic and political ideologies, both in the territories of communism and free enterprise, is crucial. For the sake of concentration, the source material is limited to the eighth-century prophets of Judah. It is in their sayings that the prophetic stance on justice receives its classic expression. They share a background of assumptions and circumstances which make a kind of overview possible, where Hosea, for instance, would have to be treated as a special case.

Justice in the Prophetic Vocabulary

Justice is a term used in three different spheres of discourse. It appears in the language of the public speaker, the one who proclaims, exhorts, criticizes. In such speaking its meaning and value are assumed. Justice is also the subject of analysis by the philosopher who seeks to uncover its coherence within itself as an idea and also with social reality. The term also belongs to the activity of the legislator in formulating particular rules for the social order and to the jurist who is responsible for their administration.

The prophets belong to the first order of discourse, and that is why their use of the word "justice" is so compelling in its immediacy and often so tantalizing in its assumptions. They hurl the word out in their messages, as though it were self-evident what it means, never lingering to analyze, justify, or explain. For them, the term seems to effect its own communication. Of course, the word has a basic currency in all the language systems of the Western culture—*mišpāt, dikē, justitia, justice, Recht.* Whatever the verbal shape, it connotes a complex of meanings like equal, fair, right, good, which, however modulated, constitute a focus of value that is understood to be essential to social well-being. Something portentous is happening when someone in a society insists on placing justice at the top of the value scale and persists in making it the primary agenda of concern. That activity alone calls in question all the other priorities and sets a criterion against every form of social process. It raises a question whether goals and practices dominant in the crucial places where a society's life is ordered do correspond in any sense to the broad intentional connotation of the word.

Imagine someone rising at the conclusion of morning worship in the First Presbyterian Church and beginning to cry, "Justice! Justice!"; or as a candidate for the presidency completed a speech and was about to leave the podium; or in a courtroom immediately after the judge had delivered his decision. The word can have a variety of definitions and imply different principles, but it has an inner core of meaning that is specific. Where someone cries out for justice, all hear in that word a claim that something has gone wrong in the relation between a society and its members.

The eighth-century prophets spoke at times in such a way and the best known of their sayings belong to such occasions. Amos spoke to a festival assembly at the royal sanctuary at Bethel, using the divine first person style:

> I hate, I despise your feasts.
> I find no satisfaction in your solemn assemblies. . . .
> Offer me your animals and grain as sacrifice,
>   but I will not accept them.
> To peace offerings of your fatted bullocks
>   I will not respond.
> Take the noise of your songs away from me.
> I will not listen to music from your harps.
> Let justice roll down like waters,
>   righteousness like an unfailing stream (5:21–24, au. trans.).

Righteousness expressed in justice is the indispensable qualification for worship—no justice, no acceptable public religion.

Isaiah, in the public square of Jerusalem, sang a song about a vineyard that belonged to his friend. The friend spared no effort, the song says, to make the vineyard fruitful—and indeed it did bear fruit—but the grapes were bitter and useless. The song was, in fact, a parable of God's relation to his people. The concluding lines interpret the parable and make its point:

> For the vineyard of the Lord of hosts
>   is the house of Israel,
>   and the men of Judah his pleasant planting.
> He looked for justice, but behold, bloodshed;
> righteousness, but behold, a cry for help (5:7)!

The entire history of Israel under God is subordinated to one purpose—righteousness expressed in justice.

Micah, provoked by prophets who tailored their oracles to the wealth of their clientele, speaks of his own vocation:

> As for me, I am filled with power, and justice, and
> might, to declare to Jacob his transgression and to
> Israel his sin (3:8, au. trans.).

To cry "justice" was to disclose the condition of the society in which he lived.

These three sayings exhibit the priority of justice for the prophets. They also point to several basic aspects of the way the notion is understood. First, justice is, in their vocabulary, a theological term. Its priority is rooted in their knowledge of Israel's God, who is himself just and requires justice of people. They would not have been satisfied with any theory of its significance which lacked a confessional dimension and did not reckon it to be inherent in divine reality. They were ready to lay their lives on the line and to live with the expectation that the end of their nation's existence was in prospect because of their confidence that justice is rooted in God himself.

Second, justice was, in their language, a moral value. It frequently appears in synonymous relation with "righteousness." Righteousness is a quality of intention and act, a characteristic of persons. It is present when a person tries to fulfill the possibilities of given or assumed relationships in a way that is fair and favorable to others. To do justice, they said, is to love good, to prefer that which makes for life. It is to hate evil, to avoid that which diminishes life. Because it was for them such a moral value, its absence would disclose a radical flaw in the whole character of a person or institution of people. It was not a separable item that could be isolated from total existence.

And third, justice, in their view, could be done. It was possible to act justly in the courts and in the economy. If they had not believed this, their criticism of their contemporaries and the judgment they announced upon them would have made no sense. Without a hint of utopian fanaticism, they assumed that concrete acts and decisions and policies which expressed justice were attainable.

The Social Context

These general features are constant dimensions of the way the prophets spoke about justice. But the notion will remain abstract and nebulous unless we learn the answers to further and more particular questions. What was it in their society that provoked them to cry "justice"? What was the nature of the social crisis which they addressed? What can be said about the content and structure of their notion of justice? What criteria mark the good society for them? Do they deal with questions like the relation between law and value? Do they have definable positions on matters like property and wealth? Do they differentiate between members of their society and take up an advocacy role for some? Did they favor some process of social change?

To gain some purchase on answers to questions like these, one must examine the sayings in which the prophets confront circumstances in Israel's society which they identify as the contradiction of the justice they have in mind. There is a consistency in their sayings, a singleness of focus which makes it possible to sketch a general and summarizing description of what they indict. Their primary point of attack was clearly an economic development. The problem was the ownership of land and the benefits and rights that went with it in Israelite society. Land was being accumulated in estates and used as a basis for status and to generate surplus wealth. Those who lost their land were deprived of status and material support. They had to become slaves or wage laborers to live. The leverage employed was the administrative apparatus of the monarchy and of the courts, where all social conflict in Israel was settled. The rights of the widow, the fatherless, and the weak to protection against the economic process were widely ignored. The result was a growing differentiation between rich and poor.

In some studies of the social history of Israel, this development has been called "early capitalism." Using that rubric can introduce ideological argument, but there are reasons for using it: the shift of the primary social good, land, from the function of support to that of capital; the reorientation of social goals from personal values to economic profit; the subordination of judicial process to the interests of the entrepreneur. The development had a long history, but there is a respectable amount of evidence to indicate its real bases were laid—one might say institutionalized—with the introduction of monarchy into Israel as a system of government. When the prophets spoke of justice, they frequently addressed specific groups whom they called "officials," "chiefs or heads," "leaders," "elders," all titles for persons who had roles of authority and power in the social and administrative structure of Judah and Israel. Some of the titles referred to offices that were present in Israel's pre-monarchical society but had been integrated into the governing apparatus of the monarchy. Others were created to extend the competence of the crown. Kings had appropriated land for the partial support of this administrative class, but they were left to some degree to manage their own support. They needed a basic capital to allow them to serve the crown. As officials, they also had the opportunity to gain from international trade. Their emergence created a group who had a vested interest in the accumulation of land and goods as capital. They were not originally an economic class, but they soon became one.

From the viewpoint of social and economic history, what happened would seem expected and explicable, the expression of forces which belonged to Israel's national development in the land they had settled. Certainly from the viewpoint of the addressees of many of the prophetic oracles (we hear echoes of their opinions in the tradition itself), the development was legal and desirable, indeed essential to Israel's emergence as an efficient and competent state. But to Amos, Isaiah, and Micah, it was a crisis. It was the specific social and economic actuality against which they cried out "Justice"!

Land as Inheritance and Possession

The central *material* issue of the crisis was land and its ownership. The traditional economy of Israel was one based on small farms held by nuclear kinship groups living in towns around which agricultural plots were spread. The families had access also to certain common public territory for grazing and water. The life-support system of most of the population depended on these two foundations. Security and freedom were derived from a relatively inclusive distribution of the two. An unfavorable redistribution of the land was the primary target of the prophetic indictment. At times it is plainly stated:

> Woe to those who join house to house,
>   who add field to field,
> Until there is no more space and you alone
>   dwell as full citizens in the midst of the land (Isa. 5:8–10;
>   cf. Mic. 2:1–2).

Many of their sayings which do not mention land are dealing with ways in which this redistribution was brought about and with its results.

In this context the prophets appear to be advocates of the private ownership of property as the right of all Israelites and as unyielding opponents of any restriction of that right. The claim that the prophets authorize the abolition of private property is simply mistaken. On the other hand, property did not have in their world the meaning or function it assumes in much contemporary argument for unqualified capitalism.

For them, an Israelite's ownership of land was not to be founded and managed on purely economic bases. They shared a theological tradition which saw the land as constitutive of the integrity of a citizen's existence. The tradition was expressed in two terms used for individually held land. The first was *inheritance*. This notion belongs to the theological interpretation of the settlement and its memory of the way in which each family had come by its land. They had received it in a sacral ceremony of dividing and assigning portions, a cultic way of recognizing that the land was not theirs as a people but came to them as the gift of their God. God was the real Lord and owner of the land, and they were his tenants. Their portion was the sacrament of their place and right in his territory. It was their inheritance from God. To lose their inheritance was tantamount to losing their identity as a member of the people and the privileges that went with that identity. The right and obligation to participate in the legal assemblies, to act in common ventures such as defense, to be present representatively at the festivals, were all grounded in the inheritance. The significance of the inheritance was the crux of the matter in the famous case of Naboth's vineyard (1 Kings 21). The king, Ahab, wanted it, offered generous terms for its purchase only to be met by Naboth's protest that the vineyard was his "inheritance" and should not be sold. It was only by the strategy of legal assassination engineered by Queen Jezebel, a Canaanite who knew how to manage such things, that Ahab secured the vineyard. The deed was denounced by Elijah with a sentence from God that was fulfilled with gruesome precision.

The other term was *possession*, another word laden with the memory of faith. The Israelites remembered that the land had come into their possession as the climax and outcome of the history of deliverance. They had begun as slaves to a tyranny whose oppression had brutally reduced their lives to the level of an economic resource. By the Exodus and the possession of the land, they were delivered, transferred from the service of Pharaoh to the service of God. Their possession of the land was the sign of salvation. By it the will of God to have free people on free land bound only to loyalty and obedience to his sole majesty was made possible. Every year at the harvest festival, the landowning Israelite took the first fruit of his ground to the shrine, announced to the priest, "I declare this day to the Lord your God that I have come into the land which the Lord swore to our fathers to give us" (Deut. 26:3). Then he would recite the creed of the history of deliverance and conclude: "And behold, now I bring the first of the fruit of the ground which thou, O Lord, hast given me" (Deut. 26:10).

When a family lost their land, all that was lost. The land was not only the basic economic good in society, essential to well-being, but it also bestowed identity; it was the instrument of participation in the society as an equal, the foundation of freedom. For the prophets, then, the right to acquire land was qualified and limited by its social role and theological significance. A share in ownership of the basic economic good was a corollary to membership in the society. A free participation in economic power by all citizens was to be maintained and protected. For the ownership of land to become the basis of power for one citizen over another was a perversion of its purpose.

The Conflict of Legality and Righteousness

The central *political* issue of the crisis was the administration of justice. The courts, the local assembly in the gate of each town and the legal apparatus created by the monarchy, were crucial social institutions because, through them, the conflicts of all kinds in Israel's society were settled. The eighth-century prophets turned repeatedly to the problem of what was happening in the courts. Amos, on the court in the gate:

> Woe to those who change justice into bitter poison
> and discard righteousness.
> Who hate the advocate of the right,
> and despise him who speaks with integrity (5:7, 10).

Isaiah, on the royal administration of justice in Jerusalem:

> How the faithful city has become a harlot,
> she that was full of justice!
> Righteousness lodged in her,
> but now murderers. . . .
> Your officials are rebels and companions of thieves.
> Everyone loves a bribe
> and runs after gifts.
> They do not defend the orphan,
> and the widow's case is not heard (1:21–26).

Micah spoke to the same audience in chapter 3, verses one through three. These bitter indictments were provoked by two problems in the judicial sphere. The first was conflict about the administration of justice in Israel's normative tradition itself. There were two distinct types of guidelines which bore on the process of deliberating and deciding in the courts. The first was a body of rules for deciding cases. These rules defined a case, stipulated how the court should rule, and often listed qualifications. They were law in the technical sense. Though they were transmitted largely as oral customary law, they represented for that culture what institutionalized law does for us—the accepted, established rules of order to give social process a consistent and regulated complex of norms. Israel shared such legal customs with the general culture to which it belonged and probably assimilated them in their absorption of Canaanite cultural tradition during the first centuries of its life in Palestine. These legal customs dealt with criminal and civil affairs and covered such matters as property, liability, debt. During the early years of the monarchy, this body of customary law would have been overlaid and expanded by powers to tax, impress for work, and appropriate land for the needs of the state and its officialdom. The law was secular and neutral, free of terms of value or appeal to faith, simply statements of what had been established as the accepted way to settle cases.

Alongside this customary law there was another body of normative tradition which was value-laden and intensely theological. Its typical forms were the command and the exhortation, and it was usually expressed as the words of God himself. It was interwoven with appeals to Israel's history of salvation, couched as arguments from the way God had dealt with Israel as analogies for the way in which Israelites had to deal with all who lived in their society. To this second tradition belong such sentences as "You shall not wrong a stranger or oppress him for you were strangers in Egypt. You shall not afflict any widow or orphan; if you do . . . I will surely hear their cry, and my wrath shall flame up. . . . If you lend money to any of my people with you who is poor, you shall not be to him as a creditor. . . . You shall not pervert the justice due to the poor in his suit. . . ." Every collection of normative material preserved in the Old Testament as what have been called codes of law (which they are not) is interwoven with this second kind of material. We must be clear that these collections do not represent official codifications of the state. They were the work of those who were attempting to bring the first type under the interpretative control of the second. The best name for the commandments is "rules of righteousness." Their function explains why the prophets usually speak of justice *and* righteousness.

So, the problem the prophets saw in the judicial practices of their time was not a failure of law. What was happening—the extraction of taxes and fines, enforcement of creditors' rights, foreclosure on land and crops, commitment of persons to bond servitude and slavery—was permitted and ordered under the customary laws that applied. It was "legal" in the sense of that word appropriate to their culture. But, by the criterion of the values they held and the social goals to which they believed Israel was committed, it was unrighteous and, therefore, a travesty of justice. Justice was a notion that was defined by values of personal intention and social consequences. Here a sentence of Paul Lehmann's applies: "Justice is the foundation and the criterion of law; law is not the foundation and criterion of justice." The prophets were a classic case of the conflict of law and value, of institutional order and justice.

The second problem in the judicial sphere can be described simply. Justice was being commercialized. The courts were not immune to the circumstances they were being used to create. As wealth grew and the difference between the rich and the rest became more pronounced, it happened that those who were rich could afford more justice than the others. Micah spoke of the corruption of judges by the love of money. Amos spoke of bribes. Isaiah said all officials run after fees. The correlation between the degree of justice available and the economic resources at one's disposal is a phenomenon which did not vanish with the end of the ancient Near East. The rules of righteousness called for a justice of equity that went beyond an evenhanded fairness to uphold and protect precisely those who could not afford justice. But such a practice of law requires righteous people for whom the social well-being of others is a higher priority than gain.

Wealth and Wickedness

It is against this background of what was occurring in the distribution of the basic economic good and in access to rights to protection and redress that the prophetic stance on other social problems is to be understood. Consider the question of wealth, for instance. Wealth, the pursuit of it and the possession of it, is a subject that appears repeatedly in prophetic indictments. Amos painted a verbal picture of a group who built houses of hewn stone and owned large vineyards, kept summer and winter places, collected furniture inlaid with ivory, were gourmets who fancied the best meat and wine. Both he and Isaiah satirized perfumed and bejeweled women who pestered their husbands for more and more and a leisure class who were heroes at drinking wine and famous for lavish entertainment. Micah accused the leaders and professionals, including priests and prophets, of the complete prostitution of their vocations to the lust for wealth.

The prophets were not primitivists or puritans. They were not members of one economic class at war against another. In all their diatribes there is not the slightest hint of an ideological rejection of prosperity in one's livelihood or of the pleasure that comes with well-being and well-doing. They saw no virtue in the poor or in being poor; quite the contrary. In fact, Amos seems to have been a successful sheep-breeder; Isaiah belonged to the upper circles of Jerusalem's urban society. But there was a kind and degree of wealth which they held to be incompatible with justice, and the nature of its incompatibility can be inferred from the way in which they describe it. If its acquisition and possession cost the economic freedom and welfare of others, they called it violence and oppression. If it fostered conspicuous consumption at a level of luxury that was enjoyed in heedless unconcern for the needs of others, it was wrong. If it was gained by violation of the rules of righteousness which set the values of personal relations above profit, it was iniquitous. If wealth became the dominant motivation of those responsible for social well-being because they held power, that was sin.

The Weak and the Poor

The motif in the social sayings of the prophets that is probably best known is their concern for the weak and the poor. The specific topic "the fatherless and the widow," a specialty of Isaiah's, belongs to this motif. The vocabulary of words and expressions with which the prophets spoke of this concern was traditional locutions rooted in an older phase of cultural history when basic social units were kinship groups like the clan. In such groups there would always be some who, by reason of misfortune or handicap, were unable to maintain their own support and status in the group. The situation of a nuclear family that had lost its husband and father was particularly desperate. The narrative of Ruth is a famous illustration. In the ethos of the kinship society, a high value and obligation were set on protection and help for the weak and the poor; and a variety of provisions for them was customary and honored.

When Israel's society changed in the course of its history, the poor and the weak were the most vulnerable. Because the social organism in which they had a place was vanishing, they were in danger of neglect and oppression. Their cause was taken up and stated in the rules of righteousness which, in effect, attempted to make this dimension of a largely personal culture normative for

154

one that was increasingly commercial. It was a valiant effort to transfer family values to the larger society.

Perhaps all that needs to be said of the prophets in this matter is that they made the treatment of the poor and the weak the functional criterion of a just society. Let Isaiah speak for all the rest in this saying:

> The Lord enters into judgment
> with the elders and officials of his people:
> "It is you who have devoured the vineyard,
>   the spoil of the poor is in your houses.
> What do you mean by crushing my people,
>   by grinding the face of the poor?"
> Says the Lord God of hosts (3:14–15).

In the prophetic oracles which broach this issue, it is apparent that principles of justice like "To each according to his merit" or "To each according to his societal contribution" or "Similar treatment for similar cases" are not adequate. The justice they advocated must be capable of exception, of responsiveness to the individual's needs, of an estimate of worth based on the simple existence of a person.

Justice, Repentance, and Judgment

These are the primary dimensions of prophetic speech about justice. It is important to remember the actual circumstance to which their sayings were addressed so that they can be heard in the context which shaped their language. That is necessary because, otherwise, their words may seem to be generalities. It is important for us to perceive that they struggled with concrete and difficult problems. That lends their stance greater power as an example. Their faith in justice as a value rooted in the ultimate reality behind all social history and their calling to make it the highest priority in a people's understanding of its common life is an example which no subsequent era has rendered irrelevant. It is true that anchoring the discussion in their environment highlights the distance between the crisis of early capitalism in Israel and the vastly more complex national and international economy whose problems confront us. There are in their sayings no solutions, no programs, no detailed approaches which can be directly appropriated and applied to our problems. In fact, of course, they themselves advocated no program of new laws or administrative correction. Nor do we hear from them any call for revolution, for the overthrow of the existing order in favour of something else, no summons to one class to seize power.

What we do hear in their proclamation is the articulation of a notion of justice whose essential structure and content have a cogency beyond their time and place. Put in a general and concise way, it says: All citizens should have a share in the control of the society's basic economic good as the instrument of their status, access to rights, and freedom. The administration of order should protect and support this distribution against economic and political processes that erode it. Institutional law should be subject to interpretation and correction by the worth of persons and moral values. Wealth which prejudices the welfare and rights of others is unjust. Treatment of the least favored in the society is the fundamental criterion of the achievement of justice. The significance of such a notion as norm and goal for every society in contemporary world history would be difficult to deny.

In the matter of what should and would happen because of the violation of justice, they made two appeals. The first was to the faith and conscience of their audience. They saw little evidence of such faith and conscience in their audience, but they, nonetheless, demand "Cease to do evil, learn to do good; seek justice, correct oppression; defend the fatherless, plead for the widow" (Isa. 1:16–17). Each of these little imperative sentences is a call to righteousness. They assume it is possible for people to change when they are confronted with a contrast between what they do and the way of righteousness. The powerful could use power in concern for the welfare and rights of others. The courts could uphold justice. The cause of the poor could be recognized and met. The social instruments at hand could serve the love of good. It would not be a perfect society, but no society escapes the character of the people who shape and control it. However it may be organized, in the long last its quality would depend on people who knew what was required: to do justice, to love mercy, and to live in awareness of one's limitations and dependence. There is a certain naïveté in that position. But where that naïveté is lost, the only alternative is a society based on the self-justification of whoever can seize and hold power. So the naïveté is a kind of realism.

The other appeal of the prophets was to history. They believed in and announced the judgment of God. There is no question that this second appeal was more central to their mission than the first. They looked for a tangible and terrible intervention from outside, a corrective catastrophe which bore the wrath and purpose of God. It would displace those who misused power, dissolve the wealth and luxury gained from oppression, interrupt the continuity and institutionalization of injustice, and clear the ground for a fresh beginning. Amos looked for an end of the northern state as an expression of Israel's existence. Isaiah foresaw a purging and cleansing of Jerusalem. Micah expected the elimination of the entire cadre of officials and leaders along with their estates and power. It is in their absolute certainty of a divine judgment which would break through and break up the dominance of injustice in Israel society that the true radicalism of the prophets lies.

It is just this concentration on the two alternative words, these two not exclusive but interdependent words about the future of the unjust society, the appeal to conviction and conscience, and the appeal to divine judgment, that leaves one in embarrassment before the prophets. For those who intend to recognize some authority in them in a purely moral sense or to recognize the authority behind them in a religious sense, they create a predicament. They do not fit any of the roles we usually play. The prophets were not ethicists or theologians or interpreters and did not go about their task in the way we pursue ours, no matter how we may share their concern for justice. Their certainty about the meaning and measure of justice in their society, about the possibility that power and justice can be united, about the intervention of God to maintain his sovereignty—these certainties are not often features of our role, nor do they offer us models congruent with the options for public action which we credit as viable. They were not social reformers or political activists or revolutionaries, certainly not conservatives or reactionaries. Their concentration on the demand for change in the lives of people and their trust in the work of God in overturning the old impossibilities to make way for the new was too unrelieved.

Perhaps it is just this embarrassment and predicament which bear their authority and meaning to us as we play our own roles and create or choose our own models. The embarrassment *can* take the form of a word that addresses our conscience and summons us to find the roles which take the word in ultimate seriousness in our time. That the prophetic tradition should work as such a word would vindicate the faith of those who created and preserved it. "For it has been shown you, O human, what is good, and what the Lord requires of you: to do justice and to love mercy and to walk humbly with your God" (Mic. 6:8, au. trans.).

NOTES

The works which were of particular value in the preparation of this article are:

K. Baltzer, "Naboth's Weinberg (1 Kön. 21), Der Konflikt zwischen israelitischen und kanaanäischen Bodenrecht," *Wort und Dienst* Neue Folge 8 (1965) 73ff.

H. Donner, "Die soziale Botschaft der Propheten im Lichte der Gesellschafftsordnung in Israel," *Oriens Antiquus* 2 (1963) 229–45.

M. Fendler, "Zur Sozialkritik des Amos," *EvTh* 33 (1973) 32ff.

F. Horst, "'Das Eigentum nach dem Alten Testament," in *Gottes Recht,* TBü 12 (Munich: Kaiser, 1961) 203–21.

H. J. Kraus, "Die prophetische Botschaft gegen das soziale Unrecht Israels," *EvTh* 15 (1955) 295ff.

R. de Vaux, *Ancient Israel: Its Life and Institutions* (New York: McGraw Hill; London: Darton, Longman & Todd, 1961).

7

The Role of the Prophets and the Role of the Church*

GENE M. TUCKER

What did it mean to be a prophet in ancient Israel? What might it mean today? What was the prophetic role or institution in Israel, and is there room for such an office in the contemporary church? Those are the questions I mean to raise and address by the juxtaposition of phrases in the title.

To talk about the relation of the Old Testament prophets to the church is to raise some very complex theological and hermeneutical issues, long debated in the church, the university and even the general society. Those questions cannot be raised here, lest we lose sight of our primary concerns, but a few preliminary remarks are called for.

First, the church settled the fundamental issue long ago, and I am convinced it was right; namely, the church needs the Old Testament—and especially the prophets—in order to shape its self-understanding and to voice its convictions about God, the world, and human existence. If we cannot read the prophets, at least now and then, as if they were speaking directly to us, then we might as well give up on the rest of the Old Testament, and most of the New Testament as well, for that matter.

Second, I am convinced that we must take seriously a prophetic role for the church in our society. Woe to us—and our nation and our world—if we do not. The model for that role, to some extent at least, must be found in the Old Testament prophets. They cannot, of course, have the last word; that must be found in the gospel. But even Jesus had a prophetic role and called his disciples to be, among other things, prophetic.

Third, to read the words of the Old Testament prophets can be disturbing. The prophets were deeply involved in the political,

* First published in *Quarterly Review* (1981) 5–22.

social, and religious affairs of their nation. They addressed not only groups and congregations, but specific individuals—often by name—including kings and princes, and even the nation as a whole. Their presumption was astounding. They called their nation to responsibility under God. They proclaimed judgment and disaster when there was false hope, and announced salvation when there was false despair. Moreover, they continue to judge us for our silence in the face of any and all forms of injustice and oppression. It is difficult to place the newspaper and the prophetic books side by side and look away with an easy conscience. In many parts of this country it is a devastating experience just to go to a law court and observe sometimes dehumanizing forms of legal process and then hear echoing in our ears the words of Amos: "Hate evil and love good and establish justice in the gate [that is, the courts]."

We ought to trust our first impressions, our intuitive sense that the prophets have something to say about the situation of our society, and our fearful sense that the church has a prophetic role to fulfill. Such impressions can be, however, no more than the starting point, not the end of our reflection. They may form the point of departure for the serious and critical investigation of the prophetic role in Israel and its implications for the church. So I want to consider first the role of the Israelite prophets by looking at what they and others said they were, by listening to what they typically said, and by examining how they said it, for the form of expression reveals a great deal about social function. Then I shall conclude by drawing out a few of the implications for the church.

Everyone has some idea of what a prophet is, but there are a great many misconceptions in the church and in society generally. In biblical scholarship the question of the prophetic role has received a great deal of attention in recent years, and a new understanding has emerged. I wish to examine here some half-dozen of the most popular misconceptions of the prophet as the basis for a new definition. The prophets have been understood variously as mystics who had special religious experiences, as great poets or literary figures, as theologians or religious philosophers, as social reformers or radicals, as seers who predicted the usually distant future, and as preachers of repentance. There is at least a grain of truth in each of these images, and in some cases more than that, but every one of them basically misses the mark.

1. It is easy to see how the definition of the prophets as *visionaries* or *mystics* arose: they regularly report their visions and even more commonly their experience of the word of God. In a sense it is correct to identify them in terms of their special ex-

periences, but that identification must be qualified in several ways. In the first place, they never emphasize the *means* of revelation, but only its reality and its contents. What they say in God's name is central, and the reported experiences vary considerably through the history of Old Testament prophecy. Ezekiel's vision reports are the most dramatic, but Jeremiah, only a few decades earlier, stressed the coming of the word. Moreover, for all the prophets the vision of the word of God came unbidden, and often unwanted: "The LORD took me from following the flock, and the LORD said to me, 'Go prophesy to my people Israel'" (Amos 7:15, RSV). An experience all the prophets seem to share is that of vocation, of being called, being compelled to speak in the name of God. Most important, the prophets themselves were suspicious of the claim that special experiences proved that one's word came from God: "'I have heard what the prophets have said who prophesy lies in my name, saying, "I have dreamed, I have dreamed!" How long shall there be lies in the heart of the prophets who prophesy lies, and who prophesy the deceit of their own heart'" (Jer. 23:25–26). The claim that supranormal or ecstatic or psychedelic experiences in themselves reveal transcendent reality is not a new or unusual one. The claim has been popularized in recent decades by a former Harvard professor named Leary on behalf of LSD and other hallucinogenics. But the prophets themselves knew that not all visions come from God.

2. Almost at the other end of the spectrum is the definition of the prophets as *poets*, thoughtful and creative literary figures. This view was popular in the literary critical era of biblical scholarship, especially in Germany in the late-nineteenth and early-twentieth centuries, and still is found, for example, in courses and books on the Bible as literature. Many prophetic words are indeed outstanding literature, filled with striking images, dramatic phrases, captivating similes, and metaphors; and most of their lines are in poetry or poetic prose. Still, it is very doubtful that any of the prophets, except possibly some of the last ones, was a literary figure at all. On the contrary, the prophets were speakers, and it is only with a generous definition of the term that what they said can be called speeches. They presented short, memorable addresses, many of them no more than two or three verses long. There may be as many as fifty such addresses in the short Book of Amos. The prophetic books, we now know, were not written by the prophets, but represent collections of the originally oral speeches, as well as reports of the prophet's activities and—in most cases—additions by later interpreters and editors. The process which transformed the short addresses into books would have been initiated by the

followers or disciples of the prophets, which groups sometimes included secretaries like Jeremiah's friend Baruch. Consequently, if we wish to hear the earliest prophetic addresses we must learn to separate the original units from one another, and from the later additions.

3. Then are the prophets *theologians* or religious philosophers? We theologians, including biblical theologians and ministers, would like to think so. Certainly the prophetic books contain theology. They constantly speak of God, the world, and human nature. They are especially concerned about the will of God, and the relationship of God to the nation and to individuals. It is a serious mistake, however, to look to the prophets for doctrines: they simply did not organize their addresses systematically, and for the most part they were not preoccupied with answering theological questions as such. They would have vigorously resisted the attempt to find in their words certain timeless truths. They seem to have been quite emphatic in denying that the word of God was a dogma. In view of what we have seen about the oral and often spontaneous character of their addresses, it is best to think of their words as messages in particular situations, addressing the problems at hand. This interpretation explains in part why it is so difficult even to translate the speeches of a particular prophet into a systematic theological summary, or even to a single message, and it explains why the messages of the individual prophets often differ so much from one another. The word of God for one time and place may not be the same for another historical occasion, which is why it was difficult to distinguish between true and false prophecy in ancient Israel, as it is today.

But not just any message, claimed to be from God, deserves to be called prophetic. For all of the differences among the prophetic messages—and even dramatic contrasts, from uncompromising and total judgment to unqualified salvation—there are certain persistent themes in the Old Testament prophets, and perhaps even more significant, certain theological assumptions which they seem to share.

Among the persistent prophetic themes is what appears to be a criticism of the status quo. (We should hasten to point out that there were exceptions; some prophets, especially some of the last ones, spoke for the established institutions.) What sounds like criticism of things as they are might more accurately be described as a reversal of expectations. To those who expect peace and prosperity they proclaim the coming of disaster. The words of Amos are not unusual:

> Woe to you who desire the day of
> the LORD!
> Why would you have the day of
> the LORD?
> It is darkness, and not light;
>> as if a man fled from a lion,
>> and a bear met him;
> or went into the house and leaned
>> with his hand against the wall,
>> and a serpent bit him.
> Is not the day of the LORD darkness,
>> and not light,
>> and gloom with no brightness in
>> it?   (Amos 5:18–20)

To those who rely on faithful observance of religious ritual they cry that such confidence is unfounded (compare Amos 5:21–27; Isa. 1:10–17). And to those whose faith and hope are fading they can declare:

> For the mountains may depart
>> and the hills be removed,
> but my steadfast love shall not
>> depart from you,
>> and my covenant of peace shall
>> not be removed,
> says the LORD, who has
>> compassion on you.
>>> (Isa. 54:10)

Another theme which must be mentioned even in the shortest list of prophetic theological motifs is represented by the frequent linking of two powerful terms: justice and righteousness. These terms, and the point of view which they summarize, are found everywhere in the prophets. The first term, *justice*, in both its Hebrew and its English forms, is originally at home in the law court. In Israel, the decision (judgment) establishing justice was pronounced at the conclusion of the trial, restoring right and fair relationships among the parties. Justice came then to be the claim each person has upon others in the society, and which God has upon the people. The dimension emphasized by the prophets is the failure of justice at the social level, specifically the oppression of the poor and the powerless. Law and order must be maintained, and that means the weak must be protected from the strong. To withhold power, or to misuse it, is a distortion of God's will, whether the power be economic, political, or military. Israel's crime, says Amos, is selling the righteous for silver and the needy for a pair of shoes, trampling the head of the poor into the dust of the earth, and denying legal due process to the afflicted (Amos 2:6–7). Righteousness, often a legal concept, also, has a somewhat broader meaning. One is righteous who fulfills the demands or established expectations in a relationship, whether with other persons or with God. Fulfillment of righteousness establishes a whole and peaceful community. In the context of the covenant, righteousness entails obedience to the law. The prophets speak of the need for or the failure of justice and righteousness when they indict Israel, but they also see justice and righteousness as the foundation for their visions of the future:

> For to us a child is born,
>   to us a son is given;
> and the government will be upon
>   his shoulder,
>   and his name will be called
> "Wonderful Counselor, Mighty God,
>   Everlasting Father, Prince of
>   Peace."
> Of the increase of his government
>   and of peace
>   there will be no end,
> upon the throne of David, and over
>   his kingdom,
>   to establish it, and to uphold it
> with justice and with righteousness
>   from this time forth and for
>   evermore.   (Isa. 9:6–7)

Justice and righteousness are not empty terms, nor are they vague concepts. They refer to the concrete and specific actions of persons in relationships when they accord others what is due to them. They are the foundations of society at its best.

In addition to these and other persistent motifs, most of the prophets share certain theological assumptions. Many of these presuppositions are taken so much for granted that they are not spelled out; they are like the air the prophets breathe. Many such assumptions deserve extended treatment, but we can mention only three of them here, their assumptions about God, history, and society. The message of every prophet was based on the conviction that Yahweh, the God of Israel, was also lord of all the earth and all history. This lord had established a covenant with Israel, was active in human events, and communicated with human beings. His purpose was to save, but he also could be counted on to judge and punish wrong. Not infrequently the prophetic vision of

Yahweh's lordship encompassed all nations. Above all, the prophets condemned any effort to practice polytheism, whether in the form of the worship of idols or in the form of giving less than full allegiance to Yahweh. In fact, one scholar has recently proposed that the impulse to "monotheize" is what distinguishes true from false prophecy.[1]

A second basic theological assumption concerns the reality and importance of history. The prophets always were historically concrete. They did not take flight to another realm of reality, either within the individual human heart or beyond history. When they speak of a kingdom of God they refer to God's rule within and among human beings in ordinary time and space. Surely they knew the difference between sacred and profane, but ordinary, profane events were sacred because it was within them that God was active. Consequently, there was a willingness to face the reality and even the terror of historical contingency. Contingent events, ever new, ever different, and finally unpredictable, could be lived because they were also where one encountered God. Nor can the prophetic view of history be called deterministic because it is the arena of divine activity. Rather, history was seen to be created by the interaction of human beings with one another and with God. Even what God does in history depends upon the actions and reactions of human beings.

Next, the prophetic assumptions about society were equally concrete and specific. The stress on the communal dimensions of reality is unmistakable. God elected a people, not individuals. The prophets spoke of justice and righteousness that could only be understood in the framework of human community. When they announced judgment it was most commonly upon the nation as a whole, for they knew that the entire body politic could suffer for the crimes of even a few. When they announced future salvation it was for a people, for they knew that no one can be completely whole unless the rights of all are respected. Above all, they were aware of the interdependence of all parts of society and of all individuals.

These theological motifs and assumptions suggest that certain central religious categories must be reconsidered. For example, salvation in Israel was never a spiritualistic or even a strictly spiritual term in our usual understanding of the word. Salvation included many facets, some of which involved some material things: having a place to live, a space of one's own, breathing room, and food to eat. That land flowing with milk and honey was a fulfillment of God's will. Salvation also meant having sufficient control over one's destiny to act out one's responsibility before God and other human beings. Judgment was equally concrete, historical, and corporate. It entailed death, destruction, enslavement, the loss of human dignity, or the loss of human community.

The prophets were not theologians, but their messages contain and are founded upon powerful theological content which is difficult to ignore.

4. What we have said about the message of the prophets might seem to suggest that they were *social reformers* or *radicals*, but not so. They do call for change on occasion, and their words sound radical in the ears of many, but they do not proclaim a new morality, or an original vision of the just society. They do not propound new laws but constantly refer to the old ones; they do not propose a new understanding of God, but constantly refer to the old traditions: Remember the God who brought you out of Egypt, or who gave you the city of Jerusalem and the Davidic monarchy. They were not radical, but conservative, calling Israel back to its roots. Israel, they remind the people, has always known what God expected of her.

On this point it is useful to review briefly the history of the interpretation of the prophets in relation to the law. Which came first, the law or the prophets? Perhaps surprisingly, the answers to this question often had profound implications for the understanding of the prophets and for their use in the church and the society. The traditional view in the church and the synagogue was based on confidence in the Mosaic authorship of the Pentateuch or the Torah. First there was the law, given through Moses, and then came the prophets, who commonly were understood as interpreters of the law. The order was reversed just over a century ago in critical scholarship and popularized by the work of Julius Wellhausen.[2] The Pentateuch, composed of some four written sources, was written long after Moses; in its final form it was composed no earlier than the Babylonian Exile, long after the classical prophets. This dating of the Old Testament literature, including the prophets, led to a rewriting of the history of the religion of Israel, and to a new appreciation of the prophets. Since they came before the law they were seen as great creative individuals. They were the ones, it was said, who established ethical monotheism, who raised religion above the level of the primitive or the nationalistic and as a matter of fact to its highest levels. They were religious and social reformers, but they failed. After they left the scene the religion of Israel was thought to have degenerated into the ritual legalism represented by the law. This view of the prophets as creative and reforming individuals was very popular in Protestantism, in part because of its antilegalistic overtones. Moreover, it was this image of the prophets as charismatic reformers which helped to give rise to and to sustain the Social Gospel.

The present situation in the study of the prophets as well as the investigation of the Pentateuch sees a much more complex relationship between the two than either of the previous views. It is, however, perhaps closer to the traditional perspective than to that of late nineteenth-century critical scholarship. On the one hand, more careful study of the Pentateuch has demonstrated that while its final form was written quite late, it is based on and contains oral traditions which are quite ancient, much older than the classical prophets.[3] Study of the prophets, on the other hand, shows that they constantly appeal to and reiterate ancient traditions. This appeal and reiteration occurs in two ways. First, as already indicated, with regard to laws or the obligations of the people, they always take it for granted that Israel has long known what is expected in the covenant with Yahweh. They rarely cite the laws themselves, but their accusations and indictments are based on old legal traditions. The problem is not that Israel did not *know*, but that Israel did not *do*. So the prophets introduce no new and higher morality, and do not even appear to radicalize the old laws, which were sufficiently demanding to begin with. Second, all of the prophets stand in certain theological traditions which had been important for centuries before them.[4] Not all, to be sure, stand in the same theological streams. Hosea, Amos, Jeremiah, and others frequently allude to the story which is told in the Hexateuch: Yahweh is the one who made promises to the patriarchs, brought Israel out of Egypt, led and cared for the people in the wilderness, and delivered them into the land of Canaan. Isaiah and Micah, on the other hand, hardly refer to those foundational events, but stress the choice of Jerusalem as a holy city and establishment of the dynasty of David as saving events. Ezekiel and Second Isaiah bring many of these themes together. So the prophets invented neither morality nor theology. What is new and distinctive is their concern with the future.

5. Are they, then, *seers* who predicted the future? That is a very popular understanding of prophecy, but it is indebted more to the interpretation of the Apocalypse of John and the Book of Daniel as prophecy than it is to a careful reading of the Old Testament prophets. It is fundamental that the Old Testament prophets are concerned with the future, but it is clear from even a casual reading of the prophetic books that their concern is with a future within

history and society as presently known, and—with a few exceptions—an immediate future.

Two other points should be stressed in this regard. First, the prophets do not *predict* but *announce* future events as divine intervention into history. That announcement may be of judgment or of salvation. This conclusion is obvious from what has come to be called the basic form of prophetic speech.[5] To be sure, the prophets were able to employ virtually all forms of address current in their society, but the most distinctive and common form was the announcement. Amos 4:1–3 is a typical example. Notice the elements in the structure of this address:

> "Hear this word, you cows of
>   Bashan,
>   who are in the mountain of
>   Samaria,
>   who oppress the poor, who crush the
>   needy,
>   who say to their husbands, 'Bring,
>   that we may drink!'
> The Lord GOD has sworn by his
>   holiness
>   that, behold, the days are coming
>   upon you,
>   when they shall take you away with
>   hooks,
>   even the last of you with fishhooks.
> And you shall go out through the
>   breaches,
>   every one straight before her;
>   and you shall be cast forth into
>   Harmon,"
>   says the LORD.

The speech begins with a call to attention—a summons to hear—addressed to a particular group, the wealthy women of Samaria. Next comes an indictment or an accusation, or reasons for punishment: "[you] who oppress the poor, who crush the needy." Then comes a transition which moves from present to future and identifies the words which follow as word of God: "The Lord GOD has sworn by his holiness/that, behold. . . ." The final major element is the announcement of judgment or punishment itself: "behold, the days are coming upon you,/when they shall take you away with hooks." The address is rounded off with an oracle formula, "says the LORD."

This is no prediction, but an announcement. It is as if a notice were posted on a bulletin board: "The meeting will be on Thursday at 3:00 P.M. in room 251." That is a far cry from what we hear from weather reporters or oddsmakers. Notice that when judgment is announced the prophet gives the reasons for it by listing the crimes of the addressees. It is theologically significant that when salvation is announced, as, for example, in 2 Isaiah, no reasons are required beyond God's initiative to save his people.

A second factor in the prophetic addresses distinguishes them from predictions. The prophet's word concerning the future, because it was believed to come from God, is powerful and effective, itself changing the future. This understanding is revealed explicitly in several texts, including a reference in Jeremiah's report of his call. It comes at the conclusion, when Jeremiah is given his commission to be a prophet:

> Then the LORD put forth his hand and touched my mouth;
> and the LORD said to me,
> "Behold, I have put my words in your mouth.
> See, I have set you this day over nations and
>   over kingdoms,
> to pluck up and to break down,
> to destroy and to overthrow,
> to build and to plant" (Jer. 1:9–10).

The conviction that the prophetic word changes history is equally strong in the motto to the Book of Amos:

> "The LORD roars from Zion,
> and utters his voice from
>   Jerusalem [through the prophet];
> the pastures of the shepherds mourn,
>   and the top of Carmel withers" (Amos 1:2).

The prophet's word is the word of God, and thus powerful. That explains why the people of Israel did not simply ignore the uncomfortable words of these spokesmen, but attempted over and over to shut them up.

6. What we have seen from these examples—and they could be multiplied—also demonstrates that the prophets were not primarily *preachers of repentance*. That is an image shaped, I suspect, by the reports of John the Baptist in the New Testament, and by the fact that occasionally the prophets do call for change. It is those occasional calls for repentance which seem to form the Protestant lectionary for prophetic preaching: "Seek the LORD and live,/lest he break out like fire in the house of Joseph" (Amos 5:6). But such calls are the rare exception and not the rule. What is missing in the prophetic

messsages, for the most part, is a positive program for reform or change, either of the society or the individual. Indictments and accusations are given as reasons for punishment, not as calls to turn aside from evil ways. According to the prophets of doom, it was too late for change. One may argue that by their indictments and words of judgment they hoped to strike such fear in the hearts of the people that they would change. In the story of Jonah that is what happened when the prophet uttered his one-line announcement of judgment on Nineveh. But as serious interpreters we are obliged first to take seriously the words themselves, before speculating on the motivations for them. Still, it is easy to see how the old words of doom could later become part of admonitions and exhortations to change. That process had begun already in ancient Israel. We see, for example, in some of the late exilic additions to the Book of Jeremiah a pattern to the speeches. The old words of Jeremiah become, in effect, the texts of sermons which say: Judgment was announced because of your disobedience, and it came in the form of the Exile. Now listen to the voice of the LORD and be obedient, lest judgment come again.

On the basis of what has been said both positively and negatively about this series of alternatives we may now summarize our understanding of the prophetic role. If that definition must be reduced to a sentence, it is this: the prophet in Israel was the one who spoke God's word for the immediate future.[6] The prophet experienced a call, a vocation or summons to speak in the name of God, and what he spoke was—for the most part—announcement of judgment or of salvation. Though they were not theologians the prophets tended to echo the same basic themes and share some central assumptions: God expects justice and righteousness now, in history and human society. Moreover, God is about to act.

What, then, would a prophetic role for the church and its ministry include or entail? At the very least we must maintain a continuous dialogue with the Old Testament prophetic words and allow them to shape our consciousness of the present and our visions of possible futures. But it is a difficult and frightening task to be prophetic. Certainly not all aspects of the Old Testament prophetic role can or should be claimed by the church or by Christian ministers. In every case our appropriation of the prophetic role or message must be through the filter of a Christian hermeneutic. Furthermore, just as the prophetic word was different depending upon the historical circumstances, no single prophetic message fits every situation. What was said recently about preaching certainly applies here: "If preaching is to be word of God, it must not only be true, but appropriate. *'Meet and right'* is still a good expression."[7] Having said all that, however, we must acknowledge that more often than we are willing to accept it, our calling, the historical circumstances, and the word of God thrust the prophetic role upon us.

Most of the other conceptions of the prophetic role are easier to cope with—one way or another—than the one which I have described here. If we see the prophets as mystics, it is easy to dismiss the role if we have had no dramatic visionary or other ecstatic experiences. If we see the prophets as poets, it is easy to sit back and admire their beautiful compositions. If we see them as religious philosophers or theologians, it is not difficult to identify them with the reflective and intellectual dimensions of our ministry. Many find it easy and even satisfying to identify with the prophets as preachers of repentance, and some seem to enjoy berating congregations for their sins. It is even relatively simple to identify with the prophets as social reformers or radicals, and either accept or reject that role for the church.

But to proclaim the revealed word of God concerning the future—that is another matter entirely. That is a terrifying challenge, but one which—on at least some occasions—must be identified with the verbal and vocal role of the church and its ministry, including preaching. Such a role appears impossible for us only if we assume that the prophetic word appears out of thin air, or comes entirely as a spontaneous, individual experience of revelation. These versions of the prophetic word as occurring independently were not true for the Old Testament prophets, and need not be for us. Gerhard von Rad's summary of the prophetic role is especially helpful—and even liberating. The prophet's experience of the word which he then proclaimed was based, von Rad demonstrated, on the particular theological traditions in which he stood, and was shaped by the specific historical circumstances of the time.[8] We have noted how some prophets live and breathe the old traditions of the Exodus and others the traditions of Zion and David.

Certainly we all stand in rich theological traditions which shape our understanding and make possible our apprehension of divine truth. For us those traditions now include the prophetic words themselves, and at the heart of those traditions stands the good news revealed through Jesus Christ, including a vision of the kingdom of God. Through such traditions we are called to view and interpret the events of our specific times and places.

All that we have said thus far indicates that it would be a mistake to give a set of instructions on how to become a prophet, or to summarize what *the* prophetic word is. Still, in particular circumstances one can proclaim the prophetic word. I heard a fine and courageous prophetic sermon in a suburban, basically middle-class church on the Sunday after the American hostages had been released from Iran. The text came from the lectionary, Matt. 4:11–17, which quotes Isa. 9:12: "The people who walked in darkness have seen a great light." What an appropriate text for the occasion! The pastor spoke of the release of the hostages, the joy experienced by them, their families, and all Americans. This event, he suggested, is not necessarily the coming of the kingdom of God, but the kingdom of God is like that. That was one prophetic word. Then he turned, with gentle concern but also with firmness, to the dark side of the American response to the events: the anger and cries of retribution which followed the reports of bad treatment of some of the hostages. Then came the other prophetic word: If we acquiesce to those feelings then we will plunge ourselves back into darkness. One may pay a price, but it is possible to proclaim prophetic words.

A prophetic ministry which looks to the Old Testament prophets will entail at least the following elements:

First, *a sense of vocation, of responsiveness to God and responsibility to and for the world.* To be sure, we have heard and will continue to hear our calls in different ways, but we must keep our ears open for still small voices. Many will hear a call to speak through encounter with biblical texts. Some have also perceived in newspaper reports of human need, or starvation, or injustice the call of God to proclaim certain words. Some have even heard God's call to speak in the daily reports of the pollution level of American cities.

Second, a prophetic ministry will have *a sense of the power of the Word, and even of human words, to change history*. We can no longer retrieve that notion as it was alive in ancient Israel, but the notion of the power of the Word to change things belongs in the traditional definition of ministerial functions. Why else would we take the time and trouble to preach, and why would anyone listen? No preacher is powerless unless he or she chooses not to speak effective words. We know the power of words in very mundane ways. Persons who say "I do" in certain prescribed circumstances find that their lives are changed. Or by choosing to eliminate the vocabulary of sexism or racism we help to build a more just society.

A third element of any prophetic ministry will be *a deep aware-*

172

ness of historical concreteness in religious life. Concrete human relationships and experiences have ultimate significance. At least as far as our neighbors are concerned, physical and material considerations—such as food and health and housing—are essential matters. Not so incidentally, that is good incarnation theology: the rule of God, including the embodiment of justice and righteousness, is not just for the world to come, but also for this world.

Fourth, any prophetic understanding of the church and its ministry will have *a profound sense of the social, corporate, and institutional dimensions of human life. Such an awareness is especially important in a society which tends to stress radical individualism, which likes to think of itself as a nation of self-made men.* These are two persistent frontier images by which we understand American life and history. One is that picture of the cabin on the frontier; standing beside it is the lonely, solitary individual with his rifle against the wilderness, and his plow to till the ground. That is the one we remember. But the other image also comes from the American drive to move West. It is the barn-raising, when all members of the community came together to help one another, to create a society, and to celebrate even their need for one another. The prophetic role will emphasize that second image, the communal dimension, reorganizing the power and importance of institutional structures. The prophetic dimension of the church's ministry will be aware that justice and righteousness, and faithfulness to God, are corporate realities or they do not exist at all.

Finally, the prophetic role entails *a moral decisiveness which is both specific and courageous.* The prophet has the courage, literally, of his or her convictions. If we do not call the society to account in the name of God, who will? If we do not hold out a vision of the just and righteous society, who will? If we see disaster coming, we should have the courage to say so because we know that, as Peter said to the high priest, we must obey God rather than men, and because we know that—perhaps even beyond judgment—God's last word is good news.

NOTES

1   James A. Sanders, "Hermeneutics in True and False Prophecy," in *Canon and Authority: Essays in Old Testament Religion and Theology,* ed. Burke O. Long and George W. Coats (Philadelphia: Fortress Press, 1977), 40–41 (also in *From Sacred Story to Sacred Text: Canon as Paradigm* (Philadelphia: Fortress Press, 1987).

2 Julius Wellhausen, *Prolegomena to the History of Israel,* trans. J. Sutherland Black and Allan Menzies (Edinburgh: A. & C. Black, 1885).

3 See, among others, H. Gunkel, *Genesis, übersetzt und erklärt,* 3d ed. (Göttingen: Vandenhoeck & Ruprecht, 1917; reprint ed., 1964); G. von Rad, *Genesis: A Commentary* (Philadelphia: Westminster Press, 1972); Martin Noth, *Exodus: A Commentary* (Philadelphia: Westminster Press, 1962).

4 See especially G. von Rad, *Old Testament Theology,* vol. 2 (New York : Harper & Row, 1965); W. Zimmerli, *The Law and the Prophets: A Study of the Meaning of the Old Testament* (New York: Harper & Row, 1965); R. E. Clements, *Prophecy and Tradition* (Atlanta: John Knox Press, 1975).

5 See especially Claus Westermann, *Basic Forms of Prophetic Speech* (Philadelphia: Westminster Press, 1967); Klaus Koch, *The Growth of the Biblical Tradition: The Form Critical Method* (New York: Scribners, 1969), 210–20; Gene M. Tucker, "Prophetic Speech," *Interpretation* 32 (1978) 31–45.

6 Tucker, "Prophetic Speech,' 44–45.

7 Fred B. Craddock, "Occasion-Text-Sermon," 35 (1981) 61.

8 von Rad, *Old Testament Theology,* 130.

Select Bibliography

Anderson, B., and W. Harrelson, ed. *Israel's Prophetic Heritage*. New York: Harper & Row, 1962.

Baltzer, K. "Considerations Regarding the Office and Calling of the Prophet." *HTR* 61 (1968) 567–81.

Berger, P. "Charisma and Religious Innovation: The Social Location of Israelite Prophecy," *ASR* 28 (1963) 940–50.

Blenkinsopp, J. *A History of Prophecy in Israel*. Philadelphia: Westminster Press, 1983; London: SPCK, 1984.

Buber, M. *The Prophetic Faith*. New York: Harper & Row, 1960.

Buss, M. "Prophecy in Ancient Israel," *IDBSup*. (Nashville: Abingdon Press, 1976), 964–67.

Childs, B. "The Canonical Shape of the Prophetic Literature," *Int* 32 (1978) 46–55 (also in *Interpreting the Prophets*, ed. J. L. Mays and P. J. Achtemeier [Philadelphia: Fortress Press, 1987]).

Clements, R. "Interpreting the Prophets," *One Hundred Years of Old Testament Interpretation* (Philadelphia: Westminster Press, 1976), 51–75.

―――. *Prophecy and Covenant*. SBT 43. London: SCM Press, 1965.

―――. *Prophecy and Tradition*. Atlanta: John Knox, 1975.

Coggins, R., et al., ed. *Israel's Prophetic Tradition: Essays in Honour of Peter R. Ackroyd*. Cambridge: Cambridge Univ. Press, 1982.

Crenshaw, J. *Prophetic Conflict: Its Effect upon Israelite Religion* BZAW 124. Berlin: Walter de Gruyter, 1971.

Cross, F. *Canaanite Myth and Hebrew Epic*. Cambridge: Harvard Univ. Press, 1973.

Culley, R., and T. Overholt, ed. *Anthropological Perspectives on Old Testament Prophecy*. Semeia 21. Chico, Calif.: Scholars Press, 1982.

Duhm, B. *Die Theologie der Propheten als Grundlage für die innere Entwicklungsgeschichte der israelitischen Religion*. Bonn: Adolph Marcus, 1875.

Eissfeldt, O. "The Prophetic Literature," *The Old Testament and Modern Study: A Generation of Discovery and Research,* ed. H. Rowley (Oxford: Clarendon Press, 1951), 115–61.

Ellermeier, F. *Prophetie in Mari und Israel*. Theologische und Orientalische Arbeiten 1. Herzberg: Erwin Jungfer, 1968.

Emmett, D. "Prophets and their Societies," *JRAS* 86 (1956) 13–23.

Fohrer, G. "Neue Literatur zur alttestamentlichen Prophetie (1961–1970)" *TRu* 40 (1975) 193–209, 337–77; 41 (1976) 1–12; 45 (1980) 1–39, 109–32; 47 (1982) 105–35, 205–18.

―――. "Neuere Literatur zur alttestamentlichen Prophetie, 1 Teil: Literatur von 1932–1939" *TRu* 19 (1951) 277–346.

————. "Neuere Literatur zur alttestamentlichen Prophetie, 2 Teil: Literatur von 1940–1950," *T Ru* 20 (1952).

————. "Remarks on Modern Interpretation of the Prophets." *J B L* 80 (1961) 309–19.

————. "Zehn Jahre Literatur zur alttestamentlichen Prophetie," (1951–60) *T Ru* 28 (1962) 1–75, 235–97, 301–74.

Freedman, D. "Pottery, Poetry, and Prophecy," *J B L* 96 (1977) 5–26.

Gitay, Y. *Prophecy and Persuasion: A Study of Isaiah 40–48*. FTL 14. Bonn: Linguisticà Biblicà, 1981.

Gross, H. "Gab es in Israel ein 'prophetisches Amt'?" *E T L* 41 (1965) 5–19.

Habel, N. "The Form and Significance of the Call Narratives," *Z A W* 77 (1965) 297–323.

Hackett, J. *The Balaam Text from Deir 'Alla*. H S M 31 Chico, Calif.: Scholars Press, 1984.

Haldar, A. *Associations of Cult Prophets Among the Ancient Semites*. Uppsala: Almqvist & Wiksell, 1945.

Hayes, J. "The History of the Form-Critical Study of Prophecy," *S B L S P 1973*. Vol. 1, ed. George MacRae (Cambridge, Mass.: Society of Biblical Literature, 1973), 60–99.

Heschel, A. *The Prophets*. New York: Harper & Row, 1962.

Hölscher, G. *Die Profeten: Untersuchungen zur Religionsgeschichte Israels*. Leipzig: J. C. Hinrichs, 1914.

Huffmon, H. "The Covenant Lawsuit in the Prophets," *J B L* 78 (1959) 285–95.

————. "The Origins of Prophecy," *Magnalia Dei, the Mighty Acts of God: Essays on the Bible and Archaeology in Memory of G. Ernest Wright*, ed. F. Cross et al. (New York: Doubleday & Co., 1976), 171–86.

————. "Prophecy in the Mari Letters," *B A* 31 (1968) 101–24.

Jepsen, A. *Nabi: Soziologische Studien zur alttestamentlichen Literatur und Religionsgeschichte*. Munich: C. H. Beck'sche Verlagsbuchhandlung, 1934.

Jeremias, J. *Kultprophetie und Gerichtsverkündigung in der späten Königszeit*. W M A N T 35. Neukirchen-Vluyn: Neukirchener Verlag, 1970.

Johnson, A. *The Cultic Prophet in Ancient Israel*. Cardiff: Univ. of Wales, 1962.

Koch, K. *The Growth of the Biblical Tradition: The Form Critical Method*. New York: Scribner's, 1969.

————. *The Prophets. Vol. 1. The Assyrian Period* (1983) *Vol. 2. The Babylonian and Persian Periods* (1984). Philadelphia: Fortress Press.

Kraus, H.-J. *Geschichte der historisch-kritischen Erforschung des Alten Testaments*. 3d ed. Neukirchen-Vluyn: Neukirchener Verlag, 1982.

Limburg, J. "The Prophets in Recent Study: 1967–77," *Int* 32 (1978) 56–68 (revised version in *Interpreting the Prophets*, ed. J. L. Mays and P. J. Achtemeier [Philadelphia: Fortress Press, 1987]).

Lindblom, J. *Prophecy in Ancient Israel*. Philadelphia: Fortress Press, 1962.

Long, B. "Prophetic Authority as Social Reality," *Canon and Authority: Essays in Old Testament Religion and Theology*, ed. B. Long and G. Coats (Philadelphia: Fortress Press, 1977), 3–20.

McKane, W. "Prophecy and the Prophetic Literature," *Tradition and Interpretation: Essays by Members of the Society for Old Testament Study*, ed. G. Anderson (Oxford: Clarendon Press, 1979), 163–88.

———. "Prophet and Institution," *ZAW* 94 (1982) 251–66.

March, W. E. "Prophecy," *Old Testament Form Criticism*. TUMSR 2, ed. J. Hayes (San Antonio: Trinity University Press, 1974), 141–77.

Moran, W. "New Evidence from Mari on the History of Prophecy," *Bib* 50 (1969) 15–56.

Muilenburg, J. "The 'Office' of the Prophet in Ancient Israel," *The Bible in Modern Scholarship*, ed. J. Hyatt (Nashville: Abingdon Press, 1967), 74–97.

Neumann, P., ed. *Das Prophetenverständnis in der deutschsprachigen Forschung seit Heinrich Ewald*. WdF 307. Darmstadt: Wissenschaftliche Buchgesellschaft, 1979.

Overholt, T. "Thoughts on the use of 'Charisma' in Old Testament Studies," *In the Shelter of Elyon*, ed. W. Barrick and J. Spencer. JSOTSup 31 (Sheffield: JSOT, 1984), 287–303.

———. *Prophecy in Cross-Cultural Perspective: A Sourcebook for Biblical Researchers*. SBLSBS. Atlanta: Scholars Press, 1986.

———. "Prophecy: The Problem of Cross-Cultural Comparison," in *Anthropological Approaches to the Old Testament*, IRT 8; ed. B. Lang (Philadelphia: Fortress Press; London: SPCK, 1985) 60–82.

Parker, S. "Possession Trance and Prophecy in Pre-Exilic Israel," *VT* 28 (1978) 271–85.

Paul, S. "Prophets and Prophecy,' *EncJud*, vol. 13, 1150–75.

Petersen, D. *Late Israelite Prophecy*. SBLMS 23. Missoula, Mont.: Scholars Press, 1977.

———. *The Roles of Israel's Prophets*. JSOTSup 17 Sheffield: JSOT, 1981.

Quell, G. *Wahre und falsche Propheten: Versuch einer Interpretation*. Gütersloh: Bertelmann, 1952.

von Rad, G. *Old Testament Theology, vol. 2. The Theology of Israel's Prophetic Traditions*. New York: Harper and Row, 1965.

Ramlot, L. "Prophétisme. II. La prophétie biblique," *DBSup*, vol. 8 (1972), 909–1222.

Rendtorff, R. "Botenformel und Botenspruch," *ZAW* 74 (1962) 165–77.

———. "Reflections on the Early History of Prophecy in Israel," *History and Hermeneutic*, ed. R. Funk (New York: Harper & Row, 1967), 14–34.

———. "*nābî*' in the Old Testament," *Theological Dictionary of the New Testament* vol. 6, ed. G. Kittel (Grand Rapids: Wm. B. Eerdmans, 1968), 796–812.

Reventlow, H. "Prophetenamt und Mittleramt," *ZTK* 58 (1961) 269–84.

Rofé, A. "The Classification of the Prophetical Stories," *JBL* 89 (1970) 427–40.

Rohland, E. *Die Bedeutung der Erwählungstraditionen Israels für die Eschatologie der alttestamentlichen Propheten.* Diss. Heidelberg, 1956 (Munich: Mikrokopie G.m.b.H., n.d.).

Ross, J. "Prophecy in Hamath, Israel and Mari," *HTR* 63 (1970) 1–28.

Rowley, H. "The Nature of Old Testament Prophecy in Light of Recent Study," *HTR* 38 (1945) 1–38.

Scharbert, J. "Die prophetische Literatur: Der Stand der Forschung," *De Mari à Qumran. L'Ancien Testament. Son Milieu, ses écrits, ses relectures juives. Hommage à Mgr. J. Coppens.* BETL 24, ed. H. Cazelles (Gembloux: J. Duculot, 1959), 58–118.

Towner, W. S. "On Calling People 'Prophets' in 1970," *Int* 24 (1970) 492–509.

Tucker, G. "Prophetic Speech," *Int* 32 (1978) 31–45 (also in *Interpreting the Prophets*, ed. J. L. Mays and P. J. Achtemeier [Philadelphia: Fortress Press, 1987]).

————. "Prophecy and Prophetic Literature," in *The Hebrew Bible and Its Modern Interpreters*, ed. D. Knight and G. Tucker (Chico, Calif.: Scholars Press; Philadelphia: Fortress Press, 1985), 325–68.

Westermann, C. *Basic Forms of Prophetic Speech.* Philadelphia: Westminster Press, 1967.

Williams, J. "The Social Location of Israelite Prophecy," *JAAR* 37 (1969) 153–65.

Wilson, R. "Form-Critical Investigation of the Prophetic Literature: The Present Situation," *SBLSP 1973.* Vol. 1, ed. G. MacRae (Cambridge, Mass.: Society of Biblical Literature, 1973), 100–121.

————. *Prophecy and Society in Ancient Israel.* Philadelphia: Fortress Press, 1980.

Wolff, H. "Hauptprobleme alttestamentlicher Prophetie," *EvT* 16 (1955) 446–68.

Zimmerli, W. *The Law and the Prophets: A Study of the Meaning of the Old Testament.* New York: Harper & Row, 1965.